AN INTRODUCTION TO INTERNATIONAL RELATIONS

An introduction to international relations

P. A. Reynolds PROFESSOR OF POLITICS,
UNIVERSITY OF LANCASTER

Schenkman Publishing Company, Inc.

Cambridge, Massachusetts

Library of Congress Catalog Card No. 73-170656

First published 1971
ISBN 0 582 48818 4 (cased)
ISBN 0 582 48819 2 (paper)
Printed in the United States of America

Preface

Until quite recently very few writers and scholars in the field of international relations had been trained in the subject as undergraduates. They began as historians or lawyers or economists or mathematicians or biologists, or perhaps as political scientists or sociologists. This is because the subject is quite new, the first chair having been founded in 1919, and effective development having begun only in the last twenty-five years. Consequently no methods of approaching the subject are universally accepted, and most teachers feel they want to set out their own way of looking at things.

Theories, models, methods of analysis have been pouring forth in the past fifteen years. The undergraduate lacks a guide through the jungle. This book does not pretend to provide a comprehensive guide. Its purpose is to elaborate some of the approaches which the author has found most helpful. The early chapters are concerned with states, what they are and how and why actions are taken on their behalf. This is one part—perhaps the major part—of what may be called micro-analysis. The later chapters offer an elementary introduction to some problems of macro-theory, using mainly the tools of systems analysis.

I should like to thank Professor Gwilym Jenkins, Martin Edmonds, and David Travers, all of the University of Lancaster, who read parts of the text or corrected me on points of detail. Discussions with students over the past ten years in Aberystwyth and Lancaster have greatly helped to clarify the ideas which are expressed in this book. The responsibility for what is written here is of course mine.

P.A.R.

Contents

Preface   v

PART I   Introduction

1   What is international relations?   3

PART II   Micro-international relations

2   The actors   13
3   Foreign policy as the pursuit of the national interest   35
4   Influences on foreign policy-making   I. The domestic
     environment   51
5   Influences on foreign policy-making   II. The international
     environment   97
6   Means of achieving objectives   123
7   The processes of policy-making   155

PART III   Macro-international relations

8   International systems   183
9   State systems   195
10   Behavioural systems   228
11   System transformation   241

Conclusion   257

Further reading   263

Index   265

PART I

Introduction

I

What is international relations?

KNOWLEDGE IS A UNITY. Total understanding of any aspect of existence is impossible without total understanding of all other aspects. So man cannot achieve more than partial understanding of anything, though this partial understanding may often be sufficient for all practical purposes of behaviour, decision and action. But even this partial understanding may be achieved only by breaking the universe of knowledge into pieces the size of which the human mind is able to comprehend and manipulate. The further the range of mankind's knowledge is extended, the more difficult it becomes for a single mind to be master of more than a diminishing segment of it. Hence the increasing fragmentation of knowledge in past decades, the emergence of ever more, and ever narrower, specialisms. Yet the expansion of knowledge has brought with it heightened awareness of the interrelatedness of the segments into which it is artificially divided. It is thus widely recognized that narrowing specialisms cause loss of opportunities for greater understanding.

A solution to this problem is as yet hard to conceive, although it may well come from the mechanical storing of facts and information on a gigantic scale, with virtually instant access as required, thus freeing the human mind to work on principles and hypotheses and their interrelationships. So far as international relations is concerned, the assembling of relevant information and data is as yet in its infancy, although the size of the data bank that might eventually be needed is beginning to be perceived.

The purpose of the foregoing is to make the obvious point that any delimitation of a field of knowledge which is then called international relations involves the making of arbitrary divisions: by some not absurd definitions of international relations the whole of human behaviour would fall within its field; and since human behaviour is affected by the physical, chemical and biological conditions of its environment, an attempt fully to explain, and not simply to describe, international relations so defined would have to range over the totality of human knowledge.

The ancient Greek philosophers did indeed do almost that. The political treatises of Plato and Aristotle derived from intellectual contexts that included all the scientific, aesthetic and spiritual understanding that was available in the Greek world. There certainly was not any suggestion of the division into 'political theory' (concerned with the purposes for which men organize themselves into political groups, and the kinds of organization best adapted to serve these purposes) and 'government' (concerned with study of the different ways in which men do in fact order their political affairs in a variety of social and cultural contexts) which has been characteristic of much political science (if science is an appropriate word) in this century. Still less were there any separate conceptions of human behaviour which might be labelled 'sociology', or 'economics', or 'international relations'. When the attempt is made, therefore, to define a field of study which may be called international relations, it is made in the knowledge that the definition is arbitrary and is also, in terms of human history, of very recent origin. The purpose of the attempt at definition is to delimit an area of human behaviour which will be small enough to be intellectually manageable and which will exclude as little as possible of other aspects or conditions of human behaviour which are significantly relevant to it.

This attempt is new. It is of course true that many of the classical political philosophers, Dante, Machiavelli, Grotius, Hobbes, Rousseau, Kant, Marx and Lenin among them, had much to say that is of relevance to what is now called international relations; but their observations were almost all directed to particular purposes, whether to advance the interest of a ruler (Machiavelli), to reduce or eliminate organized armed violence among human groups, usually known as war (Rousseau, Kant), or to stimulate and sharpen class conflict and so advance towards the historic goal of communism (Lenin). What they had to say, in other words, was based on various ethical assumptions, and they prescribed behaviour in order to achieve purposes presumed to be desirable.

This method and approach continued in the first decades of this century. The stimulus to new enquiry came from the horror and seemingly senseless slaughter of the first world war. Man's capacity for mass murder had reached such a level that the need to discover means of preventing such organized armed violence in the future seemed imperative. This was the inspiration of the work first undertaken, under the title of international politics, at Aberystwyth in Wales, soon to be followed in London and in many United States universities under the name of international relations, subsequently in Scandinavia, and more slowly on the mainland of Europe. The purpose of the study was to find ways of organizing peace; states ought to behave in accordance with the same moral principles that guided individual conduct; in order to encourage, persuade or compel them to do this the common interest of the peoples of the world in peace and prosperity should be given institutional expression on a global scale. The assumptions were that the foundations of group morality are the same as the foundations of individual morality, that a global common interest in peace existed, and that the way to preserve peace was to create international institutions.

These assumptions came under devastating attack first from the evidence of human behaviour, and secondly from academic analysts led by E. H. Carr[1] and Hans J. Morgenthau.[2] No political system commands total support of all its members all the time; but for any system to survive it must command the active support of some of the politically significant members some of the time, the acquiescence of most of the members most of the time, and a residual coercive power to constrain the remainder or to handle temporary crises. In the global system none of the politically significant members was prepared to give active support to international institutions that limited their sovereignty, few of the other members were prepared to acquiesce in directions given by such institutions, and few were prepared to assign residual coercive power to them. The creation of institutions in the absence of conditions necessary to their success was bound to end in failure and disillusion. Moreover peoples all over the world saw themselves primarily as Frenchmen or Japanese or Egyptians, not as citizens of the world community of mankind, and they expected their rulers to advance the interests, the influence and the wealth of 'France', 'Japan' and 'Egypt'. There might be different interpretations of what these interests were, and how they might best be advanced; but this was what rulers were there for and this was what they ought to try to do. It therefore did not follow that moral principles which might be appropriate for individual behaviour must also be appropriate for state behaviour: the business of state governors was to promote the interests of their peoples as best they

[1] *The Twenty Years' Crisis, 1919-1939* (Macmillan, 1939).
[2] *Politics among Nations* (Knopf, 1948).

might in the world as it was.

There was not, in other words, a common interest in peace—or at least no such common interest was universally perceived. To the peoples of the United States, or Britain, or France, who were reasonably prosperous, were politically influential, and were able to get or had got much of what they wanted (even if this was, as in the United States case, merely to be left alone), it was preferable that things should remain much as they were; but to the peoples (or at least the leaders) of the Soviet Union, of Nazi Germany, or of India, the world was not the kind of place that they wanted it to be. The Soviets were changing their own society, and thought that the rest of the world had to be similarly changed; the Germans resented their defeat in war, resented the constraints and territorial losses that the treaties of 1919 had imposed upon them, and thought—at least some of them did—that they were a superior race with a right and duty to rule the world; the Indians were beginning to be aware of, and to chafe at, their colonial status. If war was the best or the only way of changing the world, then war it must be. International peace and security, that is to say (as Morgenthau put it), is the ideology of satisfied powers.[3]

The second world conflict, after an interval of only twenty years, was taken to show the inadequacy of previous assumptions. The study of international relations now moved from consideration of the best ways of doing what it had been mistakenly assumed everyone wanted to do, to consideration of what peoples really wanted, why they were organized into particular kinds of groups, and why these groups corporately behaved in the way they did. Defined in this way international relations could be seen to subsume all the established or developing social sciences—sociology, social anthropology, economics, demography, political science, human geography, psychology and social psychology—not to mention the support required from moral and political philosophy, history and law.

Clearly such a study would not meet the requirement of manageability. Equally clearly the study of global relationships has become of steadily increasing importance as science and its technological applications have brought peoples round the world into closer and closer contact with each other. The past fifteen years have accordingly seen the emergence of numerous theories aimed at determining the significant elements or variables in these relationships in order that the mass of data may be organized in ways that will be meaningful and so will help understanding of what happens and why.

The theories may perhaps be seen as falling into two main categories.

[3] Morgenthau, op.cit., p. 83.

The first of these contains theories and methods of analysis which focus on the behaviour of those individuals, groups, or organizations that are major actors on the international stage. This may be called micro-international relations. In the second category are theories which conceive international relations as sets of interactions of many different kinds and which concern themselves primarily with the nature of the interactions and their interrelationships, and how and why and in what senses they change or remain stable. This may be called macro-international relations. This division between micro and macro will be followed in this book.

Before going further it may be worth while to compare the study so conceived with diplomatic or international history, and politics or political science, two studies which are closely linked to international relations but which differ in their methods or in the questions to which they seek answers.

The historian recognizes that his approach to the problems he finds interesting, and the issues and the evidence that he selects as being significant, will be much influenced by the social context within which he has himself developed; but he will none the less endeavour to present, within the framework of his interests, as objective an account as he can of the course and cause of events in the period or problem which he is studying. He may or may not attempt to draw from his study lessons that he thinks appropriate (Burnet described his intention as being 'to give such a discovery of errors in government, and of the excesses and follies of parties, as may make the next age wiser by what I tell them of the last'[4]), but he will not normally endeavour to quarry historical records and sources in order to produce general statements about human behaviour which are universally applicable. Many students of international relations are, however, concerned to do precisely this. Many, not all. Some maintain that human behaviour is so individual, irrational and inconsistent as to be unpredictable, and the pretence to establish 'laws' is accordingly spurious and dangerously misleading.[5] In terms of achievements in this direction so far, and of the excessive claims that have sometimes been made, the argument is not without force. But the argument is occasionally misdirected. Maybe history never repeats itself—in detail; but it is always repeating itself in general terms, and the task is correctly to identify the recurrent variables. It remains unlikely that an individual response to a particular

[4] Quoted in T. E. S. Clarke and H. C. Foxcroft, A *Life of Gilbert Burnet* (Cambridge University Press 1907), p. xxxiii.
[5] See H. Bull, 'International theory: The case for a classical approach', *World Politics*, V. xviii (1956) pp. 361-77.

situation will ever be predictable; but it is much less unlikely that the various consequences of different courses of action, or the general outcome of a set of interactions, may become predictable with a sufficient degree of probability attached to the prediction to make it worth having. To borrow an analogy used in a different context: 'I know that if I have a kettle of water at 100 degrees centigrade, it will be boiling. I know also in terms of the amount of heat I am applying to the kettle of water in the form of the gas underneath it, the rate at which molecules of water will be converted to molecules of steam.... But when I look at the separate molecules of water, each of which is at 100 degrees centigrade, I have no way of predicting which will be the next molecule of water to transform into steam.'[6] In fact, when Professor Rivett in that quotation said, 'I know', he meant 'Innumerable experiments have confirmed the hypothesis that under certain conditions the application of a certain amount of heat to water will convert it to steam, and thus have established so high a degree of probability that it will happen that I can act on the assumption that it will and for all practical purposes can say "I know".' But no scientific 'law' offers more than probability, for all involve some approximations or exclude some variables, and no number of demonstrations in the past that two variables interacted in a certain way can *prove* that they must interact in that way in the future. The problem in the social sciences (which may be insoluble) is how to identify the significant variables in situations, and having identified them, how to specify them with adequate precision, and how to test hypothesized relationships among them, in order to establish a sufficient degree of probability for action to be based on the hypothesis. I shall return to this problem in the latter part of the book.[7]

Thus the work of some scholars in the field of international relations (those indeed who have so far brought most enlightenment to the subject) is not altogether dissimilar from that of some historians; but the work of others is wholly different in object and method.[8] The comparison with politics is of another kind. As the study of politics has grown, so has the number of definitions of it. Quincy Wright differentiates four: the art of operating the state, the government, or a party; the art of organizing group power, or will, or unity; the art of achieving group ends against the opposition of other groups; the art of

[6] B. H. P. Rivett, 'The concepts of operational research', in *The University of Lancaster Inaugural Lectures 1965-67*, (1967) p. 47.

[7] See Chapter 9, pp. 212-14 below.

[8] For a further discussion of this question see M. H. Banks, 'Two meanings of theory in the study of international relations', in *The Yearbook of World Affairs* (Stevens, 1966) pp. 220-40.

making group decisions.[9] John Plamenatz introduces the normative element when he writes about the systematic examination of how governments ought to behave and what are their purposes (the study also including theories about how and why institutions and governments behave as they do, and analysis of political terms and concepts).[10] Morton Kaplan lays the emphasis on contests among individuals or groups—contests over the filling of decision-making roles, over the choice of political objects, or over the changing of essential rules of political systems (which are the rules that define the system's characteristic behaviour).[11] David Easton defines a political act as one that relates to 'the authoritative allocation of values for a society'.[12] In all cases, despite the variations, the essential element is the fact of control or government or authority, the propriety or otherwise of that control, the purposes or functions of it, and the forms and methods by which it is exercised or competed for. There is politics in this sense of all human groups, a family, a sports club, a university, a religious community, a state—but the study of politics normally takes as its primary interest that particular group known as the state, which I shall define in the next chapter. The politics of groups at levels below that of the state is conducted within a framework of convention and custom and law and authority, a framework in which restraints are accepted and enforced, and in which a monopoly of the instruments of coercion (the police and the armed forces) is in the hands of the state. Politics at the state level is concerned with exercising, or gaining control of, or influencing, the mechanism of control and coercion. But the competition to gain control is limited in scope and method, since normally all competitors desire to gain control of, but not to destroy, the state, and in established systems all competitors normally eschew the use of violence.

At the global level the situation clearly is different. The framework of convention and custom and law is embryonic only. Diplomatic procedures and immunities are normally observed; there exists a system of international law (though a peculiar kind of law) which embodies rules about such matters as movement on the seas, flying over other states' territories, neutrality in war; some even think to see the first signs of international ethics in, for example, the nearly universal condemnation of racial discrimination: but in all these cases the extent to which states' conduct is constrained is governed by the decisions of the states

[9] Q. Wright, *The Study of International Relations* (Appleton-Century-Crofts, 1955), p. 33.

[10] J. Plamenatz, in *Political Studies*, V. viii (1960), pp. 37-47.

[11] M. A. Kaplan, *System and Process in International Politics* (Wiley, 1957), p. 14.

[12] D. Easton, *A Framework for Political Analysis* (Prentice-Hall, 1965), p. 50.

themselves,[13] not by any authority external to them. Whether international law, or diplomatic immunities, will or will not be observed depends on the losses that the rulers of the state think it will suffer (from the loss of prestige or reputation, or measures of retaliation), if the rules are contravened. Similarly at the global level no person or institution has a monopoly of the instruments of coercion. There is no global authority which can make allocations of values which are generally accepted as being binding, and there are therefore no political acts in an Eastonian sense.

International 'politics' is accordingly politics of a peculiar kind. It cannot be concerned with exercising, gaining control of, or influencing the mechanism of control and coercion, for there is in the global system no such mechanism. It is pre-eminently concerned with, in Quincy Wright's third definition, the art of achieving group ends against the opposition of other groups. But the groups are unconstrained in this competition by anything other than the limits on their power, and the losses that their controllers think they might suffer from the adoption of particular courses of action. The groups are, in other words, sovereign (though this does not mean independent). There is clearly a great deal of difference between political activity within a group which has a government, and political activity within a group (the global system) which is anarchical—indeed by some definitions there is within such a group no activity which can be described as being political. To this argument also I shall return later in the book.[14]

International relations is therefore concerned with study of the nature, conduct of, and influences upon, relations among individuals or groups operating in a particular arena within a framework of anarchy, and with the nature of, and the change factors affecting, the interactions among them. No definition has at this stage been offered of the arena, of what 'international' may be taken to mean: this will be dealt with in the next chapter. The first part of the study I shall call microinternational relations, and chapters 2 to 7 will deal with questions in this area. Chapters 8 to 11 will examine some of the problems that arise in attempting to treat the subject in terms of global interactions: this part will be called macro-international relations.

---

[13] Or, more precisely, by the decisions of those who make decisions on behalf of the states.

[14] See Chapter 10, pp. 230-2 below.

PART II

Micro-international relations

2

The actors

ON ALMOST ANY DAY articles in newspapers may be found containing phrases such as the following. 'The whole question of India's non-alignment has been reopened but ... Russia's surprise decision to supply arms to Pakistan and risk its long-standing cordial relationship with India has brought many murky allegiances in Delhi into clear black-and-white tones.... Mrs Gandhi has defended the decision of Mr Kosygin, the Soviet Prime Minister.... She reminded Parliament that no formal resolution of regret was passed by the House when America entered a military pact with Pakistan in 1953.... Many members of the opposition believe that the Soviet shift towards Pakistan marks the ultimate failure of India's foreign policy.'[1] In these sentences many different 'actors' on the international stage may be seen to be named, among them 'India', 'Russia', Mrs Gandhi, Mr Kosygin, the Indian Parliament (which passed no resolution of regret), and potentially the Indian opposition. The 'murky allegiances' which were brought 'into clear black-and-white tones' might have been personal, party, linguistic, state, economic, religious or many others, and any of the more sharply defined groups so formed might have become international actors. But in what sense?

Let us begin by examining what is meant by 'India's foreign policy'. A policy is a course of action. Foreign policy would thus be a course of action, or the range of actions, adopted in relation to situations or

[1] *The Times*, 29 July 1968.

entities external to the actor. India's foreign policy thus refers to the range of actions external to itself undertaken by the actor India. This formulation raises many difficulties.

In the first place it is not clear what is meant by 'India'. The word as used above implies that there is an entity or a person called India undertaking action. Evidently there is no such person. There are persons such as Mrs Gandhi acting as if for India, but this still takes us no further towards understanding what India is. It is perhaps essentially two things. It is a geographical area with defined and generally, if not necessarily universally, accepted boundaries; and it is a group of humans who live in that area. A geographical area cannot undertake actions, nor in practice can a group of humans numbering some five hundred million. In practice action is taken by an individual or a few individuals on behalf of the group as a whole, but the group is then committed, and may be legally bound. A distinction therefore needs to be drawn between the process of arriving at decisions to take action on the one hand and the consequences of that action on the other: the former involves only a few individuals, but the latter involves the group as a whole. 'India signed the nuclear non-proliferation treaty' is accordingly shorthand for 'Persons acting on behalf of the people inhabiting the geographical area known as India signed the nuclear non-proliferation treaty and thereby (subject to ratification) committed the *state of India* to observance of its provisions.'

The legal commitment is not undertaken by the persons who signed the treaty. It is undertaken by the state. So there are senses in which the state is an actor as well as the individuals who act on its behalf: it is the legal actor. The state is a legal entity. It has no concrete existence at all. It is an abstraction. It is a corporate and legal entity representing the people inhabiting a defined territory, and it has institutions to control it which are constituted by defined processes. In just the same way as a joint stock company is not the shareholders, or the board of directors, or the plant and equipment and land, but an abstraction representing all of these, which can acquire legal rights and obligations that bind them all, so the state is not the people nor the government nor the territory but an abstraction representing all of them, which in like fashion can acquire legal rights and obligations.

Many other human groups are organized in similar ways, but the particular organization known as the state has two special characteristics. A university, or a football club, or the Law Society, are likewise abstractions representing all their members and any buildings, property or equipment corporately owned; and they all have constituted bodies authorized to act for them and able to acquire legal rights and duties which are generally binding on their members. Nearly all such groups, however, exist for a single or strictly limited number of purposes: a university exists, for example, for the advancement of knowledge and for the teaching, training, and mutual education of its members. In order to advance these purposes it will engage in many activities ancillary to lectures, discussions, experimentation, research, which are directly related to its functions: it will buy and sell property; it will provide athletic and social facilities; it will organize health and welfare services; it will undertake contract work for other bodies. But all these activities, with the possible exception of the last, are related to the primary and limited purposes for which it exists; and questions are frequently asked about the propriety of acceptance of contract work precisely because it does not evidently assist performance of the university's primary functions, and indeed may detract from them by directing enquiry along particular channels according to the temporary requirements of outside institutions or persons.

The state, on the other hand, has general functions. Its field of action covers all facets of the lives of its members (although much of this action may consist in providing favourable conditions for living, such as personal security, rather than in directly regulating its members' lives). Its virtue, according to the ancient Greek political philosophers, lies precisely in this generality of function: ... 'if all communities aim at some good, the state or political community, which is the highest of all, and which embraces all the rest, aims, and in a greater degree than any other, at the highest good.'[2]

The second special characteristic that attaches to the state is its sovereignty. A university may make and enforce regulations about the behaviour of its members, about the use of its property and equipment, about the admission of persons not members of the university to its territory or buildings, or their exclusion from them; but these regulations are made under the authority derived from the state (in the form in Britain of a Royal Charter issued by the Queen in Council), and they may not exceed the limits of delegation provided by the Charter, nor may they conflict with laws enacted by the state. No such limits operate for the state. The properly constituted governors of the state may make such regulations or laws and take such action as its institutions, procedures and customs allow within the recognized territorial limits of the state and without interference or control from other bodies. The state is sovereign also in the second sense referred to in the previous chapter, that freedom to act externally is limited only by voluntarily accepted restraints (including limits imposed by its traditions and its

[2] Aristotle's *Politics* (trans. B. Jowett, Oxford University Press, 1938), p. 25.

power), not by legal restrictions enacted by a superior authority and backed by force.[3] A state may now accordingly be defined as an abstract legal entity, representing the conceived unity of the population of a defined territory, legally sovereign, having a government to act on its behalf, and existing to serve the general purposes of its population.

So far as international relations is concerned, one further point needs to be added. One can talk about a state being legally sovereign in relation to internal affairs, in the sense that its laws, whether enacted or customary, and its allocations, are recognized by the population as being binding and as overriding all rules or allocations made by other bodies. In external affairs, however, its sovereignty and its legal status depend on acceptance or recognition by others. From the point of view of the people inhabiting that area of the Asian mainland known as China there is clearly a state called the Chinese People's Republic. This state has a government, which acts with sovereign authority and performs a generality of functions in relation to the population of a defined territorial area. But for the United States, which has not (1970) recognized the Chinese People's Republic, no such state exists. For the United States the state of China is the Republic whose government is located in, and controls, the island of Taiwan or Formosa. Relations between the United States and China are relations between Washington and Taipeh, not between Washington and Peking. No formal negotiations can be conducted, no binding agreements made, no liabilities incurred, no rights acquired, no treaties signed, no contractual arrangements such as the making of loans concluded, between the United States and the Chinese People's Republic. But the Chinese People's Republic is clearly

[3] The argument is stated simply and starkly in the text in order to make the point clear. It is of course subject to many qualifications. I have referred loosely to the 'sovereignty of the state' because the political and philosophical arguments that have raged over the centuries about the proper location of sovereignty— with a monarch, with 'the government', with a constitution, with 'the people' —are not strictly relevant to my purpose. My concern is primarily with sovereignty in the field of external relations; and since in this field sovereignty is important mainly from the legal point of view one may reasonably attach the idea of sovereignty to the legal entity, which is the state. In the second place, while it is strictly true in legal terms that 'the state' may act as it pleases within its territory, it is certainly not true in political terms: Article 2(7) of the United Nations Charter states, 'Nothing contained in the present Charter shall authorize the United Nations to intervene in matters which are essentially within the domestic jurisdiction of any state', but there is no general agreement on what matters are 'essentially within . . . domestic jurisdiction'; the behaviour of governments of states internally is in fact much constrained by their perception of the attitudes of other governments; and these constraints are much intensified by interdependence and by the emergence of widely accepted ethical principles such as the Declaration of Human Rights. Legal 'sovereignty' does not mean 'independence'.

in some senses a state. For a state legally to be an actor on the international stage it must be recognized as a state by other actors: for the government of a state to be able formally to act on its behalf, the government must be recognized as the legitimate government of the state by other governments. From the point of view of international relations a state comes into existence when it is recognized by other states, and a government acquires the ability to act on a state's behalf when it is recognized by other governments. In the Chinese case the position is anomalous, in that some governments recognize the regime in Taiwan as the legitimate government of the state of China, while others recognize the regime in Peking. There are thus two different international stages on which 'China' acts, that on which the other actors are those that recognize Peking, and that on which the other actors are those that recognize Taipeh.

This is not of course to say that in its international action the government of the United States is not affected by and totally ignores the government of the Chinese People's Republic. Far from it. The behaviour of this government is among the dominant concerns of the United States government. The United States ambassador in Warsaw, acting as an agent for the United States government, has for some years intermittently talked with the ambassador of the People's Republic in Warsaw. Speeches, statements, and action in Peking commonly provoke speeches, statements, and action in reply from Washington. Fears about the intentions of Mao Tse-tung and his colleagues in south-east Asia have been in large measure responsible for the costly involvement of the United States in Vietnam. The case of China illustrates from another angle the importance of the distinction between on the one hand the state as an actor, the entity which forms part of the network of formal and legal relationships and which continues to be bound by legal agreements, treaties and contracts irrespective of changes in the agents that act on its behalf; and the government on the other hand, which in formulating policy takes into account many aspects in addition to the legal, and which by its decisions commits the state politically and sometimes also legally.

Hitherto the word 'government' has been used as if it were a single, unchanging, and monolithic entity. This is by no means so. The government of a state consists of those persons who constitute the organs or organizations which make and enforce law, and conduct policy. The whole machinery of control is thus involved, but traditionally distinctions have been drawn among three main functions—the making of law, or the legislative function; the interpreting of, and ordering obedience to law, or judicial function; and the enforcing of law and the conducting of policy, or executive function. In some constitutions the endeavour was made institutionally to separate the three functions. In the United States, for example, not only is the judiciary independent of the executive and the legislature, but no member of the executive can be a member of the legislature, and the two branches of government have separately assigned and delimited spheres of action and powers. In other systems the judiciary may be independent but the executive and legislature may be closely linked, as in the case of the United Kingdom, where the members of the executive are normally members of one of the two houses of the legislature and the executive is formed in large part from members of the largest party in the House of Commons, and from this party support it derives its power. In still other systems all three functions may be in practice if not formally combined: this is the case in many primitive societies, where the three functions may be combined in the person of a chief or a council of elders; but it is also effectively the case in the Soviet Union where executive, legislative and judicial functions are alike controlled, if not directly exercised, by the top organs of the communist party.

But whether the attempt is made institutionally to separate the three functions or not, their performance is in fact intermingled. The Constitution of the United States represents an attempt explicitly to follow the doctrine of the 'separation of powers'. Thus the President is designated head of the executive, and Commander-in-Chief. Foreign policy-making is in large part an executive activity, consisting as it does of receiving information (much of it secret), and deciding in the light of this information on appropriate action, such as doing nothing, sending messages, opening a negotiation, offering bribes, or issuing threats. But the President can with safety do none of these things without taking Congress's attitude into account, and frequently the association of Congress with action is explicitly required. As Commander-in-Chief the President has the formal power to dispatch forces where and when he will; but the declaration of war is reserved to Congress, and the forces that the President is able to assemble, to have trained, and to dispatch will depend on the finance that Congress has appropriated for this purpose. The President's chief agents abroad in carrying out his foreign policies are ambassadors, but they can be appointed only with the approval of the Senate. Some courses of action are designed to lead to treaties, but treaties become effective only when the Senate approves them by a two-thirds majority of those present when the vote is taken. Much foreign policy is concerned with, and is affected by, economic matters; but not merely is the voting of the budget controlled by Congress, the regulation of everything connected with foreign trade is also a Congressional prerogative. Finally, and perhaps most important, since Congress has many powers in relation to domestic affairs, and since the President has domestic as well as foreign policies to advance (and indeed his popular support and so his chances of re-election will normally depend more on his domestic than his foreign record), he dare not pursue foreign policies to which too many influential members of Congress are opposed because this will affect his ability to persuade Congress to go along with his domestic proposals. For these reasons he and members of his administration constantly consult with members of Congress about foreign policy, and frequently Congressional members are directly involved in major international activities (as Senators Connally and Vandenberg were members of the United States delegation to San Francisco when the United Nations Charter was signed in 1945).

Thus even in the United States many individuals and members of many institutions executive and legislative are likely to be involved in foreign policy-making. 'Action by the United States government' is therefore a blanket phrase covering action by a single individual or by a large number of individuals acting as agents for or on behalf of a wide variety of institutions. If 'the government' is to be regarded as the whole machinery of control, then foreign policy action will be taken by a section of the government. This section will not be easily identifiable, nor will it be permanent and unchanging. The person or persons who will compose the section will vary not merely as between one state and another, but within states according to the relevance of the office that individuals hold, or the institutions that they represent, to the issue in question, and according to constitutional and changing political requirements. The composition of the section of the government that takes decisions and acts is therefore constantly changing. If the question is whether or not to attend a Soviet Embassy party on the anniversary of the Bolshevik revolution, the decision is likely to be taken (but not necessarily so) by the ambassador on the spot. On the question whether British troops were to be sent to Malaysia to aid in the 'confrontation' with Indonesia, in 1963, probably the Cabinet, certainly four or five ministers, and certainly some members at least of the Ministry of Defence, the Commonwealth Relations Office (as it then was) and the Treasury, in addition to the Foreign Office, were part of the decision-making group. On such a large question as whether Britain should apply to join the European Economic Community there was in 1960-61 wide participation in policy formulation not merely throughout most of the executive, but by members of the legislature and indeed the party machines and other bodies outside the formal institutions of government. A major element in understanding foreign policy, analysing it, interpreting it, anticipating it, is to determine precisely the composition of the section of the government that has taken, or will take the decisions—determining that is to say who in particular cases are the decision-makers. This question will be further explored in Chapter 7 below.[4]

States then are actors only in the limited sense that they are the continuing legal entities among which formal relationships and obligations subsist. Governments of states are the agents which in fact make decisions, formulate policy, and react to the decisions and policies of other governments, but varying sections of the government will be involved in different issues. But the relationships in question are normally called neither interstate, nor intergovernment, but international relations. A further distinction now needs to be drawn.

The state, as we saw, is an abstraction, representing many empirical elements, but having itself no concrete empirical manifestation. The word 'nation' is likewise an abstraction, but it is concretely manifested in the individual humans who compose it. But to define a nation is not as easy as it seems. Many writers, particularly in the United States, use the terms state and nation as if they were synonymous. This is a confusion, and an important one. Of course it is frequently the case that the people who are represented by a state form a nation, and in those circumstances the confusion caused by using state and nation synonymously is less serious. But there are numerous cases where the people within the frontiers of a state would be generally held to comprise more than one nation: certainly a majority of the people who live in the western fringe of central Great Britain would protest vigorously at the suggestion that there is no Welsh nation. But not merely is there frequently more than one nation within a state, but nations may be scattered among many states: Italian nationalism, presumably referring to an Italian nation, was thought to have been one of the main factors bringing into existence the Italian state in 1859-60, and there existed something which appeared to be a Jewish nation for nearly nineteen centuries after the dispersion until a Jewish state was created in 1948. So a nation cannot simply be defined as the inhabitants of a state.

Nor can a nation be identified by racial differences or by common racial origins. Apart from the biological difficulties of defining race, which are considerable, there are many cases, of which the Brazilians and the West Indians are perhaps the best examples, where nations have emerged out of great and continuing racial admixture; and on

[4] See pp. 155-65.

the other hand there are instances, such as the Czechs and the Slovaks, where the nations exist but where it would be impossible to identify any racial distinctions. Similarly with language: few would deny that a Swiss nation exists, yet within this small country German, French, Italian and Romansh are all spoken, and some Swiss will speak only one of these. Geographical or economic or religious criteria are equally insufficient: West Pakistan is divided from East Pakistan by more than a thousand miles of Indian territory, but a single Pakistani nation exists; perceived economic interests have, among other factors, drawn together the six states now forming the European Economic Community, despite strong national differences, and the powerful economic ties of the Sudeten Germans to Bohemia and Moravia could not make them in the interwar period members of the Czech nation; religions span national 'frontiers', and many if not most nations contain adherents to more than one religious faith.

None of these criteria will serve to differentiate one nation from another. Nations can only be defined subjectively: a nation consists of those people who feel themselves to be members of it. The reasons for this sense of nationhood may be found in any or all of the considerations listed above. It is likely that at some time in the past, if not now, people feeling themselves to be members of one nation will have lived in geographical proximity to each other; economic or religious ties may provoke a sense of common interest and so perhaps of nationhood; common language is a powerful factor; belief in common racial origins is often derived from common language and so, with however little justification, may also be a powerful factor; the fact of being governed through the same institutions and procedures may act to produce a sense of nationhood where none existed before. But the only way to define a nation is somewhat tautologically—that a nation is a group of humans who have a sense of nationhood, who feel mutual affinities, who believe themselves to be members of that nation. The group must of course be sufficiently large for the use of the word not to be absurd. It is not possible precisely to say what 'sufficiently large' means; but it would clearly be nonsensical to describe as a nation two individuals who declared themselves to be a nation.

There is therefore no necessary coincidence between a nation and the population of a state. Where virtually the whole population of a state does in fact feel itself to be a nation, then and then only is it appropriate to speak of a nation-state. Moreover this idea of a nation-state is in historical terms very new, and only in the last decade or so has it been relevant in any political or cultural tradition other than that of so-called western civilization. Until recently boundaries of states usually did not coincide with boundaries of nations: Austria-Hungary, for instance, before 1914 was certainly a state, but contained within its borders many nations or parts of nations. The idea of a nation-state is either absent from, or directly alien to, the political philosophies and traditions of Africa, India, China and Islam. The distinction between nation and state is of great importance for a state's foreign relations, for the existence of different nations within a state is likely to affect its internal cohesion and so the quality of its government's foreign policy (perhaps by undermining it, perhaps by making it aggressive to mask or distract from internal unrest); while the existence of national links across state frontiers may impose virtually unbreakable constraints on a government's action, and may provoke or give excuse for aggressive action by the governments of other states.

The twentieth century has seen three crucial developments in this relationship between nation and state. The process of industrialization and 'modernization' that took place in western Europe in the nineteenth century increased interdependence and interrelationships among peoples within states, and correspondingly required and made possible the extension of governmental activity. Where different national groups existed within the frontiers of one state, increased contact stimulated consciousness of national differences; and increased intervention by governments frequently thought to be alien stimulated feelings of repression or discrimination. These were some of the reasons for the rise of 'nationalism' in Europe in the nineteenth century, and one of the manifestations of this nationalism was the struggle to create a state for each nation—to give each nation, that is to say, a defined territorial area controlled by a legally recognized government composed of members of the nation. This idea that each nation should have its own territory controlled by its own government reached its apogee in Europe at the Paris Peace Conference of 1919. By endeavouring to settle frontiers on the basis of 'self-determination' Woodrow Wilson and those who thought like him believed that many causes of conflict would be removed and the preservation of peace would therefore be made much more likely.

But it was in practice impossible to draw neat state frontiers separating one nation from another, partly because in many parts of Europe (Transylvania and Bessarabia are good examples) members of different nations are in a geographical sense inextricably intermingled, and partly because the only way of determining which people were members of which nations would have been by asking them. Clearly this was impracticable, and would have been valueless since the results could not have led to the drawing of national frontiers. Various expedients were accordingly adopted. In a few cases plebiscites were held, as for instance to decide the destination of Silesia to Poland or Germany. But the results of plebiscites are greatly influenced by the ways in which the constituencies for the voting are delimited: in the plebiscite in Wales in 1961 on the question of opening public houses on Sundays, for instance, had there been a single vote over the whole of Wales, undoubtedly there would have been a majority for Sunday opening; but since the voting was county by county some had majorities in favour of Sunday opening and others majorities against, so that Cardiganshire in 1968 was dry and Radnorshire wet; but again had the voting been by town or village it is likely that some communities within Radnorshire would have been wet and others dry. So in the Silesian plebiscite the constituencies were drawn in such a way as to maximize Poland's gains.

A second method used to determine frontiers at Paris was to apply strategic and economic criteria: thus Czechoslovakia's north-west frontiers were drawn partly so as not to impose a political frontier between the industries in the Sudeten-German-inhabited area and their traditional markets in the Bohemia-Moravia plain, and partly to give Czechoslovakia a powerful strategic frontier against Germany in the mountains of the Erzgebirge, Isergebirge and Riesengebirge. But the criterion most commonly used was linguistic and ethnic: there were people called Romanians, who by language and ethnic (Latin) origin were different from the Bulgars, and Yugoslavs, and Hungarians, and Ruthenes, and Poles, and Ukrainians who surrounded them, and these people must therefore be members of the Romanian nation. The frontiers of the Romanian state should be so drawn to include as many Romanians so defined as possible and exclude as few.

The first modern development, then, was the growing strength of the idea that each nation must have its own state. The second development was the growing belief that nations are identified by race and language. The assumption was that if peoples had 'self-determination' they would opt for linguistically and ethnically defined states and that therefore this was how state frontiers ought to be drawn. Hitler skilfully used this assumption to inhibit opposition to his expansionist policies, but it is still not sufficiently recognized that self-determination does not necessarily mean the drawing of linguistic and ethnic frontiers, and that such frontiers frequently cannot be drawn, at least without large-scale transfers of populations. If in the exercise of 'self-determination' the choice were put in the form 'Join state X and move fifty miles from here, or stay in state Y and stay here' the supposed strength of linguistic and ethnic ties might well be found to be less than assumed.

At least this would very probably have been so in Europe in

1919. But since that date there has been a third development. It has not been the case in the past, as we saw, that people speaking the same language, or having the same ethnic origins (whatever that means) necessarily formed a nation. But since it has come increasingly to be thought that race and language do form the basis of nationhood, so it has increasingly come to be so. A nation being composed of people who believe themselves to be members of it, the more people believe that speaking German makes them members of the German nation, the more it does so (though many Austrians—probably the majority—still have not come to that view). The growing strength of this belief is to be seen in increasing tension between Walloons and Flemings in Belgium, and between French- and English-speaking Canadians in Canada; but the most striking example is the powerful fissiparous tendency in India, which very largely derives from linguistic divisions. *tending to divide*

The nation-state philosophy has rapidly spread over the globe from its European home. The most tragic recent example of its influence was the civil war between Biafra and the remainder of the Nigerian Federation. The leaders of the Somali republic believe that Somalis in Kenya and Ethiopia should be united with them in a single state. The peoples in the northern part of Uganda resent the frontier that divides them from other peoples in the southern Sudan, whom they conceive to be members of the same nation as themselves. This is not to suggest that the frontiers of the new states of Africa have everywhere been wisely or rightly drawn. On the contrary, many of them are the purely arbitrary legacies of former colonial rule. All that is being said is that the belief that nations should each have a state to represent them is widely held around the globe and this has important effects on state cohesion, on interstate relations, and on the behaviour of governments. For this to be clearly understood, accurate appreciation of the distinction between state and nation is essential.

Three different types of actor have now been identified. States are actors in the formal diplomatic and legal network of relationships. Governments are actors in that they make the decisions and formulate the policies by which the states' roles in the formal network are determined. Nations are actors, though they usually lack formal structures, in the sense that their aspirations and their antipathies affect the behaviour of governments, and that relationships among their members may cross state frontiers.

The unsatisfactory nature of the word 'international' may now appear. The word means 'between nations'. But nations may not have institutions, procedures and individuals to act for them and enable them to act as corporate entities: they will have these in those cases in which the nation is identical with the population of a state, but probably not otherwise. 'International' can then properly be used to describe relations between states only when they are nation-states; and it is misleading precisely for this reason, in that it encourages the assumption that is already too generally made, that all states are in fact nationstates. If there are difficulties in the word 'international' because nations may not be able to act corporately, there are even more striking commonsense difficulties in using the word to describe relations between members of nations : if a Frenchman sells a car to a German this might well be regarded as an 'international' transaction, but almost no one would see an international transaction in the sale of a car by a Welshman to a Scot.

It seems therefore that the essential element of an 'international' relationship is that it is a relationship between individuals or groups who are members of different states, or between the states themselves. But to rename the subject 'interstate' relations would have even greater disadvantages. In the first place, as we have seen, relations between states are of a formal and continuing legal character only : relations in a dynamic sense of action and interaction are relations between governments. Secondly, interstate relations would imply that states are the permanent and proper units of the global system, whereas questions about the basis and appropriateness of this assumption may be among the most important that the student of the subject needs to ask. Thirdly, many transactions that would customarily be thought of as falling within the field of study are not between states but between individuals or groups other than states. ('Intergovernment relations' would be no less restrictive, and in addition would obscure the important element of the relationships with which we are concerned that derives from continuity despite the fall of governments.)

The least unsatisfactory solution seems to be to retain the customary 'international relations'[5] as the name of this segment of knowledge with which we are concerned, while keeping constantly in mind the fact that the relationships in question are sometimes intergovernmental, sometimes interstate, sometimes intergroup or interindividual, but rarely international except in those cases where the interacting entities are nation-states (where they are simultaneously international and inter-

[5] In a recent article Dr M. B. Nicholson and I tried out the word 'global' as a substitute for 'international', but this had the disadvantage of suggesting, and was read by some as meaning, that we were interested only in interactions which were global in the sense of 'operative all round the globe'. This word is thus also unsatisfactory. 'World' would have the same effect. See M. B. Nicholson and P. A. Reynolds, 'General systems, the international system, and the Eastonian analysis', *Political Studies*, xv (1967), pp. 12-31.

state). The distinguishing characteristic of the relationships in question is that they cross state frontiers, physically or notionally, that they are between individuals or groups who are members of different states, or between the states themselves.

The state, the government, the nation. As the foregoing discussion suggests, these by no means complete the catalogue of international actors. The state and the nation are particular kinds of human groups. Other groups than these operate internationally in the sense that they have relationships and interact across state frontiers. Such groups may be 'international', 'supranational' or 'transnational'.

International or supranational groups are composed of states. The word supranational is of relatively recent origin, and refers to institutions which have been created for the performance of specific functions, and which have power to take decisions binding on the members whether they have participated in the decision or not. The word is typically applied to institutions that have been established in Europe since 1950, but many earlier international institutions had a supranational element about them in the sense that their supreme organs might by majority vote take decisions that were binding on all members. Thus in the Rhine Commission established by the Congress of Vienna in 1815 equality and unanimity were the normal rule, but in certain administrative matters voting power varied with the length of the river bank of the member states; while the European Commission for the Danube, established in 1856, frequently acted upon a majority vote.[6]

These two institutions were limited in their range of action both functionally and geographically. Since the middle of the nineteenth century institutions have slowly emerged with large numbers of members, or with a wide range of different functions, or with both. No universal association has yet been formed, in the sense that every state has been a member; and indeed no such association could be formed so long as differences about recognition exist. But some associations are frequently called universal because they come close to universality, and to distinguish them from associations clearly and intentionally of a regional character.[7]

The first quasi-universal international institution was the Interna-

[6] See D. W. Bowett, *The Law of International Institutions* (Methuen University paperbacks, 1963), p. 6.

[7] 'Regional' is a word that appears in the United Nations Charter, but it is by no means clear that definition by geographical 'regionality' is always either possible or intended. For a stimulating discussion of the identification of 'regions' by socio-cultural, United-Nations-voting, international-organization-membership, trading-pattern, and geographical-proximity criteria see B. M. Russett, *International Regions and the International System* (Rand McNally, Chicago, 1967).

tional Telegraphic Union, established in 1865, the second, the Universal Postal Union nine years later. They symbolized recognition of the fact that certain functions—the routing and dispatch of telegrams, the international movement of mail—could be more effectively performed if there were a body to standardize costs and procedures so that, for example, a letter posted in France and stamped with a French stamp would be accepted and delivered in Germany without the levying of any additional charge. The second of these had a clearly supranational element in that proposed amendments to the Convention of the Union could come into force and be binding on all members if they received a majority vote in their favour conveyed by letter to the permanent bureau. The former also adopted majority voting, but in this case the bureau had power to act only *ad referendum*, so that members could not be bound against their will.[8]

The League of Nations represented the first attempt to create a universal political organization (though it failed not merely to achieve universality, but even membership of all the major powers). By the Covenant of the League the member states bound themselves to take specified actions in specified contingencies; but they did not surrender their sovereignty, for their decision to bind themselves was their own and they did not establish any body able to order or compel them to adhere to their obligations. When the League concept was fatally undermined by the failure of the United States Senate in 1919 and 1920 to ratify the Treaty of Versailles and the League of Nations Covenant, and so to permit the United States to become a member of the League, the other members swiftly limited their obligations under the Covenant by resolving that though the principle of automatic reaction to certain specified actions remained, how the principle was to be implemented was for subsequent decision. Under the auspices of the League a series of Committees was established, Economic, Financial, Health, Communications and Transit, Intellectual Organization, and for various social and humanitarian activities; and in addition an International Labour Organization and two *ad hoc* Commissions on Mandates and on Disarmament were created.

After 1945 the model of the League was followed but revised to produce the United Nations Organization; and a large number of specialized agencies for economic, financial, social and cultural purposes were founded under the auspices of the Economic and Social Council. In the United Nations, however, a new principle was introduced in that certain decisions of the chief peacekeeping agency, the Security

[8] Bowett, *op. cit.* pp. 7 and 325.

Council, were made binding on all members, provided that the Council voted by a majority including the five permanent members of the Council. While it is the case that few such binding decisions have been taken, and all members have not in practice always acted in accordance with their obligations, this principle in fact abrogated the legal sovereignty of all but the five permanent members, at least as far as a limited class of decisions is concerned. However small the effect has been, the United Nations in the Security Council is an international organization that contains a clear element of supranationality.

In addition to the quasi-universal organizations, there have emerged many groups of states with limited memberships determined by various criteria. The British Commonwealth, as an association of equal and independent states, freely associated under the symbolic titular headship of the British Crown, is the loosest of such groups and has been formed of those former colonies of Britain which on achieving independence chose to become members. The Organization of American States is a slightly more formalized association of states geographically located in the American continent. The membership of the Arab League, also a loose association, consists of states whose populations are supposedly members of the Arab nation. The North Atlantic Treaty Organization and the Warsaw Pact Organization, very much more tightly structured, were designed for strategic, economic and ideological purposes against specific perceived threats.

These international organizations may be seen as actors in three main ways. In some cases their role is clearly institutionalized. When United Nations Secretary-General Dag Hammarskjöld, acting on the basis of loosely framed Security Council resolutions, assembled armed forces, appointed commanders and political advisers, and despatched them to undertake military action in the Congo in 1960, the United Nations through the agency of the Secretary-General was clearly acting on the international stage no less than any state. When the Council of the North Atlantic Treaty Organization in December 1950 announced in Brussels their agreed view that 'German participation would strengthen the defence of Europe'[9], the statement from its collective nature carried much greater significance and weight for the government, for instance, of the Soviet Union, than if the fourteen states members of NATO had individually made statements to the same effect. When the Directors of the International Monetary Fund announce the making of a loan to

[9] North Atlantic Council, Sixth Session, 18-19 December 1950, Brussels, final communiqué, quoted in Lord Ismay, NATO, *the First Five Years* (Netherlands, Bosch-Utrecht), p. 187.

support a currency in difficulties, this has repercussions on transactions, not only financial, around the globe. In all these cases institutions are actors, although, as in the case of states, they act through appointed agents.

They may be actors, however, in two other, more subtle ways. Whether an institution is or is not corporately acting, and so producing consequences on the international stage, is immaterial: what matters is whether the governments of other states, or other actors, believe it is so behaving. There is an association called the British Commonwealth, probably the loosest of all international associations. If at the United Nations it appears important to the government of say the Soviet Union whether the countries of the Commonwealth are or are not in agreement and acting collectively, what will affect the behaviour of the Soviet government is the belief the members of the government form about the 'action' of the Commonwealth. An association, however loose, can therefore from the fact of its existence produce consequences, and thus in a sense act, even if in fact it 'does' nothing at all.

Secondly associations may be actors in the sense that they affect the behaviour of their members. To the extent that the government of a state-member of an association values maintenance of the association and its own membership of it, to that extent the fact of existence of the association will cause the views of other members of the association to have greater weight. It is difficult to believe, for example, that Britain's interest in maintaining good relations with certain individual states of Africa would have so significantly affected the policy that Britain adopted towards Rhodesia after the unilateral declaration of independence in 1965, had it not been for Britain's desire to preserve the Commonwealth. This made the African members' voices much more important for Britain, and in this sense again the Commonwealth was 'an actor'. I am not of course suggesting that it was the views of the African state-members alone that produced the British policy, merely that the existence of the Commonwealth had as it were an autonomous influence.

International institutions that have 'supranational' characteristics are much more evidently actors on the international stage. Many federations are supranational institutions in the sense that the federal form of government frequently is adopted when many national groups wish to preserve their identity but recognize the advantages of acting together for certain purposes such as foreign affairs, defence, or mutual free trade. Here evidently the federal authorities are the international actor, since normally state-members of federations do not themselves conduct external relations.[10] The term 'supranational' is, however, more usually applied to institutions which have been established for the performance of specific and limited functions and which contain special agencies with defined powers. The prototype of institutions of this kind was the European Coal and Steel Community, which, in the words of the original public announcement by the French government on 9 May 1950, was to be controlled by 'a new higher authority, whose decisions will bind France, Germany and other member countries'.[11] It was precisely over this supranational element, the binding force of the decisions of the future High Authority, that disagreement on the proposal arose between France and Britain; and Britain's refusal to participate in the negotiations was predicated on France's insistence that the binding quality of the High Authority's decisions was not negotiable. (This was not the only reason why the British government reacted somewhat coolly to the proposal, and in fact during the negotiations the starkness of the High Authority's power as originally outlined was much attenuated : the Anglo-French skirmishes over the proposal reflected a deep-seated political division between France and Britain about the leadership of Europe, and about the kind of Europe that was to be led.)

The European Coal and Steel Community was followed by Euratom and the European Economic Community, each of which had supranational elements, though more circumscribed than in the case of the ECSC. The extent to which the powers have in fact been exercised has varied with changes in the political, strategic and economic environments within which the Communities work. But that they are international actors is undeniable. Not merely does their existence, whether action is being taken or not, very much affect the behaviour both of their members and of other states outside, but they do directly engage in international activity. They have diplomatic missions formally accredited to them, and thus are recognized. The Council of Ministers of the EEC acting corporately, takes decisions on such matters as the admission of new members. The Commission of the EEC engages in negotiations with governments of states about, for instance, questions of tariffs. The Commission does not of course act without regard to the interests of the member-states of the Community. These interests have to be recon-

[10] One of the attributes of 'states' as defined above was legal sovereignty. Units in a federation do not of course have sovereignty, and therefore are not states for my purpose. In many federations, however, India and the United States being examples, the component units of the federation are called states. This causes a further confusion which cannot be avoided, but which should be borne in mind.

[11] *Anglo-French Discussions regarding French proposals for the Western European Coal, Iron and Steel Industries* (Cmd 7970, HMSO, 1950), p. 4.

ciled by hard negotiations among the members of the Community in which the members of the Commission assist; but the Commission acts, and with some discretionary powers, to implement agreed policy in negotiation with states outside the Community.

The European Communities offer the most striking examples of institutions with evident supranational characteristics. The Western European Union seemingly carried a supranational feature in the undertaking of the United Kingdom not to withdraw its forces from the mainland of Europe against the wishes of the majority of the Brussels Treaty Powers; but the escape clauses relating to 'an acute overseas emergency' and to 'too heavy a strain on the external finances of the United Kingdom'[12] have been more than once invoked and have thus undermined the supranational quality of the Union. Some supranational elements are perhaps to be seen in the working of the North Atlantic Treaty and Warsaw Pact Organizations, at least as far as the defence aspect of foreign relations is concerned, where decisions may be taken by organs in which some member-states are not represented. But attachment to state sovereignty continues to be strong, so that institutions with a supranational component are rigidly limited in their functional range, or, where in recent instances this has not been so markedly the case, their activity has often been more circumscribed than original intentions or blueprints suggested. None the less such institutions as do exist are clearly international actors in their own right.

Four types of actors have so far been identified, international institutions (of which some have a supranational character), governments, states and nations. Apart from the last of these it is the state that in each case is the critical element: international institutions are composed of states, governments represent states. But there is another class of human groups which contains international actors in the sense that transactions take place (again physically or notionally) across state frontiers, but which are not emanations of states. These may be called transnational institutions. There now exist several hundred non-governmental organizations: these consist of persons of similar interests or concerns, and their purpose is to advance the particular interests which the members share. Many of these non-governmental organizations are scientific, educational or cultural, and are linked with the United Nations Educational, Scientific and Cultural Organization (UNESCO). They are sometimes consulted as corporate bodies by governments or by international institutions, but they are international actors also in the sense that they organize conferences, discussions, the exchange of infor-

[12] *Final Act of the London Conference*, 3rd October 1954 (noted in Ismay, *op. cit.* p. 239).

mation, and personal meetings, among people who are members of different states, and they thus promote transactions across state frontiers.

As science and technology shrink the globe, the number of these transnational institutions continues to grow. The Roman Catholic Church has long been such a body: indeed the Pope has for centuries headed a state as well as a church (though he ceased to be a temporal ruler during the fifty-nine years between the occupation of Rome and Mussolini's signing of the Lateran Treaties in 1929); but he does of course exercise authority not merely over the inhabitants of the Vatican City, but over all adherents to the Roman Catholic faith. No other church is so effectively institutionalized, but membership of other churches has moderated or stimulated international transactions, and should the Christian ecumenical movement grow, this could not but have effects on relations among the peoples of eastern and western Europe.

Cartels, trade unions, internationally based industries, political parties, are other examples of transnational groups. International cartels have perhaps played less significant roles in recent years with anti-monopoly and antitrust legislation in many industrialized countries, and international trade union associations have acted only spasmodically. The development of major companies spanning state frontiers has on the other hand proceeded apace as increasingly costly and complex technologies have created demands for larger capital resources and larger markets. Oil, computers, chemicals, and vehicles are only a few examples of enterprises which have become in substantial degree internationally based and financed, and such companies are international actors both because of the international transactions that they conduct and because of the influence that they exert on the behaviour of other actors on the international stage. Their requirement for easy movement of capital at the international level has tightened economic links among developed economies, and this has been one of the factors making for central bank cooperation in stabilizing currency exchange rates, cooperation which has made banks increasingly important international actors.

Among political parties, the last of the examples of transnational groups quoted above, the communists have been both the most effective and the most institutionalized. The first attempt at transnational party cooperation was made by Marx with the foundation of the First International in 1864, but internal disputes led to its collapse, while its successor, the Second International, succumbed to state loyalties on the outbreak of the first world war. Lenin's Third International, or Comintern, however, founded in March 1919, established during the Stalinist period effective control over most communist parties outside the Soviet

Union, though admittedly at heavy cost; so that six years after its formal dissolution in 1943 as a gesture indicating lessened hostility to the United States and Britain during the second world war, the leaders of the French and Italian communist parties, Maurice Thorez and Palmiro Togliatti, could still say that in the event of invasion of France or Italy by the Red Army, they would welcome the Soviet forces with open arms. These declarations contrasted with the attitude of Tito of Yugoslavia in 1948, or of Dubček of Czechoslovakia in 1968; but they demonstrated how effective the Comintern had been in establishing transnational loyalties to communism more powerful than loyalty to state or perhaps to nation.[13] The Comintern was clearly a significant international actor, probably more important by reason of the fears and suspicions it aroused than the numbers or quality of its adherents in fact warranted.

These are examples, but examples only, of transnational groups or institutions that act on the international stage. Finally a word should be said about the individual as an actor. His actions will rarely be significant. It is unlikely, for example, that the intervention in the Cuba crisis of 1962 even of so well-known and so self-confident an individual as Bertrand Russell had much importance. But individuals are none the less actors in some small degree. The author of a book which sells in a foreign country; the tourist who spends foreign currency and meets 'nationals'[14] of other states; the runner who competes in the Olympic Games; the doctor who first transplants a human heart —all these are international actors, though the isolated activity of each is not likely to be of much international consequence.

'Much international consequence': the phrase suggests an obvious criterion to use in order to make selections from this great complexity of interaction so that the study may be manageable. States, governments, and nations, international, supranational, and transnational groups or institutions, and individuals, have been proposed as actors on the international stage. Clearly an enormous amount of time and energy could be spent examining the nature and significance of individual action; but the time and energy would be likely to be ill-spent, for the results of the enquiry would almost certainly be insignificant. Much time could also be spent on studying the activity of transnational groups,

[13] Thorez and Togliatti would doubtless have argued that there was no disloyalty to the nation since the nation's interest would best be served by communization. I am of course making no value judgments on the propriety or otherwise of these declarations.

[14] Another indicator of confusion. The citizens of Britain are known as British nationals and have British nationality: the Welshman who gives his nationality as Welsh has no legal foundation for doing so.

and this might well prove less unrewarding, though still probably not of major importance. Many scholars do in fact spend time analysing the behaviour of international and supranational institutions, and here an important part of international action is surely involved. But it remains the case that the greater part of significant action on the international stage continues to be that of states and of the governments that represent them. Much of the effect of action by others is important for its impact on the behaviour of governments; most of the action by international and indeed supranational institutions is the consequence of decisions made by governments. There is therefore good reason for using the behaviour of governments on behalf of states as the focus for the study of micro-international relations, taking the behaviour of other actors into account primarily as it affects the governments of states. In making this deliberate decision, however, the student must remain aware that this is a simplification and so a distortion. The simplification rests moreover on the assumption that states are the most significant actors, and while this is doubtless true in 1970, it is unlikely to remain true for all time. In the succeeding chapters on micro-international relations, however, this assumption will be accepted. The behaviour of the governments of states will be taken as central, and the chapters will accordingly deal with the goals of and influences upon what is commonly called foreign policy, the means that policy-makers use, and the the processes through which policy is made.

3

Foreign policy as the pursuit of the national interest

IN THE LAST CHAPTER it was suggested that, although there is a considerable variety of actors appearing on the international stage, there is advantage in concentrating at the micro-level on the performance of states, since in the present condition of international relations they are the leading players who dominate the action. But it must also be remembered that though it is the states that are committed and bound by action, that action is in fact taken by members of governments, whether of their executive or legislative sections, or of both. This chapter is concerned with the nature of the goals the governments of states seek to achieve in their foreign policies.

A more precise definition of foreign policy than was previously offered is perhaps desirable as a preliminary. It was suggested that foreign policy consists of a range of actions taken by varying sections of the government of a state. The actions are taken with reference to other bodies acting on the international stage, of which the most important are other states, but which include, as we have seen, international, supranational, and transnational groups, and occasionally also individuals. The word 'policy', however, like its adjective 'politic', carries overtones of prudence or wisdom, and thus implies something about the purposes for which actions are taken. A policy therefore is frequently taken to be not simply a range of actions, but also the principles influencing those actions, or the purposes they are intended to serve. So far as the international actions of the government of a state are concerned, the purposes the actions are supposed to serve are usually summed up in the concept 'the national interest'. One might accordingly distinguish two quite different senses in which a policy might be good or bad: first, that the objectives the policy was designed to attain accorded well, or accorded ill, with the national interest; or secondly that the actions taken were well-judged, or ill-judged, to attain the objectives. A policy may be well conceived in terms of goals, but ill-executed; and frequently excuses for bungling are proffered in the phrase, 'He was acting in the national interest'. Wise selection of goals is of little value if action in pursuit of them is ineffective, and the distinction between the goals and the action is worth preserving. I shall therefore use 'policy' to refer to the actions designed to achieve goals but not including the goals themselves. This chapter deals with the latter, the goals; the succeeding four chapters will deal with the kinds of action that may be taken, and with the factors that determine the choices of action that are made. Foreign policy may now accordingly be defined as the range of actions taken by varying sections of the government of a state in its relations with other bodies similarly acting on the international stage, supposedly[1] in order to advance the national interest.

The words 'the national interest' are among those most frequently to be heard from the lips of politicians. Many of them, if pressed, might be hard put to say with precision what the words mean, still less to define the criteria by which the interest is to be determined. The term commands such obeisance that to claim an act to be in the national interest immediately, if sometimes spuriously, increases the act's acceptability; and consequently groups in all polities endeavour to identify with the national interest the interests which the groups exist to serve. Such groups may be economic, military, political, racial, ethical, religious, or for the forwarding of any other purpose to which humans attach themselves. French farmers maintained, with substantial success, that it was in France's national interest for cereal prices in the European Economic Community to be fixed sufficiently high to promote the rejuvenation and expansion of French agriculture. When British bicycles made large inroads into the United States market in the 1950s, United States bicycle manufacturers persuaded the Eisenhower administration that it was not in the national interest for an important industry to be driven to the wall, and tariffs on imported bicycles were accordingly

---

[1] I say 'supposedly'; because although it may be that members of governments ought always to act to further the national interest, they may mistake what that interest is, or they may act in part in the interests of their own political position. This would be furthering the national interest only to the extent that their remaining in power accorded with it.

raised. During the prolonged controversy within the British Ministry of Defence between 1964 and 1967 over Britain's commitments east of Suez, the Royal Navy's view that the national interest required the maintenance of Britain's presence in that area temporarily prevailed, though not the Navy's case that that interest could be most cheaply and effectively served by the aircraft carrier. British Conservative leaders claim, though rarely explicitly, that the national interest is served by Conservative party rule because Conservative governance increases international confidence in sterling. German national interest was declared incarnate in Hitler, for he alone could formulate and realize German aspirations. Some Negro leaders in the United States adduce disservice to the United States national interest from the damage done to the image of the United States by discrimination against the Negro. The Campaign for Nuclear Disarmament claims that Britain's national interest would be served by a unilateral renunciation of nuclear weapons.

The national interest is not simply to be seen in the goals of such subnational groups as these, however stridently the groups may claim that advancement of their interests means advancing the national interest. On the other hand it does not follow that, because the interest of a subnational group may not be the same as the national interest, it never can be: the fact that United States oil companies have an interest in the United States maintaining a position in the Levant (or the Middle East[2]) does not of itself mean that it is *not* in the United States' interest to maintain such a position. More importantly, however, the national interest is not to be found from a process of adding up together the various interests of subnational groups, for of course they do not coincide. They may conflict simply—in the sense that across the board reciprocal tariff cuts will be in the interest of some industries in a country, but against the interest of others; or they may conflict complexly—as for example some political, diplomatic, economic, and defence groups in Britain would have an interest in maintaining special relations with the Commonwealth, but if these relations were in some ways to be adversely affected by new ties between Britain and the European Economic Community, some of these groups would feel their interests threatened and would be wholly opposed, some might find political interests pulling one way and defence interests another, some might judge new European ties to contain the potential of much greater advantage. The national interest cannot be conceived of as having no connection with subnational interests, but it is not to be identified by a simple process of trying to put them together.

Just as the national interest may not be found in the sum of sub-

[2] For a comment on this term, see Chapter 4, p. 61 fn. 10.

national interests, so it may likewise not be found in the sum of national objectives. These (frequently confusingly called 'national interests' in the plural, which should be sharply distinguished from 'the national interest' in the singular) comprise the range of particular ends, usually of a relatively short-term nature, which policy-makers at a given moment in time are trying to achieve. In 1967 United States objectives may, for example, have included among others the reduction of tension in relations with the Soviet Union, the signature of a nuclear non-proliferation treaty, the sustaining of NATO, the defence of West Berlin, the overthrow of Castro, the strengthening of relations with the states and peoples of Latin America, the maintenance of prestige and the containment of communism in south-east Asia, especially Vietnam, the defence of Chiang Kai-shek in Taiwan, the reduction of instability in Africa, the reduction of foreign aid, the expansion of trade, the defence of the existence of Israel, the maintenance of oil companies and their supply of oil from the countries of the Arab world. Merely to list interests or objectives in this way shows the incompatibility of some with others, and the national interest is not therefore to be found in either a partial or a comprehensive inventory of national objectives. The precise requirement indeed is for a criterion or criteria for selecting or giving priority to some of these objectives as against others, for determining, for example, that even though the people of the United States should suffer damage and loss if South Vietnam were abandoned, nonetheless if intervention in Vietnam should excessively impede the reduction of tension in relations with the Soviet Union, and the latter objective should be more important than the former, then South Vietnam should be abandoned. As Pierre Mendès-France said: 'To govern is to choose.'

What criteria may be discovered? I would suggest that action by authorized decision-makers, and so by a state, might be taken to be in accordance with the national interest if it served the real interest of a community as it would be seen by an omniscient observer. Such a formulation raises a host of difficulties. In the first place no such 'real interest' may exist. If it were the case that assent to a sufficient commonalty of values and aspirations were universally commanded from every member of a community, then such a real interest might be said to exist; but in every community there are differences of aspirations and values, and one cannot say more than that the community exists primarily because the differences internally are in some senses less than the differences of values between the community in question and other communities. The particularity of a community may however be in large part identified by the degree and manner in which differences in values and aspirations between the community and others exceed such differences internally.[3] The concept of a 'real interest' commanding universal assent contains similar philosophical difficulties to Rousseau's *volonté générale*, and perhaps to Plato's Form of the Good. It is not for that reason only to be assumed to be wholly valueless, for as an ideal, if unrealizable, it forces attention away from the partial or subnational interest, and the limited or particular or short-term objective.

The second difficulty can be seen in the problem of how to identify such an interest, even if it could be conceived to exist. The problem of identification is twofold—the problem of identifying general ends or goals of which the national interest may consist, or which may offer approximations to it; and the problem of determining the extent to which a particular action in the real world would accord or conflict with it. Both aspects of the problem present acute difficulties.

In the third place the word 'community' was used, thus deliberately begging the question of which the group was whose 'real interest' was referred to—the group within a defined territory represented by the state; or 'the nation' (whose limits may or may not coincide with the boundaries of a state); or some other group larger or smaller or in some other way different from either of these. These two latter difficulties can best be considered in the light of a discussion of the basic reasons for the existence of human communities, of which three in particular have been identified by western political philosophers.

Plato and Aristotle argued existence in a social environment to be natural to man. 'No individual is self-sufficing; we all have many needs ... having all these needs, we call in one another's help to satisfy our various requirements.'[4] To Aristotle society was natural, in the main because of man's peculiar ability to communicate, and this ability to communicate, and so to act in accordance with his nature, could evidently not be exercised if he lived in isolation. Communities therefore exist, on this reasoning, to make possible and to facilitate social intercourse, and only through such intercourse can man develop his capacities to the full. If this reasoning is accepted, then it may also be the case that the fullest development of capacities requires the widest

---

[3] Karl Deutsch makes a similar point in cybernetic language: 'The limits of an autonomous organization can be described in terms of a *communication differential*: among members or parts of an organization there should be more rapid and effective communication than with outsiders'; but he nowhere suggests that there can be *totally* effective communication of such a kind as would be necessary—in my language—for a universal agreement on a commonalty of values. See K. W. Deutsch, *The Nerves of Government* (Free Press, 1963), p. 205.

[4] *The Republic of Plato*, ed. F. M. Cornford (Oxford University Press, 1961), p. 54.

range of social intercourse that is practically possible. In the state of technology, of transport and of communications of the world of ancient Greece the limits imposed by practical possibilities were very sharp, and were conceived by Plato and Aristotle to enclose communities of about the size of the Greek city-state; but in the last third of the twentieth century, where no place is physically distant by air more than twenty-four hours from any other, and where verbal communication round the world is virtually instantaneous and visual communication is rapidly becoming so, the setting of proper limits, and indeed the appropriateness of limits at all, presents a difficult problem. Possibly other criteria than practicality must be applied. It is to be noted, however, that these reasons for man to live in a community would not be acceptable to all philosophers or theologians in all cultures throughout the world. To some Hindus, for example, the supreme capacity possessed by man which must be developed above all others is the spiritual capacity, and the fullest development of this capacity requires abstraction from the world, and the realization of identity with Brahman. So even this most general of reasons for the existence of communities would not be universally acceptable, and this presents a further problem in the application of the idea of the national interest which will be explored below.

A second reason why man should live in a social framework was also identified by Plato, namely the material (and subsequently other and superior) advantages to be derived from the division of labour, '... more things will be produced and the work be more easily and better done, when every man is set free from all other occupations to do, at the right time, the one thing for which he is naturally fitted.'[5] The industrial and technological revolutions in modernized societies have developed and extended this principle, far beyond any possible conception of Plato's, to the point where not merely would high standards of living be jeopardized (standards, moreover, to which people have become accustomed, and so expect as their right), but the very survival of large numbers would be threatened, if the process of exchange upon which industrial society depends were totally disrupted. This is a more compelling reason for the existence of communities: the very survival of many depends on the maintenance of processes of exchange, and so on a substantial measure of certainty of supply of materials and of markets for selling products. Political organization, and political and social procedures, are therefore necessary to ensure the political and social conditions in which the processes of economic exchange may operate in security, and the almost universal aspiration to maximize wealth may

[5] Cornford, op. cit. pp. 55-6.

be satisfied. In most societies different political groups, or groups with different economic interests or different theoretical panaceas, will dispute the best methods of achieving the purpose of maximizing wealth, and perhaps whether the maximizing of wealth is more important than, for example, the maximizing of strategic security (these issues are the very substance of political debate); but from the view that the maximizing of wealth is one purpose which the community exists to serve, almost none will dissent.

A third reason for the existence of communities is man's need for security. The argument has two aspects. It was Thomas Hobbes who most coherently and forcefully presented the view that the desires of men, in competition with each other, in face of a shortage of resources, or of shared desires for the same thing, must lead to an intolerable and unfruitful existence in a state of perpetual fear of conflict or violent death. The only remedy for this condition was for all to accept over them an absolute sovereign to impose order on them so that all could live in peace and security. It is not necessary to accept the totality of the Hobbesian thesis to acknowledge that the existence of a community with a governmental structure provides means (not always, or always equitably, employed) for increasing the safety and security of the individual in relation to his fellows. But the actual historical process of evolution of groups or communities shows their emergence in terms of shared values; and the more closely the values of its members are assimilated to each other, the more clearly delineated a community becomes, and the more it is felt to differ from other communities. The development of social exchange within communities, and the rise and extension of political authority, normally act further to sharpen the boundaries between the community and others which then, as 'outgroups', tend to be conceived as alien and in some sense hostile. The community thus comes to be something that has to be defended against others, its survival guaranteed, its 'independence' assured. The security which communities exist to serve accordingly has two aspects, the security of the individual within the community, and the security of the community as a whole against others perceived as enemies. It is to the latter that most theorists of international relations mistakenly limit their attention.

The difficulty of giving identifiable content to the idea of the national interest is already exemplified in this discussion of the three most general purposes that communities exist to serve, for even these purposes evidently conflict with each other. The defence of the community against others may well require, or be thought to require, the incarceration of some individuals (and thus restrictions on their freedom of social intercourse), and even the execution of others (and thus denial to them of their security and safety); this implies, possibly erroneously, that an individual's interest must be held subordinate to that of the community.[6] As between the two purposes of maximizing wealth and maximizing security, however, the difficulty of determining where the national interest lies is more obvious and even more intractable: the complexity of the variables involved in decisions about defence requirements makes it exceedingly difficult to prepare reasonably reliable estimates of the defence capability that will result from a given expenditure, and in these circumstances the value judgment whether defence has a stronger claim than welfare on the community's economic resources may lack even the factual data to which the judgment has to be related. (In some conditions of course the two may not conflict at all but may complement each other.)

Despite the likelihood that pursuit of one of these purposes may lessen the extent to which another may be achieved, it is none the less widely recognized that without a community none can be realized at all. The preservation of a community is therefore thought to be a prime goal which must form part of the national interest. In addition, however, the national interest is frequently taken to include the preservation or promotion of the values which are specific to particular communities. These values, which are widely variant, derive from past interaction of geographical, economic, demographic, racial and sociopolitical influences. The communities called western democracies, drawing on Greek, Judaic, and Christian philosophy and ethics, conceive the individual human to have inalienable rights and an innate unique value, and have developed political institutions and procedures, and social processes, which are intended to maintain these rights and values. In particular it would be generally held in such communities that the members should themselves have the power of determining the size and structure of the community, and the nature and broad composition of the government set over it. The national interest of such a community, as for instance the United States, would be almost universally thought to include the defence of this power of the citizens against any who would threaten it, internally or externally. The belief may be taken further. Some Americans (of whom Woodrow Wilson seems to have been one) have conceived man to be naturally virtuous, so that happenings deemed to be evil, such as war, would not occur if states were controlled by the people; both because if they had self-determination and so decided the

---

[6] I do not wish to rehearse familiar arguments on this hoary topic of political philosophy. The aspect of the question that is relevant to the subject of this chapter is dealt with on pp. 45-7 below.

boundaries of the state in which they should live they would be content, and because if they chose their own government they would reject irresponsible or aggressive or warlike leadership. Since wars carried dangers for all, the promotion of self-determination and democracy was in the national interest of the United States, quite apart from being good for the peoples to whom the principle was to be applied.

National interest may therefore be conceived as requiring not merely the defence of the community's ability to maintain its values internally, but also their promotion externally. The Soviet Union has in the past offered (and perhaps still does offer) the best example of such a view of national interest. Soviet values and beliefs are Marxist. Conflict is the dynamic of all development. In human society conflict occurs between classes, which are groups defined according to their relationship to ownership of the means of production. Human history is the record of the quantitative accumulation of conflicts between two classes to the point where a qualitative leap occurs by the revolutionary overthrow of the previously dominant class by the previously subjected one. The victor in its turn becomes faced by a new class opponent. This historical evolution is inevitable. It is moral to act in accordance with, and promote the advance of, the inevitable course of history.

This class conflict is projected on to the international scene so that, as between modern industrialized societies of the twentieth century, states which serve the interests of the capitalist class which owns the means of production (for example, the United States) are bound to come into conflict (assumed until 1956 to mean inevitable war) with states which serve the interests of the proletariat which has no share in ownership of the means of production (for example, the Soviet Union). Soviet national interest therefore required action in all modernized countries to encourage socialist revolution (i.e. overthrow of the capitalists by the proletariats), both because according to Soviet values this was the morally correct way to behave, and because there could be no lasting security for the Soviet Union, and certainly no freedom from war, until at least a major part of the modernized world ceased to be controlled by capitalists.

Values may require external action in a still more direct way. To many of the Italian Fascists, as to the German historian Treitschke, the greatest human virtues could find expression only in war. To the Nazis the history of man was the history of conflict between superior and inferior races. All progress had come from the Aryan race, of which the Teutons were the highest form, and Germany's and the world's destiny could accordingly be fulfilled only through a Teutonic mastery of mankind, and so through world conquest. Each of these sets of values required for their satisfaction the exercise of military violence against other states or peoples.

Goals conceived in terms of promotion of values externally may however be thought to be in some circumstances irrational. When international relationships are of such a kind that the values of different communities have a degree of homogeneity, and the values of none require action with unlimited aims, then conducting policy in accordance with the national interest conceived in terms of values may make sense. An example of such relationships is perhaps western Europe in the eighteenth century. But the more heterogeneous and unlimited in aim values are, the more costly is pursuit of policy in terms of the national interest as defined likely to become. Communities will resist the imposition of alien values, and the more insistently values require external promotion the more certain it is that war will result.

Before the twentieth century it was still possible to judge that armed conflict would produce greater gains (if only in the sense of suffering smaller losses) than could be achieved without it. In these circumstances war could be in the national interest. But in a set of international relationships such as those since 1945, where actors have or are acquiring the technical ability totally to destroy themselves, pursuit of policies carrying substantial risks of major armed conflict becomes of questionable rationality. The national interest cannot be served by self-destruction. Since self-extending heterogeneous values of unlimited range must almost certainly lead to major armed conflict, national interests must require their limitation. National interest cannot therefore always in all circumstances be identified with the values of the community; and when to this is added disagreement about the basic general purposes for which humans exist (as for instance that between the Hindu and the liberal democrat referred to above) the difficulty of giving any generally applicable empirical content to the notion of the national interest becomes apparent.

No attempt has yet been made to define the community whose interest it is intended to serve. It is normally assumed that the community in question is that represented by the state, on the grounds (not always made explicit) that it is within this community that social intercourse most effectively flourishes, that it is within the state that economic affairs are mainly organized, that it is the state that offers protection and security to the individual and to the way of life that he cherishes, that it is for all these reasons to the state that primary loyalty is accorded, and finally that it is the state (or its government) that is the main actor on the international stage. Making the grounds of the assumption explicit perhaps helps to bring into question the assumption itself.

If it were the case that there were to be a substantial widening of human experience, knowledge, understanding and wisdom from an extension of social intercourse between the peoples of two states, but that such an extension would undermine the cohesiveness upon which the existence of one of the states depended, would it be in the national interest to prevent such an extension of intercourse (as the Soviet government has hitherto tended to maintain), or would it not rather be the state (or its particular form) that was an obstacle to the national interest? If a major advance in scientific knowledge, or a wiser application of it, were attainable by an intermingling of scientists of two states, but the sharing of 'secrets' would reduce the ability of each to defend itself, would it be in the national interest to ban the intermingling, or would it be that the states were obstacles to the respective national interests?

The answers to these questions depend on the referent to which the national interest is taken to be linked. If the purposes of political organization are to meet the requirements of individuals (which must include, on most western philosophical assumptions, the existence of organized communities), states exist not as ends in themselves, but as means for facilitating or promoting the ends of their citizens. If these ends can best be served by the state as it exists, then the national interest requires that it should stay so. If the defence, security and survival of the individuals within the state can best be assured by the state, then it is in the national interest that the state should exist, but it exists for the defence of them and not of itself for its own sake. There is here a point of major theoretical and practical importance. Micro-international relations, which tends to concentrate on the behaviour of states, encourages the implicit assumption that the survival of the state is primary. Many of the theorists of foreign policy as the pursuit of the national interest state this explicitly; in the words of Hans J. Morgenthau: 'The survival of a political unit ... in its identity is the irreducible minimum, the necessary element of its interests vis-à-vis other units ... its content ... encompasses the integrity of the nation's territory, of its political institutions, and of its culture.'[7] In practical terms, as a description of the way decision-makers normally act, this is correct: statesmen normally assume that the survival of the state over which they preside is the supreme national interest. It is not so. If attempts to preserve the

[7] H. J. Morgenthau, 'The national interest of the United States', quoted in W. C. Olson and F. A. Sondermann, *The Theory and Practice of International Relations* (Prentice-Hall, 2nd edn, 1966), p. 244. Morgenthau uses the words state, nation, and nation-state interchangeably.

state lead to the destruction of its people, then these attempts could not be in the national interest. In the age of thermonuclear weapons this is evidently not an unreasonable hypothesis.[8] But though the argument is strengthened by the existence of these weapons, it does not depend wholly on them: in March 1939, for example, when Hitler delivered his ultimatum to President Hacha of Czecho-Slovakia, if he had in fact had the air strength to overwhelm the Czech air force, destroy Prague and kill the great majority of the Czech people (which he had not), and also had the will to do it in the then-existing international situation (which he probably had), it could hardly have been in the Czech national interest to have refused to submerge the Czech state in the Nazi empire. Submergence of the state would have retained the possibility of the survival of something. Refusal would have left no chance for the survival of anything.

The almost universally accepted purpose of maximizing wealth might also require the death of the state. It may be that the standard of living of the British people can continue to rise only if Britain gains entry to the European Economic Community, but that if she remains outside it, the standard of living will remain stationary or will decline. If this were so, and if entry into the Community would eventually involve the disappearance of the British state (and this could well be the case), then probably here also the national interest would be served by the demise of the British state. Probably, not certainly: the answer in practice would depend on an assessment, first of the effect of such an entry and such a demise on other values and goals and their importance relative to wealth maximization, and secondly of whether other values and goals in addition to wealth maximization might be adversely affected by a failure to gain entry. If Britain became part of a continental political system, for example, the behaviour and modes of operation of the British police might well become more distasteful; but if Britain's remaining out of the Community brought eventually a substantial lowering of the standard of living, this too could make untenable the methods of the British police because of the breakdown of the social mores of tolerance and moderation which have made these methods hitherto practicable. In practical terms the two questions again arise of choice among ends, and choice of courses to achieve ends.

The theoretical point that must be clearly recognized, however, is that the 'national interest' which is at stake is that of people, not of the

---

[8] This statement of course makes no judgment about the slogan, 'Better red than dead': it says nothing about what the empirical conditions might be in which attempts to preserve the state might in fact mean the destruction of its people.

state, which is an abstraction. Service of the ends and values of people may require the submergence of the state. The state is not a person. It has no innate moral attributes. It has no honour. It has no inherent right to survive.

There remain two observations to be made. In the first place, although in theoretical terms it is necessary to recognize that the national interest *may* require the destruction of the state, in the world of the 1970s it remains the case that the general ends and values which people desire to be served will probably in fact still best be served through the state's machinery and by its survival and action. In the second place, the destruction of the state, should the national interest require it, would eventually have consequences for the values of the community within it. It could be that these consequences might be so far reaching that the values by which the community was distinguished became merged in other values through a process of mutual influence and interaction. The community would then itself have become absorbed in a larger one. This is to say that not merely the state, but the community within it (which may be a nation) is of value only so long as it serves individual purposes. Clearly it is probably true that some losses would be suffered if the community were merged with another: the argument is that the national interest would still be served if these losses were less than those that would be suffered if the community were not merged. In the Czech case instanced above the question would be whether it was better that all Czechs should die, or that some proportion of Czech individuals should survive even though everything that made them and their descendants 'Czech' would eventually be obliterated. In practical terms the choice, as so often in politics, would be between two courses of action, each of which would produce undesired consequences. In theoretical terms, the logical conclusion of this argument is that the national interest is to be taken to refer, not to the values of the state (which has none), nor to the values of the community, but to the values of individuals within communities. Normally preservation and advancement of these values will best be served by the survival of the state. Even greater is the likelihood that they will be served by the survival of the nation or other communities within the state. But conceivably their service may require the merging both of state and nation into other entities, so that ultimately national interest relates to individual values.

The philosophical problem of whether there can exist a 'real interest' of a community (given that the individual members of it have conflicting values and aspirations) is thus generalized on to a world scale. Though the major actors on the international stage are states, their actions ought to serve the purposes of individuals, and individuals exist in a variety of groups, including the global group. The Platonic and Hobbesian problems reappear at the world level. It could conceivably be or become the case that threats to individual survival in the global community could become so acute that a global political authority with a monopoly of force had to be established. There is probably a greater likelihood that it is or may become the case that individual security should require, if not the full starkness of a Hobbesian solution, at least a substantial transformation of the near-anarchy that at present characterizes international relations. Similarly the maximization of wealth might require some kind of global political community for the most effective organization of the processes of production and exchange. Finally the full richness of social intercourse may now perhaps only be realizable within the framework of a global community. All the problems of conflict of aspirations among individuals and among groups thus reappear at the global level; but the 'real interest' in accordance with which policy ought to be conducted should take into cognizance the interest of individuals not merely as members of groups within society, or of nations or of states, but as members of the global community also. Our omniscient observer, that is to say, would have to judge whether real interest would be served if states and communities remained as they were, or whether they should be changed, and in what ways.

The concept of the national interest is therefore an unfortunate and on the whole an unhelpful one. It is normally attached to the notion of the state and so sanctifies state goals. It directs attention to a particular human group as that into which humans ought to be organized and the preservation and advancement of which accordingly ought to be the criteria for judgment of action. But if individuals are the proper referent, a distinction needs to be drawn between strictly state goals and the goals that national interest prescribes. In this case foreign policy would be defined as the range of actions taken by varying sections of the government of a state in its relations with other bodies similarly acting on the international stage, properly with the intention of advancing the continuing purposes of the individuals represented by it. Normally these purposes would require preservation and advancement of the state, but they *might* require action leading towards the weakening, submergence or abolition of the state itself, or even of the particular values of the community within it.

The conclusion of this argument appears to be that the concept does not effectively encapsulate state goals and encourages the begging of a crucial question. But if attention is for the moment being concentrated on micro-international relations (a concentration which begs the same question), some normative concept is required if state goals are to be seen in a broad and long-term, rather than limited and short-term perspective. This is desirable both for decision-makers and for observers. It may be that the term national interest is now so universally used that there is little point in trying to eliminate it from the vocabulary of international relations. But if the student continues to use it, he should be aware of its conceptual weaknesses, of the impossibility of applying it to real-life situations, and of the inappropriate slant that it gives to his thinking. Moreover, even if a 'real interest' is conceivable, and should exist, no practical decision-maker in an actual situation, and no observer of that situation afterwards, could have the totality of knowledge necessary correctly to identify it. This does not of course mean that action may not chance to be 'right' (if there exists in the situation a right action to be taken), merely that action cannot be known to be right, either at the time or afterwards.

Using the national interest to represent state goals requires therefore that state goals may include the goal of merging or accepting the destruction of the state. If that is admitted then the idea of the national interest as the guide to policy may be not without value with its connotation of the general and the long-term, and in relation to classes or categories of actions.[9] The decision-maker may not be able to tell whether an agreement by which he grants a 5 per cent reduction on the tariff on butter for a 3 per cent reduction in another state's tariff on margarine is or is not in accord with the real interest of the community; but in his approach to the general question of trade relations he should remember that the economic welfare of his people should be one of his main concerns. He may not be able to judge to what extent particular actions should be influenced by his desire to maintain himself in power, but it may be possible to identify general situations in which such action would be in greater or less degree justified: in view of the declared goals of the Nazis, for example, Brüning in Germany in 1932 could properly have selected a greater range of action, internal and external, designed to keep himself in power than might, for example, Baldwin in Britain in 1923. The concept of categories of action may also help in the identification and selection of objectives, though it will usually not be of much assistance in trying to determine priorities among them.

In sum therefore, goals are normally seen as including state survival, wealth maximization, and preservation and promotion of values. The national interest is intended to be a concept summing up goals, but the first and third of these goals may occasionally be incompatible with

---

[9] I am indebted for this idea to Dr Margaret Leslie, who made the point during a seminar discussion of the subject.

it, and the second may be incompatible with the other two. In essence
it should relate to the real interest of people, and this interest is not to
be seen as being necessarily contained within the state context. This
notion of a 'real interest' is difficult to conceive, but there may be value
in a concept which draws attention away from immediately pressing
urgent problems and causes them to be viewed in the light of the long-
term and the general. But even if it can be seen as a theoretical norm,
it cannot in practice be identified, and will not serve as a means of
judging particular decisions or particular actions. State decision-makers
who claim to be acting in the national interest misuse the notion, cannot have the perfect information necessary to validate their claims, and
so are pulling the wool over other people's eyes, and possibly over their
own.

4

Influences on foreign policy-making
I. The domestic environment

FOREIGN POLICY CONSISTS OF the external actions taken by decision-makers with the intention of achieving long-range goals and short-term objectives. Action is constrained by the perceived circumstances of the state on behalf of which the decision-makers are acting—its geography, its economy, its demography, its political structure, culture and tradition, its military-strategic situation. This I propose to call the domestic environment of decision-makers. But action is taken with reference to other bodies similarly acting on the international stage, and is likewise constrained by their action. This may be called the international environment of decision-makers. Elements within environments interact with each other, and interaction takes place between environments as well. Various means are available to policy-makers in their endeavours to achieve goals. Within the constraints of the decision-makers' domestic and international environments, who the decision-makers are in particular questions will much affect the selection made among the means available. The choices will also be affected by the procedures and processes through which selections are made. These matters will be dealt with in this and the three following chapters.

The logically primary influence on foreign policy lies in the goals that policy seeks to achieve. These as we have seen are normally security (usually in practice taken to mean security of the state), welfare, and preservation or promotion of values. The search for security is perennial. All foreign policies of all states are basically influenced by it. For three centuries and more, for example, French decision-makers sought to establish France's eastern and north-eastern frontier on the Rhine. That France had natural frontiers formed by the English Channel to the north, the Atlantic to the west, the Pyrenees, the Mediterranean, and the Alps to the south, and the Rhine to the east, was no new conception of the kings of the newly united France that emerged from the Middle Ages: in Roman times Tacitus and Strabo had seen the Rhine as the natural limit of Romanized Gallic influence. Between the northern reaches of the Rhine and Paris was no easily defensible natural feature, and so France's security was thought to require the attainment of the Rhine as a frontier. The theme is fundamental in the wars and schemes of Louis XIV, it forms part of the policies of Napoleon, Louis Philippe, and Napoleon III, and it reappears in muted form in 1919 and in 1945 after the two world wars. The search for security is primary.[1]

For some states, such as Switzerland, for example, security consists solely in defence of the metropolitan territory. For others security includes the defence of interests outside the metropolitan territory thought to be vital to its existence or to the welfare of its people. Before 1939 the maintenance of a system of imperial communications was taken by British decision-makers to be vital to Britain (I am making no judgment about whether their view was right or wrong). From this it followed that a navy of a certain size and composition had to be maintained, and this had profound consequences for Britain's relations with the United States, Japan, France, Italy and Germany.[2] It also meant that Britain needed bases and coaling stations round the world and these had to be located in territories that were securely controlled by Britain, whether as colonies (Malta, Gibraltar, Aden, Simonstown—in a former colony—Trincomalee, Singapore, Hong Kong), or in a sphere of influence (Suez). The colonies were necessary, in part, so that the bases should be secure:

[1] I have used the term 'natural frontier'. To the geographer there is no such thing. A geographical feature is not 'naturally' anything. It becomes significant in human terms only as a result of the activity of human beings in relation to it. Rivers, mountain ranges or seas can act equally as barriers or as uniting influences. Before 1492 the Atlantic was a barrier so formidable that nobody (or almost nobody) had hitherto crossed it: now the ocean is seen by some as the focus of an Atlantic Community. Before 1945 the river Oder was a main artery of east Germany on which much of the life of the people of that part of Germany centred: now it is a barrier between Germany and Poland in a psychological as well as a physical sense. But if for a geographer no such thing as a natural frontier exists, for the student of international relations it exists in so far as decision-makers think it does. Because French decision-makers fought to extend French authority to the Rhine, seeing it as France's natural frontier, so in international relations terms it was so. See Chapter 7, pp. 172-3 below.

[2] See S. Roskill, Naval Policy Between the Wars (Collins, 1968), passim, but particularly pp. 83-4.

the bases were necessary, in part, to safeguard communications to the colonies. Of course there were other reasons for both, but the security argument was self-sustaining.

The basic goal of maximizing welfare may also act as a major influence on policies. No state is now autarkic, or self-sufficient, at least in the only sense that is politically relevant. Self-sufficiency is meaningless except in relation to the aspirations of the inhabitants of a state or region. Every state can be economically self-sufficient in the sense that the territory in question could support some number of people at some standard of living, even if only the most primitive. But a state could be regarded as being self-sufficient in a political sense only if it could from its own resources provide for all the needs and desires of its people—which would include, for example, the demand on resources made by the people's desire for security. Since no people ever feels entirely secure, since aspirations and expectations mount with opportunities and means of fulfilling them (expenditure rises to exceed income, as any housewife knows), and since no state has unlimited supplies of all materials and resources, no state is self-sufficient in politically meaningful terms. Some are, of course, more nearly so than others. But to the extent that deficiencies are felt to exist, whether of materials, or food, or markets, or capital, or technical skills, foreign policies will endeavour to supply them. Shortage of the last two is a characteristic of underdeveloped or developing countries, and agreements designed to rectify these shortages may well act as limits on their governments' freedom of manoeuvre. Shortage of the former three is more characteristic of modernized countries, and policies seeking to rectify them may take the form of trading agreements, of colonization, or of conquest and annexation. In either case the desire to maximize wealth is a major influence on policy-making.

Thirdly among basic goals is the desire to preserve or promote values. Examples were given in the last chapter of values that required external activity for their satisfaction: these included the values of the Bolsheviks, the Nazis, the Fascists, and the Wilsonian apostles of self-determination.[3] Anticolonialism and nationalism are two other frequently related sets of values that seek to bring about external change. The values of some states, however, may encourage decision-makers to endeavour to preserve things as they are; and values may have much effect on the methods by which change or no change is sought—by negotiation, by 'peaceful' pressures, by subversion, or by open military action.

The foregoing suggests one main way in which foreign policies may be classified. Policies may be revisionist, in the sense that the decision-

[3] See pp. 42-4 above.

makers aim to bring about change in the relationships among the actors on the international stage, or change in the actors themselves; or they may be antirevisionist, in the sense that decision-makers are essentially satisfied both with the number and nature of the actors, and with their mutual relations. Of course it is the case that no set of international relationships is ever static, so the exact *status quo* can never be preserved, and few statesmen attempt this (it has been one of the most frequently made accusations against Metternich in the period after 1815 that he attempted precisely this, and the attempt could not succeed). It is also the case that most decision-makers will try to make limited changes when they perceive the possibility of deriving some advantage in doing so. But there is a distinction worth making between the policies on the one hand say of Louis XV and Louis XVI of France, who were willing to make only such advances as might be possible within the limits of their assumption that the system as a whole should be preserved; and the policies on the other hand of Danton and Robespierre, of the Directory, and of Napoleon, who desired totally to transform the condition of Europe. Are the current policies of the United States or of the Soviet Union essentially revisionist or antirevisionist? The question in this form evidently opens up important and fruitful lines of enquiry, the answers to which may not be so obvious as initially they may seem.

Two further general comments should be made about goals as influences on foreign policies. In the first place, foreign policies may be adopted for purposes other than those to which they are ostensibly or immediately directed. The use of foreign policy to strengthen the internal political position of particular leaders is well enough known; from major attempts, like that of Sukarno to divert attention from the acute internal economic and social problems of Indonesia by his 'confrontation' with Malaysia, to minor excursions, like those of Harold Macmillan seeking by trips to Moscow to build himself up as the indispensable international statesman. But equally, foreign policies may be adopted in part for other rather more fundamental purposes: one of the arguments adduced by protagonists of Britain's entry into the European Economic Community is that only the shock of competition which would thereby result can shake the British people out of their 'I'm all right, Jack' philosophy, their restrictive practices, their apathy, their desire to take the maximum and give the minimum, their envy—their general social malaise, in other words, which if not cured will lead to the end of the way of life that most' Britishers prize. Whether or not the diagnosis and the prescription are accurate is again not my concern here: I quote this as an example of a foreign policy being advocated for ends other than those to which it seems immediately to be directed.

From this follows the second general point that should be borne in mind, the distinction between short-term objectives and long-term goals. In an ideal world all decisions in relation to short-term objectives should be consistent with each other and with long-term goals. Frequently in the real world neither of these desiderata can be satisfied. Short-term objectives are very often mutually incompatible, and in relation to incompatible objectives it will be very difficult, if not impossible, to maintain a consistent pattern of decisions. But even if such a pattern were, improbably, maintained, the compatibility of the pattern with long-term goals is even less likely; partly because immediate pressures are usually such that the long-term can hardly be thought about at all, and partly because the effect of decisions can never be precisely calculated, and in the long term their effect will be modified both by the actions of others and by subsequent action by the decision-makers of the state in question. It should never be assumed therefore that a decision in relation to a short-term objective is organically related to a long-term goal : usually it will not be, often it cannot be, and sometimes it will directly prejudice the achievement of the long-term goal. The appeasement policies of successive British governments from 1931 onwards achieved successive short-term objectives of settling issues without Britain being involved in war, but only at the cost of eventual involvement in a far more prolonged and damaging war than it otherwise would have been, with profound adverse effects on Britain's international position, economy, and internal social cohesion. Long-term goals were prejudiced, probably irremediably, by decisions in relation to short-term objectives; and a majority of the British people, and a substantial proportion of the informed elite, at the time thought the decisions were right and wise.

Policy is thus a process. A major constraint on decisions at any one time is decisions that have been taken previously.[4] The taking of an initial decision may carry with it the taking of many subsequent decisions if the purpose of the original policy is not to be abandoned (and that may not remain possible). Roosevelt in 1939 thought it not in the interest of the United States that Britain and France should be defeated by Germany. He therefore persuaded Congress in November 1939 to revise the Neutrality Act so that Americans could sell arms to Britain and France provided that they were paid for before they were shipped, and

---

[4] President John Kennedy's first act on the morning of the first of the seven days in 1962 before his public announcement of the placing of Soviet missiles in Cuba, was to send for copies of all his earlier public statements on Cuba (see T. C. Sorensen, *Decision-making in the White House*, Columbia University Press paperback, 1964, p. 34).

were carried in British or French ships. In September 1940, recognizing that Britain's shortage of destroyers in face of German submarine power was resulting in excessive losses of American supplies destined to arm Britain in Washington's defence, Roosevelt agreed to the transfer of fifty overage destroyers, receiving in return leases of bases in British territories in the Caribbean. By November 1940 Britain was on the brink of bankruptcy as far as foreign exchange was concerned, so in order that Britain could continue to acquire arms, and so not be defeated, Roosevelt persuaded Congress to pass the Lend-Lease Act by which Britain was able to get the arms without paying dollars. Increased shipping losses in the summer of 1941 led to convoying by United States vessels into the Atlantic, German retaliation, the arming of United States merchant vessels, and finally the order to shoot at German submarines on sight. The United States was thus virtually in the war two months before Pearl Harbour and the German and Italian war declarations: each of these decisions producing in the end effective though not formal belligerency flowed relentlessly from the November 1939 revision of the Neutrality Act if the policy which motivated that decision was not to be abandoned.[5]

The effect of past decisions, and of the reactions of others to them, is to set limits to possible policies which can be exceeded only at the cost of abandonment of policies previously thought wise, and on which considerable resources may have been expended. United States involvement in Vietnam offers a clear illustration. This suggests a classification of influences upon policy into those that primarily set limits to possible policies, and those that act primarily to stimulate the adoption of policies. Previous policy decisions are among the most important influences in the former category, which includes most of the geographical, economic, demographic and strategic elements of a state's situation.

[5] The logic was clearly put in a 'Joint Board Estimate of United States Over-all Production Requirements' dated 11 September 1941: '... United Kingdom ... defence depends on the safety of sea communications. The sea communications can continue to support the United Kingdom only if the damage now being inflicted upon them is greatly reduced through increases in the strength of the protective sea and air forces based in the British Isles, Iceland, and positions in the central and eastern Atlantic. Unless the losses of British merchant ships are greatly reduced ... it is the opinion of the Joint Board that the resistance of the United Kingdom can not continue indefinitely, no matter what industrial effort is put forth by the United States. Therefore, the immediate and strong reinforcement of British forces in the Atlantic by United States naval and air contingents, supplemented by a large additional shipping tonnage, will be required if the United Kingdom is to remain in the war. These contingents must be manned by Americans, since the reserves of British manpower for employment in Europe are practically exhausted.' Quoted in Robert E. Sherwood, *The White House Papers of Harry L. Hopkins* (Eyre & Spottiswoode, 1948), p. 420.

Goals, values and ideologies are likely to operate mainly as stimuli to the adoption of particular policies. The categories are not exclusive, for each of the influences may in different circumstances operate in either sense; but again the distinction is analytically useful in that it poses a general question which it is helpful to ask.

Among primarily limiting influences on policy, geography has long been recognized as being of major importance. Some geographers have indeed adopted a near-determinist position which has seen all human activity as being inexorably conditioned by the geographical circumstances of human existence.[6] More modern geographers and political scientists maintain that geography of itself can have no influence: it allows or impedes activity, but it can have no influence on human behaviour independent of human decisions to exploit or not to exploit its possibilities.[7] This is not to deny that impediments offered by geography have frequently been perceived by humans as being so severe as to make not worth attempting the efforts that would be required to overcome them. Thus, in the most general terms, the latitudes of extreme climates, whether polar or tropical, erect fearsome obstacles to human existence and activity, and since the land masses of the Southern Hemisphere (Africa, South America, Australia, Antarctica) are mainly tropical or polar, and much of the rest desert, the major population of the world has hitherto been concentrated mainly in the Northern Hemisphere. This has accordingly been the major hemisphere for world politics. It is significant that the Arctic polar region, where the Soviet Union and Alaska are in close proximity, has become of major strategic importance, while the Antarctic polar region is so far removed from the main areas of world conflict that it was the subject in December 1959 for one of the rare international agreements for cooperative activity which have been signed both by the United States and by the Soviet Union.

True as it may be that geographic elements of man's environment are significant only to the extent that he perceives them to be so, and reacts accordingly, none the less it is the case that these geographic elements have in the past been perceived as being among the most

[6] See, for example, E. C. Semple, *Influences of Geographic Environment* (Holt, 1911), and especially Ellsworth Huntington, *Civilization and Climate* (Yale University Press, 1915) and *World Power and Evolution* (Yale University Press, 1919).
[7] For a thorough discussion of these arguments see H. and M. Sprout, *The Ecological Perspective on Human Affairs* (Princeton University Press, 1965).

important factors in foreign policy making. Decision-makers see the state on whose behalf they act as being of a certain size, situated in a certain location, characterized by a certain topography and terrain, enjoying a certain climate, and possessed of certain natural resources. Each of these affects foreign policy.

A good big 'un will always beat a good little 'un. Whether large size is an asset or a liability as far as foreign policy is concerned will depend upon the use made by the inhabitants of the facilities size offers. The Soviet successor to the Tsarist empire is the largest state in the world, covering one-sixth of the land surface of the globe. Because of its size it has land frontiers with Norway, Finland, Poland, Czechoslovakia, Romania, Turkey, Iran, Afghanistan, China and Mongolia, and it is in close maritime proximity to Sweden, Germany, Bulgaria, Japan and the United States (Alaska). Widely dispersed interests are normally a source of weakness in relation to a given level of resources. Britain in 1939 was simply unable effectively to defend her important interests in the Far East against Japan because of the threats that were being presented to her in Europe by Germany. The Russian Tsars had endeavoured to deal with the problem of dispersed interests by concentrating first in one area, and then if checked switching to another. Thus the policy of pressure westwards towards the Black Sea was checked by defeat in the Crimean War in the 1850s, was followed by the building of the trans-Siberian railway and pressure eastwards until checked by defeat by Japan in 1904-05, and this in turn led to new pressure in the Balkans and revived conflict with Austria-Hungary, which was one of the main causes of the first world war. Similar tactics have not been wholly absent from Soviet foreign policy since 1917, and the continuing importance of dispersed interests resulting from great size is illustrated by the fact that Stalin's first concern in discussing a non-aggression pact with Germany in August 1939 was whether such a pact might lead to a reduction in the hostility of Japan to the Soviet Union.[8]

Size has fundamental implications for strategy. The Soviet Union has an enormously long perimeter to defend; and even though much of this has in the past been virtually unassailable because of the Arctic wastes in the north and the deserts and mountains in the south, none the less the strategic problems are formidable. The concentration of forces necessary for offensive action could be achieved only at the risk of denuding other areas, and the enormous distances and poor communications intensified the dangers by making swift transfer of forces exceedingly difficult. Only the huge Russian manpower in part compensated for these difficulties.

[8] See *Documents on German Foreign Policy*, ser. D. vii (HMSO, 1956), p. 225.

But size can also be a source of great strength strategically, particularly in the nuclear age. Should the Japanese think to develop a nuclear deterrent it would have only limited credibility, because the small habitable area of Japan and the heavy concentrations of population into very few vital regions, mean that Japan is highly vulnerable to thermonuclear attack. For Japan to threaten to use thermonuclear weapons against any adversary with a second-strike capability[9] is barely credible, since the retaliation would cause the destruction of Japanese society and the death of the great majority of the Japanese people. The Soviet Union, on the other hand, is able to disperse its industry and so its population over the vast spaces of its territory and thus could be destroyed in the same sense only by a very much greater offensive effort. This advantage of size in modern strategic circumstances parallels the advantage that Russia traditionally exploited, of withdrawing forces deep into the Russian interior and so extending the enemy's lines of communication and placing them in a hostile human and climatic environment. Napoleon and Hitler alike learned the effectiveness of this strategy.

Large resources are important if the population has the capacity and the will to exploit them, and a large country is more likely to have these. Even though there may be instances where this is not the case, as for example Greenland, the converse is true, that a small country can have only limited resources. A large country is likely to be able to support a larger population than a small country. Finally size creates political problems: until the development of modern means of communication and transport (and even still to some extent), size created problems of political organization and control which had consequences both for political structures, and for the effectiveness of political decision-making. Again the Tsarist empire, and to a lesser extent the Soviet Union, offers the best illustration.

This discussion of the first aspect of the first element of decision-makers' domestic environments clearly illustrates a general point which is relevant to all elements of that environment. Although for the purposes of study and analysis it is desirable to isolate and to examine individually each of the influences on foreign policy-making, none in practice operates in isolation from any other. All interact. Thus it was not possible to talk about size except in relation generally to human activity, and specifically to diplomatic expedients, strategic planning, technological development, exploitable and exploited resources, population numbers and skills, and political structures and processes. The

[9] That is, with the ability still to launch a major retaliation even after receiving a major thermonuclear assault.

discussion of each of these in turn will draw on many of the others; and it must always be borne in mind by the student, as by the statesman, that all influences on policy are interrelated, and the omission or gross misunderstanding of any may make analysis or action wholly misconceived, even though all other influences were accurately assessed and taken into account. Examples of this are difficult to suggest, because it will usually be the case that inaccurate assessment, or omission, of more than one influence will cause an action not to have the effect intended; but a possible example is Hitler's persuasion of the Yugoslav government to accede to the Tripartite Pact in March 1941, which would have been likely to have achieved all the purposes he then had in mind, had it not been for a group of Serb leaders who were no longer prepared to tolerate the dictatorship of Prince Paul and his government, and who had already in train the *coup d'état* of 27 March which overthrew Paul and which was taken as an annulment of the Tripartite Pact signature. This one insufficiently appreciated internal element in Yugoslavia caused Hitler's plans to be drastically revised, possibly with critical effect on the whole course of the second world war; for the attack on Yugoslavia which Hitler then thought necessary caused a delay of six weeks in the invasion of the Soviet Union, and so enabled winter to overtake the Nazis just before they reached Moscow.

Foreign policies are, secondly, much affected by the ways decision-makers conceive their states to be located. To the first leaders of the United States at the end of the eighteenth century and the beginning of the nineteenth, a major fact of existence appeared to be the great expanse of the Atlantic Ocean to the east, the great expanse of the Pacific Ocean to the west, the small and quarrelling Spanish colonies to the south, and the sparsely populated British colony of Canada to the north, itself protected by Arctic ice. Once the war of 1812 had been fought, and the Spanish colonies had been helped to independence by the doctrine of Monroe and the support of Canning, the United States seemed to exist in such a condition of isolation that virtually no foreign policy was necessary. In fact this isolation was possible only because vast resources lay ready to be exploited in the North American continent (which British capital assisted the Americans to develop), and because the British navy gave to the Monroe Doctrine its effective backing, which United States forces alone could not have given. But under this shield, and with these riches to hand, the location of the United States appeared so enduring and so obvious in its advantages that it took two world wars, the decline of British power, the rise of the Soviet Union, and the technological revolution which made possible flight over the polar ice-cap and submarine navigation under it before the people of the

United States realized that they were not divinely cut off from the rest of the world. Effects on foreign policy have been profound and lasting.

Similarly the foreign relations of the peoples inhabiting the area significantly called by westerners 'the Middle East'[10] have been critically affected by the way their location has entered into the calculations of statesmen. The Straits control a warm-water outlet for the peoples of Russia, whether for trade or for offensive naval marauding; Palestine, Mesopotamia and Persia formed a land route to and from the riches of the east; likewise Turkey, Syria and Palestine formed a land bridge from the north to Egypt and Africa; the Suez isthmus when cut by canal offered an even more convenient route to the east, soon conceived to be vital, for commercial or strategic purposes. So this area has been one of the storm centres of politics from the time of Alexander the Great intermittently until today. The foreign relations of Turkey have been in large part governed since the eighteenth century by the attempts of the Russians to gain control of the Straits, and the efforts of Britain and France (and lately the United States) to stop them. Egypt's foreign relations have been dominated by the endeavours of Britain and France, usually in rivalry but eventually in partnership, to control Suez from the time when the cutting of the Canal was started to the *débâcle* of 1956. And in the major jockeyings among the powers, whether Russia or France or Britain or the United States (with Italy occasionally trying to join in), influence or control over this area has seemed a major prize; so that in the conditions of stalemate that have developed in the past fifteen years, Egypt in particular has been able to derive much advantage from the unwillingness of either Washington or Moscow to allow the other to gain too firm a foothold in the area. The crowning folly of the Anglo-French assault on Suez in 1956 was perhaps precisely this, that Eden and Mollet failed to recognize that the Soviets could not tolerate so serious a shift in the balance as re-established western control over Suez would have brought, and the United States could not risk the consequences of such a provocation to the USSR.

Third among geographical elements that enter into foreign policy-making is topography and terrain. In almost all states the obstacles and

---

[10] The term 'the Middle East' is of course a geographical nonsense. It might not be totally absurd for an inhabitant of the eastern seaboard of the United States to call the area the middle east, for following the circle route eastwards it is about halfway to Japan, but it is not helpful to describe areas from one arbitrary standpoint only. The Indians call the area south-west Asia. This is geographically meaningful but it loses sight of the fact that the politically significant region includes Egypt, which is in Africa. Perhaps one should revive the term the Levant, and give it appropriate definition.

opportunities arising from topography have entered into the calculations of statesmen. The gentle shelving of the Italian coast towards sandy shores on the Adriatic littoral, offering few harbours, has been seen by Italian leaders as posing strategic threats of invasion from the sea which could be countered only by influence over the countries on the eastern side of the Adriatic, and particularly over the area around Valona in Albania commanding the narrowest point of entry to the Adriatic sea. Similarly, the Apennine mountain range, with its western spurs running down to the Tyrrhenian sea, has impeded communication and move-ment of the Italian peoples, and so has enabled strong local patriotism to persist, with notable political consequences. The fact that the state of Brandenburg, and later Prussia, had no evident geographical (or religious or ethnic or linguistic or cultural) limits meant that its survival was seen as being dependent on a powerful military establishment, and when Germany became unified under Prussian control in 1870-71, this had major consequences for the political and social structure and mores of the new German state, and hence for its foreign policy. Perhaps more fancifully, the limitless open spaces of the Russian steppe, the sense of isolation and loneliness which this encourages, have been found by some to have much to do with the Russian predilection for the infinite, his weak sense of form, and his Messianic consciousness, whether Greek Orthodox or Marxist.[11]

The most familiar and frequently quoted example of the importance of topography, however, is the insular character of Great Britain. From this many consequences have been seen to flow. As an island Britain until recently could not be attacked except across the sea. Adequate naval strength could therefore give Britain total security. Alfred the Great was the first to see this, but not until the Tudors and Cromwell was the policy developed fully. But having a navy naturally en-couraged maritime activity, and so the British began to explore over-seas, to develop trading links, and to establish bases and colonial outposts which gradually expanded into great empires. These empires brought wealth and power, but also created widely dispersed interests and led to conflict with many other states, both in Europe and in other parts of the world. But Britain's insular character and strategic security enabled her to stand aside from quarrels on the mainland of Europe, intervening only as necessary to serve her overseas imperial ends, or to prevent the establishment of a dominant position by one power on the mainland which might then be able to threaten the British metropolitan territory. Moreover the water divide between Britain and the mainland in some degree insulated her people from the movement both of ideas

[11] See for example N. Berdyaev, *The Russian Idea* (Bles, 1947), pp. 2-8.

and peoples on the mainland, and enabled her without interference to develop her own political and social structures, to become steadily more homogeneous in ethnic composition and in outlook, and so to conduct affairs with moderation, tolerance and pragmatism in the knowledge that disagreements were limited in their scope, and extremism was rare. Thus the major themes, and the character, of British foreign policy are derived from Britain's island condition.

The argument is clearly carried beyond the limits within which it can be sustained. It is reasonable to argue that a state with a seaboard has greater opportunities to develop overseas activity than a state which is landlocked: such activity has been a feature of the policies of France, Holland, Spain and Portugal in Europe, but not of Austria-Hungary, Prussia, or Switzerland. But none of the four first-named countries is an island, so the opportunity derives from the seaboard, not from insular character. And the case of Japan demonstrates that even being entirely surrounded by water does not mean that overseas activity is sure to be undertaken: for two and a half centuries after the establishment of the Tokugawa Shogunate at the beginning of the seventeenth century Japan had no contact of any kind with any people outside her territory, with the exception of one Dutch ship a year which was permitted to call. So to explain the development of empire and all that flowed therefrom as resulting from Britain's insular character is mistaken. All that can be accurately said is, first, that Britain's high degree of security, derived from the creation of naval power which enabled her statesmen to exploit her island status, gave her a freedom of manoeuvre in foreign policies enjoyed by few other states; and, secondly, to the extent that the Channel discouraged immigration and checked the flow of revolutionary ideas (though it did not altogether prevent either), to that extent the self-satisfaction, complacency, and unity of the British people may have been fortified, and these characteristics certainly were reflected in the customs and values of British society, and in the *style* of foreign policy.

Less can be said about climate, for (*pace* Ellsworth Huntington) it has less specifically identifiable relationships to foreign policy-making than the other geographical aspects of a state's situation. Its importance may perhaps be observed, other than in very general terms, only in association with other geographical features such as size and location. The continental character of the United States, for example, lying approximately between the thirtieth and fiftieth northern parallels of latitude (i.e. from Algeria and Libya to Germany and Poland) and extending over nearly sixty degrees of longitude, means that the climatic variations are wide from the north-western seaboard (with a north-European

temperate climate), to the Californian coast (with a sunny Mediter-
ranean-type climate), to the hot interior near-desert conditions of the
south-west, to the continental-type climate similar to parts of the Soviet
interior with 120 degrees (F) variations from winter to summer in north
central states such as Minnesota. Climatic variations make different
kinds of activity more possible and profitable, so typical occupations in
the United States are dairy-farming and industry in the east and parts
of the mid-west, merging into cereal-growing and thence cattle-raising
further west and south (with tobacco and cotton in the south-east),
reaching citrus fruits and tourism and industry again on the Pacific
coast. With different types of occupation go different patterns of social
structure and behaviour, and different economic interests. Climate thus
joins with size and location to encourage diversity of occupation, outlook, and interests; and since the United States political system is designed to reflect diversity and to give voice and weight to minority
interests and regional views, these characteristics have much effect on
United States foreign policies and sharply limit the freedom of manoeuvre of decision-makers in Washington.

Last among geographical aspects of the foreign policy context is
economic geography—the natural resources within the frontiers of the
state, and how they are disposed. Again it is clear that the relevance of
natural resources to foreign policy-making is conditional upon awareness that they are there, awareness of the use to which they can most
profitably be put and ability so to use them, and availability of means
(human, financial, or mechanical) to exploit them. Whether resources
are available is affected by their location: their value is dependent on
the cost of transportation to points of use or sale and on the cost and
feasibility of the effort needed to exploit them. The existence of oil in
the Sahara or iron in Labrador or gas in the North Sea has long been
known or suspected, but as means for serving the political purposes of
states these resources did not exist until methods had been devised for
tolerably sustaining life in the regions in question, and for economically extracting the materials. Chinese foreign policy will be able to work
within different limits when complete and accurate geological surveys
have determined what resources are located within China's frontiers,
and when human skills, capital, and technological means have been
developed to exploit them, and to improve the productivity of known
agricultural possibilities. Other things being equal, possession of extensive natural resources increases a state's freedom of manoeuvre, among
the more important resources being iron and other metals, coal, oil, gas
or hydroelectric power, and food. The high level of economic activity
which some states have now achieved, and to which all aspire, is more

attainable the more resources are under immediate control; and desire to remedy shortages by a variety of means (the most important being trade) is among the most fundamental influences on foreign policy.

This latter point suggests a second way in which economic geography is important in foreign policy-making. The attention of governments will be attracted towards areas in which large reserves of valuable materials are located, particularly, though not exclusively, when governments do not have adequate supplies of the materials within their own territories. The Levant—meaning by this term south-west Asia and Egypt [12]—has in recent years been a focus of international activity not only because of its historic locational importance but also because it contains the largest known world reserves of oil. The absence of oil resources in Britain and France had much to do with the Anglo-French attack on Suez in 1956, both because Nasser's Arab nationalism was thought to threaten the security of oil deliveries, and because guaranteed passage of oil tankers through the Canal was thought to be vital. But the Soviet Union and the United States have also deeply concerned themselves with this area on account of its oil; not because they themselves lack oil resources, but mainly in order to deny the accretion of strength to its rival which would follow a mastery of these resources by the other. Each has in addition desired to draw upon these resources in order to conserve their own, but the determination to deny control to the other has been a primary motive for action. One reason for the tenacity of both in the struggle over Germany has likewise stemmed from determination to deny to the other the enormous acquisition of strength that control of the whole of Germany would bring—though here the assets are less natural resources than developed industrial strength and skilled manpower.

Each of these aspects of geography is thus relevant to foreign policy-making, but each aspect, it will be observed, is made relevant by man's reaction to it. Thus although geographical 'facts' change only rarely, or slowly, their political significance may change more frequently or more rapidly because of man's behaviour in relation to them. Many of these changes result from science and its technological applications. The Atlantic Ocean has ceased to be regarded as a barrier and is by some seen as the centre of a community because the ease with which men may now communicate and travel across it has lessened its effectiveness as an obstacle to intercourse among likeminded peoples of similar cultural origins. The strategic disadvantage of size has been lessened by new means of swiftly transporting men and equipment, while the advantage of possible defence in depth has been reinforced by ability to

[12] See p. 61 fn. 10 above.

disperse vital centres. The security which the United States enjoyed because of its geographical location has been in large measure destroyed by swifter means of travel, by ability to fly over or navigate under the polar ice-cap, and above all by the development of missiles of inter-continental range. The high degree of freedom of manoeuvre which British foreign policy acquired from her insular character and naval mastery of the seas has been totally destroyed by Britain's peculiar vulnerability in face of twentieth-century weapons. The effects on political affairs in the United States of climatic diversity and diversity of occupation have been lessened by greater wealth, greater ease of movement, greater interdependence of regions, and so greater government intervention. Industrial technology makes possession of some resources more valuable, others less so, and changing needs redirect the attention of the governments of major states from one area to another. Deliberate modification of geographical features, such as the cutting of the Panama and Suez canals, have major consequences for international relations.

But although the political impact of geographical considerations is not permanent and unalterable, the rate of change is relatively slow. This is partly because very considerable efforts or very substantial technological advances are necessary before the significance of geographical conditions is modified, and partly because there is usually a timelag between the effecting of changes and their recognition by statesmen. Although Woodrow Wilson and a few of his supporters recognized in 1919 that the isolation of the United States was effectively ended, the majority of the American people did not, and the 'internationalists' were defeated. Baldwin could say in July 1934, 'When you think of the defence of England you no longer think of the chalk cliffs of Dover; you think of the Rhine. That is where our frontier lies';[13] but the opinion was not sufficiently firmly held, or widely supported, for action to be taken to sustain it. Thinking is still conditioned by generations of use of Mercator's projection, so that few realize that New York is 400 miles nearer to Leningrad than it is to Rio de Janeiro.

Since therefore the relevance of geographical considerations changes only slowly, and perception of them even more so, in any particular international situation, and over substantial periods of time, the geographical element in foreign policy is constant and unchanging. Influences on foreign policy may be arranged on a continuum, of which constant is one extreme and volatile the other. No influence is permanent or constant for all time, but some are constant over a relatively long period, others are constant over shorter periods, and others change from

[13] Speech in the House of Commons, 30 July 1934, *Parliamentary Debates* (*Official Report*), ser. 5, vol. 292, col. 2339.

day to day or hour to hour as a crisis unfolds. Geographical facts lie towards the constancy end of the continuum. It is not enough accurately to identify and to observe influences on foreign policy: it is necessary if policy is to achieve the goals to which it is directed for influences to be judiciously located on this continuum. To take once more the 1956 Suez example: Nasser was a relatively swiftly changing influence upon Anglo-French policy, but Arab nationalism was to be located towards the constancy end of the continuum. One of the surest ways to cause policies to fail, though not necessarily in the short term, is to base them on swiftly changing elements to the exclusion of those influences which are relatively long-lasting.[14]

Reference has already been made to economic geography. The quantity and availability of resources within the frontiers of a state evidently is a central element of the economic influence on foreign policy-making. This influence is relatively new, at least in its scope and range. The more primitive an economy, the more it is able to sustain itself without dealings with others, and the less susceptible it is to natural or human disaster. A flood wiping out half an African tribe need have only negligible economic consequences for the survivors; but a strike in Britain by a small number of workers making components for motor-cars may in a fairly short time have consequences that will make themselves felt throughout the economy. This has implications for foreign as well as for domestic policy, as will be seen below.[15]

The first and major economic influence on foreign policy derives from the extent to which a state is dependent on trade for its 'survival'— more exactly, for maintaining or improving its standard of living and its wealth. 'Dependent' is an imprecise word concealing a variety of interrelationships. To say that in the 1920s Japan was dependent on the United States market for silk may mean, first, that in no other market could enough of the silk be sold at any price; secondly, that in no other market could enough of the silk be sold at a price bringing an adequate return; thirdly, that the variables 'enough of the silk', and 'an adequate return' were not susceptible to changes in the costs of produc-

---

[14] I am not asserting that Arab nationalism was in fact ignored in 1956. Some supporters of the action maintain that one of the reasons for overthrowing Nasser was precisely that this was the most effective method of checking Arab nationalism.

[15] See pp. 90-2.

tion (labour costs, management skills, capital investment and so on) or in standards of living; fourthly, that the imports purchased with the foreign exchange accruing from silk sales could not be reduced or re-placed by internally-produced substitutes; and fifthly, that no substitute products could be developed that could be sold abroad and so produce for Japan 'sufficient' foreign exchange to purchase abroad the com-modities and manufactures that she 'needed'. The facts of the matter were that Japan was very poorly supplied with natural resources, only about one-fifth of her land surface was cultivable, and her population was expanding rapidly. Apart from coal, which though expensive to mine, was adequate for the domestic demand, Japan lacked sufficient supplies of most metals and most fertilizers, and had to import almost all her oil, rubber, raw cotton and raw wool. The means to buy these could come only from sale of her one major indigenous product, silk, or from the sale of manufactures, many of the raw materials for which would themselves have to be imported. The vital processes of the Japan-ese economy in the 1920s were sale of silk in the United States, purchase of raw cotton in the United States, manufacture of cotton textiles, sale of cotton textiles in world markets, purchase of raw materials and manufactures with the proceeds. (This was not of course the only economic activity, but it was the crucial one.) When the world economic crisis broke in 1929, the level of world trade fell catastrophically, the price of silk (a luxury commodity, and so with an elastic demand) dropped sharply, access to the United States market was curtailed by the Smoot-Hawley tariff of 1930, so the bottom dropped out of the Japanese economy. The standard of living fell sharply, hardship became acute, especially in rural areas where pressures could no longer be relieved by dispatch of children, particularly girls, to industry, and dis-content mounted. These were economic elements of the decision to conquer Manchuria, whose iron resources would enable economic activity to be diversified, and whose soya beans would make up for the one serious deficiency in Japan's food supply. (This is not to say that economic reasons alone caused the attack, or indeed that they were the most important; merely that these were reasons that entered into the calculations of some of those concerned with the decision, and that were subsequently used as justification for the attack by many more.) In cases of this kind economic influences in a given political context may act as a stimulus to the adoption of policies by governments.

This example illustrates how an undiversified economy can limit the options available in foreign policy. Brazil (coffee), Cuba (sugar), Vene-zuela (oil), were other examples of states which relied very heavily on the disposal of a single commodity, while in contrast United States foreign policy acquires great freedom for manoeuvre from the fact that her economic activity ranges from food crops through cash crops and light industry to heavy industry and the most advanced technologies. Restriction on freedom in foreign policy through restriction of economic range is not confined to primary-producing countries: one of the arguments advanced for a British application to enter the European Economic Community has been that in the current state of the international economy the only exports that Britain can hope to produce competitively and so to sell (she no more than Japan can feed her people or supply her industries from indigenous resources) are those with a low import and high skill component, such as vehicles, engineering goods, electronics, chemicals, computers; and goods of this kind can be sold only in developed economies such as those pre-eminently of the United States and western Europe. If declining sales of, for instance, textiles in Asia, were not compensated for by rising sales of other goods in Europe, then Britain's standard of living must fall, possibly severely; and sales in Europe would be unlikely to rise in face of an external tariff against Britain and other states round the Community and tariff-free movements of goods within it. Whether the argument is valid or not, it illustrates the point that foreign policy may be limited by production only of a class of goods for which the market is limited, as much as by a high degree of reliance on sales of a single commodity.

States which are heavily dependent on trade are in addition more generally affected in that, except in the most desperate circumstances, international stability is made more desirable. Trade flourishes more easily when the level of international economic confidence is high, when capital moves across state frontiers easily, and when confidence in currencies is adequate for forward dealings in foreign currencies to be freely undertaken. International conflict reduces international confidence, and in major war the weapon of economic blockade is now normally used. For a people whose food supply and level of industrial activity is in substantial degree dependent on purchases from abroad it is vital to keep supply routes open. The most serious danger of defeat for Britain in each of the two world wars came from the German submarine campaigns which in 1917 and 1942 came close to reducing supplies across the Atlantic below a tolerable level. A major world trader such as Britain has therefore a real interest in the maintenance of peace, as in war vital supply routes are always liable to be endangered.

The first aspect of the economic element in foreign policy, then, is the degree of dependence on external trade. This is related to and affected by the quantity and availability of natural resources, the commodity composition of exports, the range of markets for them, the size and trends of population, and the standard of living and expectations about it. Again the interrelatedness of different elements is evident. Moreover, it is once more the political implications of economic considerations that are relevant to foreign policy making. For centuries the peoples of Asia, and to a less extent those of Africa, have lived in conditions of squalor and poverty which they have accepted with varying degrees of fatalism or resignation. Colonization by Europeans, introduction of examples of higher living standards, and the undermining of traditional customs and values by the impact of western culture, have gradually created awareness of and dissatisfaction with poverty. The sense of deprivation emerges where in similar or worse conditions it did not exist before. The governments of all 'underdeveloped' states are therefore faced with demands for economic betterment, and the capital and technical skills are everywhere insufficient to meet them with the speed that is required. Governments are accordingly driven to seek economic assistance in the form of gifts, or loans without interest or at concessional rates, or technical assistance. Transactions of this kind in greater or less degree impose restrictions on the freedom of manoeuvre of governments, although the pretence is always maintained that economic or technical assistance is 'without strings'. The degree of constraint resulting from economic assistance has been less since 1945 than it otherwise would have been, because of the rivalry between the United States and the USSR: each, but more particularly the former, has been hesitant in trying to use aid to influence the recipient's foreign policy lest it should be driven to turn for assistance to the other, and so fall under the other's influence. Nor is it the case that constraints of this kind operate only for underdeveloped or developing countries: there can be little doubt, for example, that one of the reasons why the Wilson government in Britain gave high priority to the maintenance of good relations with the United States was the seeming dependence of the pound sterling on international financial support in which the United States had to play the leading role.

Foreign policy is then affected secondly by the extent to which a country's economy is a deficit or surplus one in terms of capital, technical skills, and finance. The degree to which an economy is thought to be stable will also be relevant for the raising of capital internally, as well as for the investment of capital or the granting of technical aid from external sources. But the making of loans or the investment of capital carries with it consequences for the creditor country as well as for the debtor. 'Economic interests' are created which then are seen to require defence. The interests of the United Fruit Company in Guatemala were widely thought to have had much to do with the intervention of President Eisenhower in that country in 1954. French investments in Syria and the Lebanon increased de Gaulle's reluctance to grant these countries independence at the end of the second world war. The concern of the Soviet Union with internal developments in the countries of the Warsaw pact is doubtless the result in part of strategic and ideological considerations; but it also in some degree derives from the advantages in terms of exports and raw materials acquisition which the Soviet Union obtains from its dominant position in east European economic cooperation, advantages which would be largely lost if economic windows were more freely opened towards the west.

The third economic element which enters into foreign policy making is the degree to which a state's industrial capacity is adequate to sustain the military forces and equipment necessary to its defence. This will be dealt with below.[16] One further point should be made at this stage. Foreign policy decisions are taken in relation to some expected or desired future state of affairs, whether long-term or short-term. Influences on foreign policy are relevant not merely in terms of their present or actual nature, but in terms of their future or potential. Although this is a general point, it may perhaps most usefully be made in the context of economic considerations. In judging the action that is appropriate in relation to desired trading relationships or to compensating for some deficiency, for example, the decision-maker should always take into account not merely the actual but also the potential economic strength or weakness of his state. (He must also, of course, take into account the potential as well as the actual economic strength of the states with which he is dealing; but this is an element of the external environment which will be dealt with in the next chapter.) This is a matter of great difficulty, for economic forecasting is an activity little more precise than political forecasting, particularly in the relatively long term and when the rate of technological change is high. The ratio of the potential human and material investment required for participation in the development of advancing nuclear weapons technology and delivery systems to the potential rate of growth and size of the British economy (modified by possible side benefits) was one of the considerations that should have been weighed (and possibly was) when the original decision to go ahead with independent British production was made. It may well be that in practice forecasts are as yet likely to be subject to such large margins of error that a decision-maker can hardly afford to be influenced by them; but in analysis the point must be made, and it indicates an area in which research directed towards the creation

[16] See pp. 90-2.

of sharper aids to understanding is very much required if policy-making is to become more effective in achieving its intended goals.

Another way of viewing the ratio mentioned in the previous paragraph is in terms of what the economist calls opportunity cost. The economic wisdom or folly of the British decision to develop an independent nuclear capability was not to be assessed only in relation to the potential capacity of the British economy, but also in terms of the other things that could not be done—the other opportunities lost—because of the resources devoted to this particular project. There can be little doubt, for instance, that the role of the German Federal Republic in world affairs in the 1960s was in very large degree affected by the strength of the Federal economy, and that the strength of the economy was in part the consequence of the fact that for more than a decade after the end of the second world war no German resources were allocated to defence. The United States, Britain, France and NATO conducted their defence for them, and with varying degrees of conviction insisted on doing so. The Germans were thus able to devote themselves to other activities, and they seized their opportunities with characteristic energy and determination. This is not to say either that the British decision to develop nuclear weapons was wrong, or that Germany ought to have been allowed or required to rearm earlier : the examples are given to illustrate the concept of opportunity cost and to show its relevance to the economic element of foreign policy-making.

The economists' language of profits and costs, or more generally of gains and losses, is indeed helpful and appropriate language to use in relation to foreign policy. Almost never will it be the case that a choice between two courses of action can be seen in simple terms of one being likely to succeed and the other being likely to fail. Every course of action will almost always involve some gains and some losses, the gains frequently being the negative ones of preventing some other losses. Whether or not a particular action will be undertaken will therefore depend on whether the particular gains that it is expected to achieve are thought to be greater or more desirable than the particular losses that are expected to be suffered. The argument can be put more formally in the language of game theory.[17] In some situations gains are almost certain to be made at least in the short term, and then it is a question of maximizing them. In other situations losses are almost certain to be suffered, and then it is a question of minimizing them. The Soviet decision to invade Czechoslovakia in the summer of 1968, for example, was presumably made on the basis of judgments that the losses to be suffered by the invasion (setback to *détente* with the United States, new

[17] See Chapter 9, pp. 215-25 below.

consolidation of NATO, new hostility of Yugoslavia and Romania, further weakening or alienation of communist parties not in power, general loss of reputation in world opinion, direct military and economic costs) were less than the losses to be suffered by allowing the Czech liberalization to continue (disruption of communist solidarity under Moscow's leadership, loss of Czech economic strength from Comecon, spread of the liberal virus, possibly in the Soviet Union itself, but certainly in other eastern European countries, and particularly in East Germany conceivably leading to the fall of the Ulbricht regime and the reunification of Germany under capitalist control). These particular anticipated losses from not invading (mostly long-term) were judged to be less tolerable than the particular expected losses from invading (mainly short-term). The losses to be suffered from each course of action were of different kinds, and balancing each group against the other was accordingly exceedingly difficult. Most foreign policy decisions will involve this kind of comparison of unlike elements.

The third major component of the domestic environment of decision-makers is the demographic—the limits thought to be imposed on policies, and the impulses imparted to them, by the size, skills, structure, distribution, and increase or decline of the population of the state. If states are ranked in order of size of population China in 1967 headed the list, followed by India, the Soviet Union, the United States, Pakistan, Indonesia, Japan, Brazil. Clearly while the list includes the two states generally thought to be the most influential or significant in world politics, the United States and the Soviet Union, it does not include many others which would widely be thought to rank higher than all but these two and possibly China in the scale of powers, such as Great Britain, the Federal German Republic, and France. Alternatively one could reasonably say both that the size of China's population inevitably makes her one of the great states of the world, and that the size of her population drains away wealth and economic improvement into the sands so that she will never be able to realize her potential until the population numbers are controlled.

Evidently statistics of the size of a state's population by themselves are of little value in the analysis of foreign policy. They are significant only in relation to all other elements of a state's situation, but particularly the territorial, the economic, and the technological. One may therefore conceive an optimum population for a given territory, a given

level of resources broadly defined,[18] a given level of technological development, and a given international environment. This optimum would
be exceedingly difficult to determine in practice in a particular case,
and of course it would change rapidly as the other variables themselves change. The concept is useful none the less as a shorthand expression of the elements that must be taken into account in judging
whether a state's population is 'too large' or 'too small'. Japan's population had in some senses become too large in 1931 when it had not been
too large in 1929, as a result of the change in the international trading
system between these two years. Britain's population was considered
by some to be excessive in 1967, but the degree of that excess if it
existed was susceptible of reduction by the effective exploitation of
North Sea natural gas. After 1922 the main criterion for judging the
number of Jews that should be allowed into Palestine was the economic
absorptive capacity of the country, a criterion that soon proved itself to
be meaningless because of the skills, the capital, and the technological
advances particularly in irrigation that the Jews introduced. Simple
figures about the sizes of populations do not therefore themselves offer
any clue to the importance of population numbers to decision-makers.

In two senses however population numbers are important. In the
first place they indicate limits and potential. Norway can never be
among the great powers of the world, and the freedom of manoeuvre of
her decision-makers in foreign policy must accordingly remain restricted,
if only because her population is little more than $3\frac{1}{2}$ million. China
on the other hand could become the greatest state in the world if the
relationship between the size of her population on the one hand and
the capacity of her economy and the level of her technological development on the other could be brought into better balance. In the second
place, size of population is frequently taken by decision-makers as a
reason or a justification for the adoption of policies which for other
or additional reasons seem more desirable than different courses of
action. Control of immigration into Britain in the 1960s was justified
by some on the grounds that Britain was over-populated, an argument
likely to be more acceptable to many than one based explicitly on the
social problems of absorbing increasing numbers of coloured people.
Hitler asserted that there were or would be too many Germans for the
territory contained within the German frontiers, and they must therefore have more 'living-space' to the east in Poland and the Ukraine. The
desire to preserve the flow of British immigrants to Australia to en-
large the population has been one of the reasons for the strong attach-

[18] Including, for instance, education, skills, natural resources, capital, interest-
bearing external investments, credit-worthiness.

ment of Australia to the Commonwealth despite developing economic links with Asia and growing strategic dependence on the United States. Size of population is thus in association with other elements one important index of the power of a state,[19] and it is a factor cited by politicians as a reason for action perhaps more often than it is in fact a major motivation.

The importance of numbers is likewise affected by the population's level of education and technical skill. Few would dispute that for much of the nineteenth century Britain was among the most influential, if not the most influential, of the states of the world; yet her population remained below that both of some of her European neighbours (France, Austria-Hungary, and after 1870 Germany) and of territories overseas that she either directly controlled (such as India) or extensively influenced (such as China). Many factors contributed to this ascendancy, but among them was the relatively high level of technical skill of the population which in part compensated for its relatively small numbers. Technical skill cannot by itself be an adequate compensation for small numbers. It is one of an interacting complex which includes quality of original research, availability of finance for research and for the exploitation of its results, and flexible industrial practices and a mobile social order which offer little resistance to processes of change. The level of technical skill and the quality of scientific research in Britain in the last third of the twentieth century is probably little less high in relation to those of other states than it was in the nineteenth, but industrial practices have become increasingly ossified, and the availability of finance for research and still more for development of the results of research has steadily declined in relation to needs, with the twin consequences that the level of skill has in less and less degree compensated in the world power scale for the relatively small size of Britain's population, and the territory and the economy have seemed steadily less able to support at the expected standard of living even the population that the islands now contain. This has social and political consequences which in turn affect foreign policy.

Skills are thus closely related to the level of economic activity. In a primitive economy the individual and his immediate dependants are likely themselves to consume virtually the whole or the equivalent of the whole that he in a full day's labour is able to produce. As skills improve individual productivity increases, and although personal expectations and demands also rise an increasing surplus of individual production over individual consumption is likely to appear which can

---

[19] For the concept of power, and the relationship between the power of a state and its policy, see Chapter 5, pp. 115-22 below.

be used, among other ways, for foreign policy purposes (larger defence establishments, increased propaganda activities, extended diplomacy, greater aid programmes) or for increasing leisure. The skills of a population thus form an important component of a social and economic complex that has much effect on foreign policy limits, capabilities, and potential.

Population composition forms part of the same complex. Ethnic homogeneity is normally a source of strength, heterogeneity normally a source of weakness except in so far as it is subordinated to the sense of nationhood, as has hitherto been the case in large degree in the United States. But to the extent that the sense of nationhood is associated with ethnic consciousness, and nationhood is deemed to require political expression, so ethnic differences affect state structure and foreign policy. The effects are many and various. In the first place internal cohesion may be undermined, with consequences for political structure and political behaviour. The autocratic and centralized nature of Tsarist government resulted in part from ethnic diversity. In the words of Count Witte, the great statesman of the pre-1914 period: 'The world should be surprised that we have any Government in Russia, not that we have an imperfect Government. With many nationalities, many languages and a nation largely illiterate, the marvel is that the country can be held together even by autocracy. Remember one thing: if the Tsar's Government falls, you will see absolute chaos in Russia, and it will be many a long year before you will see another Government able to control the mixture that makes up the Russian nation.'[20] The Bolshevik revolution saw the swift emergence of separatist movements in Finland, Latvia, Estonia, Lithuania, the Ukraine, Georgia, Azerbaijan, Armenia and the Turkish provinces in central Asia, and the integrity of the empire was restored only by treachery and brutality (as in Georgia), by military invasion (as in Latvia, Estonia and Lithuania in 1940-41), by imposition of rulers of Russian nationality (as in the Turkish republics), and by wholesale transfer and dispersal of populations in order to destroy consciousness of national identity. Policies of this kind can be carried out only in political systems of a certain character, and the character of political systems affects foreign policy.

In the second place lack of correlation between ethnic divisions and political divisions may be used as a means or an excuse for foreign policy actions. Internal ethnic diversity may have created political difficulties and had effects on the nature of government within the Soviet Union, but links between the Azerbaijani within the Soviet Union and the Azerbaijani in north Iran have more than once served

[20] Quoted in B. H. Sumner, *Survey of Russian History* (Duckworth, 1944), p. 122.

as effective means of pressure on the government in Teheran. The foreign policy of Romania is critically affected by the intermingling of Magyars and Romanians in Transylvania. Hitler's use of Czech-Slovak antipathies, and of the Sudeten German group in Bohemia and Moravia, to destroy the Czechoslovak state in 1938-39, is a familiar example. For a state which is strong in relation to its neighbours, different ethnic groups which have links with similar groups across its frontiers may serve as means for advancing foreign policy goals. For a state which is weak in relation to its neighbours, internal ethnic diversity will always be a cause of concern, and may prove fatal to its existence.

In the third place ethnic groups may act directly to promote particular foreign policies. It was primarily the Magyar interest within the Austro-Hungarian empire that so disastrously pressed for a total humiliation of the Serbs in 1914, in part because of the links between the Serbs and the other south Slavs in Croatia who formed part of the Hungarian section of the Dual Monarchy. In the United States, despite the generally overriding sense of nationhood, the influence of the 'hyphenates' has at times been significant—the German–Americans in the main opposed to intervention against Germany in the first world war, and again, this time with the Italian–Americans, in the second world war; the Irish-Americans hostile to association with Britain; the Scandinavian-Americans desiring to preserve isolationism and neutrality; the Jewish-Americans pressing for action against Hitler, and after 1948 for support to Israel. Ethnic diversity can thus lead to the emergence of a particular kind of pressure group activity which can have direct impact on policy.

Geographical and occupational distribution is perhaps of less importance than ethnic diversity. The former has none the less strategic implications. Among the many reasons why German chiefs of staff have planned offensive strategies in the event of Germany becoming involved in war has been the location close to the frontiers of most of Germany's vital population centres—Berlin, Silesia, the Rhineland and the Ruhr. The strategic significance on the one hand of the concentration of Japan's population and on the other of the dispersal of that of the Soviet Union has already been noted. Occupational distribution, together with output *per capita*, is one index of the level of economic efficiency and economic development, and is very relevant to the economic component of the military power of a state, but is perhaps more conveniently considered in that context.[21]

Much more significant are demographic trends, and age and sex structure. The rate of increase or decline of a population, considered

[21] See pp. 90-1 below.

in conjunction with the availability of resources, the intensity and extent of economic mobilization, and the level of technology, is one major indicator of the power of a state. France's population in 1815 (29 million) was greater than that of any other of the neighbouring states of Europe although Austria (some 26 million) came close. The population of Britain was 13 million, and of Prussia under 11 million. By 1870 Britain's population had increased to almost 32 million, Austria-Hungary's to nearly 36 million, and Prussia's to 40 million (admittedly with dramatic changes in territorial size due to the unification of Germany), while France's had increased only to 38 million. The figures are even more striking by 1914 when they were respectively Britain 41 million, Austria-Hungary 51 million, Germany 65 million, and France 40 million. In the absence of other compensating changes (in fact the rate of economic growth and technological advance was also greater in Britain and Germany than in France) these population rates of change in themselves in considerable degree account for the transformation from 1792-1815, when France alone was almost able to master the whole of Europe, to 1914-18 when France before 1917 was almost defeated by Germany (with little assistance from Austria-Hungary) despite support from Russia, Britain, and many small states. Since, to make the point again, foreign policy decisions relate to future situations, long-term as well as short-term, decision-makers ignore at their peril demographic statistics, rates of change, and projections of future trends.

But this is not the whole story. Rates of population change have effects on age structure. A population with a high birth-rate which over a period of years slowly declines will have a steadily ageing population as the earlier large birth-classes grow old and the later smaller birth-classes form the younger elements in the population, even though, other things being equal, the total population may continue to increase. If the birth-rate falls far enough the population may indeed actually start to decline when the effects on age structure are likely to be even more marked. Age structure is important, because the productivity *per capita* and the innovating capacity of a population 80 per cent of which is under fifty is likely to be greater than one 60 per cent of which is under fifty. Moreover the ages twenty to thirty-five are those of primary importance for the armed services. In 1970 the Soviet Union had probably more men in the critical military age group than all her six nearest European neighbours combined, including both Germanies; while in France, where the formerly stagnant birth-rate has since 1945 shown sharp increases, the average age of the population is falling.

Death-rates also enter the picture. A population will increase when there is a high birth-rate and a high, though slightly lower, death-rate.

It will also increase when there is a low birth-rate and an even lower death-rate. The experience of Asia over millennia has been of high birth-rates and high death-rates, so that average life expectancy may have been about thirty-five years, and population increases have been contained. The introduction of better health and hygiene has produced dramatic falls in death-rates and so, with no corresponding falls in birth-rates, the so-called population explosion has occurred. Some rates of increase exceed 2 per cent per annum, which means a doubling of population in about thirty-five years, or, in China's case, perhaps 100 million more mouths to feed between 1970 and 1976 (that is to say an increase in six years greater than the total population of any but the seven other most populous states of the world). These figures cannot but be of crucial importance to foreign policy decision-makers.

It was stated earlier that absolute numbers of people become significant only in their economic and social context. The same applies to trends. A population that is expanding more rapidly than resources, as previously broadly defined, will be a source of weakness. But a population which is expanding rapidly within an even greater expansion of resources and technological development will be a source of great strength. It is one of the striking contrasts between the population explosions of the earliest-industrializing states (in western Europe and the United States) and the mid-twentieth century 'developing' countries, that in the former the expansion of resources tended to be followed by the population growth, whereas in the latter the population growth has in general been brought about by other factors (particularly health measures) and the expansion of resources has followed desperately behind. Moreover as between the two ways in which populations may increase (high birth-rate and high but slightly lower death-rate, and low birth-rate but even lower death-rate) the increase which results from low rates in each case is overwhelmingly more efficient: a far lower proportion of women's time is spent 'unproductively' in pregnancies and confinements so that they are freed for other activities, and a given level of educational investment produces far higher returns if a life contributes forty-five or fifty years of trained effort to the community (even if followed by ten years of community-supported old age) than if it contributes only fifteen years of effort. The so-called developed countries have passed through this demographic transition from the wasteful high rates of birth and death to the economic low rates, while the developing countries still have higher death-rates, even though they have fallen.

These are some of the reasons why population trends are a critical variable in foreign policy decision-making. But it will be observed that population questions are less important for their direct impact on policy-making than for their effect on other considerations that decision-makers must take into account, though they have some direct effect also. Population numbers, trends and structures affect economic growth and technological change, they affect the proportion of economic output that can be devoted to other activities than simply keeping people alive and fed, they accordingly affect the proportion of resources than can be used for foreign policy or defence purposes, they affect the manpower that can be made available for military recruitment (a surplus of females will affect this likewise), they affect social structures, they affect the extent to which a political system is able to satisfy the demands of its members, and they thus affect political stability and the extent to which from the processes of decision-making can emerge acceptable and accepted decisions. Demographic considerations are therefore among the most important elements of the decision-maker's environment, both domestic and international; but since their effects usually take time to make themselves felt, the attention given to them is frequently too little and too late.

In the previous chapter reference was made to various groups which on occasion claim to represent the national interest. Spurious though their claims may be the decision-maker can ignore them only at some political risk. The size of the risk will vary according to the nature of the group, the nature of the issue, and the nature of the political and social system; but in all systems the domestic political context in some degree constrains foreign policy makers. The constraint may derive simply from events, or from the aspirations of politically significant groups, or from social mores, traditions, and morale. The first of these is too obvious to need more than mention : evidently a study of British foreign policy in the Manchurian crisis in 1931, for example, would miss an essential component if it omitted to observe that the political cataclysm which resulted from economic crisis, and which produced the national government and disrupted the Labour party, occurred on 23/24 August; the naval 'mutiny' at Invergordon against the new government's proposed pay cuts broke out on 15 September; the Mukden incident which sparked off the Japanese invasion took place on the night of 18/19 September, and Britain went off the gold standard on 21 September. Equally French policy towards the *Anschluss* of Austria with Germany in March 1938 is not fully explicable without reference to the fact that the French government was defeated in the Chamber of Deputies on 10 March and resigned. The historian of foreign policy must clearly have the chronology of domestic events always in mind.

An important skill of the political leader is the ability to detect and to predict movements of public opinion. Of course he plays some part in shaping those movements; but in the delicate interplay of opinion influencing leadership and leaders moulding opinion, the successful leader is the one who is sensitive to the movement of opinion and who diverts or reorients it perhaps, but who does not set himself in direct opposition to it. The proposition formulated in this way, however, is so oversimplified as to be wholly misleading. It suggests that opinion is a monolithic entity which moves as a unit in one direction or in another. This cannot be so, if only because there are always many issues simultaneously in question. If desired ends in relation to one question can be achieved only at the sacrifice of desired ends in relation to another (and we have seen that this will very frequently be the case), it is certain that members of the public will differ among themselves as to which of the desired ends is more important, and which are the means likely to achieve any of the ends, in just the same way as do the political leaders who have to make the decisions. In the United States in the 1960s, for example, it is evident that some opinion believed that in the allocation of resources which were not unlimited a greater share should go to aid developing countries and a smaller share to fighting the war in Vietnam; while among those who agreed on the aim of preventing the spread of communism in south-east Asia some believed that the best way of achieving this was by military action in support of a South Vietnamese non-communist government, while others believed that a military presence was counterproductive as it caused nationalism to join communism, and a better way of achieving the containment of communism would be by military withdrawal and support thereafter to the independently-minded governments which would eventually emerge. When more than two issues are in question, as is always the case, it is likely that the movement of opinion, in relation both to the priority of ends and to the means of achieving any of them, will be confused and complex in the extreme.

Even if there were only one issue, or if (which is more possible) one issue were very widely thought to be more important than all others, it is still unlikely that opinion would move consistently and unitedly about the actions that should be taken in relation to it. Differences will almost certainly emerge because some people have more information or knowledge or greater intelligence than others, because some people have economic or other interests that will be served by one course of action and other interests that will be served by other actions, because some people have strongly held beliefs or convictions that a particular course of action would outrage, or because some people interest themselves in public affairs and others do not. In Britain in the late 1930s it was very widely, though not universally, believed that the problems presented by Hitler dominated all other foreign policy questions: but many thought that Britain's interests (which included the maintenance of peace) would best be served by meeting Hitler's supposedly reasonable grievances; some opposed the economic losses that they might suffer if south-east Europe were entirely surrendered to German economic domination; some out of moral conviction opposed any participation in any war even in ultimate self-defence; a few believed that Hitler's behaviour and intentions were such that he must be resisted and overthrown, by force if necessary, and the strongest possible combination should be assembled to achieve this as quickly and as painlessly as might be; while many continued to think only of getting or holding on to a job, of keeping the children happy, or of football on Saturday afternoon or the pub on Saturday night.

Thus when a politician speaks of his inability to do something, or in the past to have done something, because he had not the support of public opinion, he is using language of extreme vagueness. Some might be hard put, if pressed, to explain what they meant. Others may use the language deliberately to justify policies adopted for other reasons. There is nothing necessarily wrong with that. But the analyst of the nature of the constraint imposed on foreign policy decisions by public opinion must isolate the kinds of opinion that exist. There is, in the simplest analysis, political opinion (by which I mean opinion organized and canalized by parties) both at the parliamentary level (if there is a parliament) within the decision-maker's own party and within his opponents', and outside representative assemblies; informed opinion—that of journalists, commentators, academics, or others who seek to influence opinion on public affairs; pressure-group opinion—that of groups formed to advance a particular interest or cause, and endeavouring directly to influence action; and mass opinion, ill-informed, inarticulate, and with little influence except as a slow-moving ground swell which sets very broad limits to possible policies and forms very general judgments about a government's competence or incompetence. So far as foreign policy is concerned, the last of these has singularly little impact. Uninformed opinion moves in response to immediately experienced concerns such as the cost of living, wage levels, food supplies, or housing conditions and rents. Foreign policy questions by their nature seem remote, irrelevant, or unintelligible, and the ordinary person can do nothing about them anyway. In countries where multi-party elections are held foreign policy issues only rarely play much part in influencing the majority of voters, and even more rarely does a major threat to a government during its term of office arise from a question of foreign relations. Exceptions to this general statement are perhaps the Hoare–Laval pact of 1935[22] which in Britain produced a sufficient outcry for the Foreign Secretary to be jettisoned from the Cabinet (though only temporarily), and the Vietnam war which in the United States in 1968 certainly influenced President Johnson's decision not to run again and played a considerable part in the presidential campaign. In general, however, the most that can be said is that an impression may become widely shared that foreign policy is being broadly well handled, or broadly bungled, and this will add up with more immediate concerns in determining an electorate's attitude to a government. It is probable that the seemingly uncourageous and muddled handling of the Iranian oil crisis in 1951 played some part in strengthening a widespread feeling that the Labour government was tired and had become incompetent and needed a rest.

Apart from these very vague and general considerations, then, mass opinion acts only in the sense of setting very broad limits to the behaviour of policy-makers. They have to pay much more attention to political opinion, to informed opinion, and to pressure groups. But even these influences will vary in their importance according to the nature of the political system within which decision-makers are operating. In a system like that of the Soviet Union where opinion-leaders and groups or organizations that in other systems might form pressure groups are alike under the control of the sole political group, the communist party (though perhaps slightly less so than before the death of Stalin in 1953), decision-makers need pay little heed to any opinion other than that within the party; and even within the party a variety of rewards and pressures lie to the hands of the ruling oligarchy which may make the expression of opinion contrary to that of the party leadership not worth while. The political system of the United States, to take the other extreme, is designed to reflect and facilitate the expression of the great diversity of the fifty states which results from their varying climates, resources, occupations, economic

[22] A draft agreement between the British and French foreign ministers, Sir Samuel Hoare and Pierre Laval, attempting by the cession of a large chunk of Abyssinian territory to Italy to buy Mussolini off from his war upon Abyssinia. The plan appeared to reflect an abandonment of pledges by the government at a general election a few weeks previously to resist aggression by collective security through the League of Nations.

interests, ethnic composition, and social structure and mores. It is the intention of the constitution that states rights and minority opinions shall not be suppressed. In a system of this kind policy must constantly take account of conflicting interest groups and lobbies, and must moreover pay more attention to the cultivation and to the views of opinion-leaders because of the opportunities for action that are open to those who are spurred to take it. From this in part derives the great authority that has attached to leading journalists such as Walter Lippmann or James Reston.

Having said this one must immediately qualify it by the observation that even in the United States the policy that evolves under the constraint of proliferating pressure groups is less affected by them in the field of foreign affairs than in domestic affairs. Fewer interest groups perceive so direct a connection between their interests and particular actions in foreign policy that they are impelled to expend much energy or resources in trying to influence policy-makers. There are of course exceptions. In 1934 in the late stages of the world economic crisis representatives of the state of Nevada at last succeeded in persuading the federal authorities to give a boost to the economy of Nevada by raising the price of silver, with the consequence that silver flowed into the United States, the stability of the silver-backed Chinese dollar was undermined and the Chinese economy brought to the point of collapse—all this at a time when a major purpose of United States foreign policy was to sustain China against Japanese pressures. United States policy towards Israel has without doubt repeatedly been affected by the pressures of American Jews, who are able to exercise an influence disproportionate to their numbers because they form a significant element of the population of New York State, one of the two largest states and so commanding a critical voting block in the presidential electoral college.

The influence that pressure groups can exercise in foreign policy-making, when they seek to exercise it, thus varies with the nature of the political system, the general political strength or weakness of an administration, the proximity or distance of an election (in systems where contested elections are held), and the extent to which an unsatisfied group is able politically to harm leaders who resist it. The nature of foreign policy issues, their remoteness, their secrecy, their complexity, and the fact that the prestige, the authority and standing of the whole nation are involved, diminish the scope and opportunities for interest group activity in this field.

Some interest groups do now operate in a further dimension. Many are organized across state boundaries. The Roman Catholic Church, internationally based companies, international peace groups, non-governmental organizations are examples of such groups, and their influence as a result has an additional aspect. If an internationally organized group of scientists, for example, simultaneously launched campaigns in many countries opposing the atmospheric testing of nuclear weapons, at least some of the governments concerned would wish to find out how others were reacting to this pressure, lest, for instance, they should find themselves isolated. The effectiveness of pressure groups is not necessarily increased if they are internationally organized—it may indeed be diminished—but governments will need to react to them in different ways. This is an example of the interrelationship of the domestic and international environments of decision-makers and more will be said about it in the next chapter and in Part III of the book.

The extent to which informed opinion influences policy is exceedingly difficult to judge. Its impact too will vary according to the nature of the political system and its particular condition at a particular time, to the political strength or weakness of an administration, and to the nature of the issue. It will also vary according to the personalities of decision-makers. Those who are possessed of great self-confidence and certainty (such as Neville Chamberlain or de Gaulle) are much less susceptible to the influence of informed opinion than those who are able to see many sides of a question (such as John F. Kennedy). But even the arrogant ones are likely to be less assured on questions about which they know nothing, so generally speaking the more obscure and recondite a question the more influence informed opinion is likely to have. On questions that persist over a long time, also, informed opinion is likely to make itself more effectively felt than if an issue is settled by rapid decision. When a government is politically insecure it is likely to feel less able to fly in the face of informed advice. But all these propositions are loose and imprecise in the extreme, and an immense amount of empirical investigation is needed before any of them can be accepted with confidence.

The remaining segment of the division of opinion made above is political opinion. Here another term enters into the equation. All other segments of opinion are concerned to influence action in ways which they consider to be right, or in ways which will benefit themselves or their affiliates, or in ways which they believe to be in the national interest, or in some combination of these. Political opinion is concerned also with the relationship of policies to the possession of power to make policies. Political groups such as parties differ from other groups in the sense that they aim to gain power while other groups aim to influence those in power. The influence of political opinion will therefore depend not only on many of the other factors previously mentioned but also upon the extent to which the political group can make or unmake its leaders, and *vice versa*.

In the United States the President is independently elected and thereafter virtually irremovable for four years. Moreover he has immense patronage and his popular appeal will usually have much effect, at least in quadrennial presidential elections, on the election of members of his party to the Senate and the House of Representatives. The President, that is to say, can greatly affect the fate of members of his party. They, once they have nominated him, can do virtually nothing to him. The influence of political opinion in the sense of a party group is thus minimal. Of course party members in the Congress have great influence, but this derives from their place in the institutional structure of the United States and not from their party membership.

In Britain the situation is subtly different. Here too the top decision-maker, the Prime Minister, has substantial ability to unmake his party through his power to recommend dissolution of the House of Commons, although in so doing he risks his own position as well. But he depends for his leadership on the support of a sufficient majority of his party in the House of Commons and he could not persistently ignore them with impunity. His patronage, however, is also sufficiently large for attempts to unseat him to be exceedingly rare, although whispers that such attempts are in the making may bring about modifications in policies to prevent any movement growing. But while his own position is relatively secure, that of his colleagues, including the Foreign Secretary, is much less so. A Foreign Secretary has a constitutional position in his own right; but his political position depends on his relations with the Prime Minister and on the support he commands within his party (and to a less extent on the attitude to him of the opposition and of the electorate in general). A Foreign Secretary not powerfully backed by his Prime Minister cannot afford to persist in policies to which too many of his party are opposed; and even a Foreign Secretary pursuing policies in close harmony with his Premier is less secure, because if political opinion is outraged to the point of the government being threatened, one way in which the Prime Minister may save it is by jettisoning his Foreign Secretary even though policies are not changed. Thus, as was mentioned above, Baldwin saved himself by obtaining Hoare's resignation over the Hoare-Laval pact in December 1935, and Macmillan endeavoured to save himself by sacking Selwyn Lloyd, among others, in July 1961. Decision-makers below the Prime Minister, that is to say (and of these the Foreign Secretary is the most important in foreign policy), must pay more attention to political opinion, though the Prime Minister cannot persistently ignore it with impunity.

The Third and Fourth Republics in France, contrasting more sharply with the United States, illustrate cases where political opinion is a major constraint on foreign policy-making. The atrophy of the presidential power of dissolution of the Chamber of Deputies, and the steady concentration in the Chamber of decisive authority over governments, meant that governments changed easily and frequently, and in the reshuffling of many of the same cards that took place on each occasion a minister who had attempted to pursue unpopular policies would find himself left out in the cold. In such circumstances as these political opinion is likely to be of decisive importance in the making of policies, despite the secrecy of much of the information upon which foreign policy is or ought to be based, and this includes opinion not only in the minister's own party but in all other parties out of which some future coalition might be involved. In these circumstances the conduct of foreign policy may be severely hampered, and it is remarkable that despite this domestic political environment most of the major constructive foreign policy initiatives in Europe after 1949 and before de Gaulle's return in 1958 came from France. On the other hand the constraints were too strong for any government in the Fourth Republic to be able to evolve a satisfactory policy for Algeria, and this failure was primarily responsible for the Republic's fall.

More general and more nebulous than these considerations is the influence exerted upon the decision-maker's behaviour by his understanding of the social mores, ethics and traditions of his society, and of the character of the people who compose it. The newer a society, the less this influence is likely to be felt. The longer a society has existed the more likely it is to have developed a tradition and a pattern of behaviour emerging from the interacting geographic, economic, ethnic and politico-social conditions of its life. As a tradition and a behavioural mode emerge they will normally attach to themselves ethical norms and beliefs about right and wrong ways of doing things. Traditions and behavioural patterns and moral beliefs are sustained through written history, through education, and by the official policy-making machine the members of which before entry have themselves been brought up in the cultural environment and after entry follow the precepts and practices of their seniors. Thus the United States—by reason of its high degree of geographical isolation and so of strategic security, its great unexploited reserves of wealth enabling aspirations for increased wealth and prosperity to be satisfied by intracontinental expansion, the refugee origin of many of its people seeking to flee the injustices or oppression or poverty of the old world—developed a behavioural pattern of withdrawal, and ethical principles of non-intervention, freedom of the seas, and peaceful settlement of disputes by arbitration, mediation or diplomacy. For the interlocked rival states on the mainland of Europe, on the other hand, moral principles had to yield to physical means of defence, and *raison d'état* was its own sufficient ethic.

For Britain, to whom as the major naval power blockade was a main means of enforcing her will, freedom of the seas was an unacceptable principle. Traditions of this kind, once established, take a long time to change : whether they act to limit the freedom of manoeuvre of decision-makers depends on their nature. The sense that the intervention in Suez in 1956 ran counter both to British principles of action and to traditional methods of action which had proved their wisdom in the past, had much to do with the internal opposition to the action and so something to do with its abrupt termination. Significantly, almost no such internal reaction occurred within France, whose traditional modes of behaviour and rules of conduct for state action are quite different. The violence thought to be done to United States principles of behaviour by the intervention in Vietnam limited the action, and was illustrated by the nature and strength of the opposition to it and the depth of self-questioning that the operation provoked. In contrast Soviet treachery and brutality in Hungary in 1956, and invasion of Czechoslovakia in 1968, were not in any way inhibited by behavioural norms, for behaviour of this kind fits the Russian pattern that emerged from the seventeenth century onwards.

The 'Russian' pattern, or the 'Tsarist' pattern? Do peoples, that is to say, have their own special characteristics which inhibit, or stimulate, or have negligible effect on their rulers? This is another area where understanding is limited and empirical evidence is sparse; but it appears at least *prima facie* probable that upbringing in a cultural environment in which certain characteristics are valued will cause these characteristics to be emphasised, that those highly endowed with these characteristics are likely to reach positions of authority, and thus the valuing of the characteristics and the stamping of the society with them will be self-sustaining. It is difficult to doubt, for example, that clearly expressed instructions appropriate to circumstances will be implemented with greater organizing skill, attention to detail, and incorruptibility in Germany than in Italy, and in Italy than in India. If this is so, it will affect both the kind of decisions that will be taken, and the degree of success in achieving purposes that will result from them. The people of the United States, in contrast with the Germans, are widely thought to have an unrivalled genius for improvisation and a concomitant distrust for intellectualism and planning. Things are good or evil, right or wrong, black or white, and people should go for the good and crush the evil. To the pragmatic British, however, most things are of varying shades of grey, and one should seek to act as closely to the white end of the grey as may be, but recognizing that a compromise position is proper since there is something to be said on the other side of the case as well. To the French the principle *solvitur ambulando* is anathema: the logical consequences of decisions must be foreseen and analysed, and action thereby determined. Spanish pride is not to be insulted. Russian endurance is inexhaustible. Most peoples are widely thought to have a national character of which these are some familiar examples. If decision-makers are aware or believe that the people of their state are of a certain character, this will be another in the range of considerations that will influence their action.

All the elements of the domestic environment which have been discussed in this chapter come together to form one part of the framework within which the strategy of policy must be determined. But they have a direct bearing also on the last element of that environment, the military-strategic situation of the state. Decision-makers of almost every state perceive as one of their goals the maintenance of the 'independence' of their state—the control, that is to say, of the internal affairs of the state by an authority accepted as being indigenous. Provision for the defence of that independence is the major task of military strategy, though it may not be the only task that the military are called upon to perform. Military advice derived from analysis of a state's strategic situation can therefore be ignored by decision-makers only at very great risk.

Such analysis should include consideration of each of the elements already discussed. A state's geography is clearly fundamental. Britain's insular character meant that before the days of air power her security could be guaranteed if she could acquire and maintain mastery of the seas surrounding her. The naval arm in consequence was of primary importance, and the navy commanded admiration, status, and social prestige. A state with a long perimeter to defend, such as Tsarist Russia or the Soviet Union, needs massively large forces to guard it. Brandenburg-Prussia, as mentioned above, illustrates in the most extreme form the effect of strategic vulnerability. This state in the eighteenth century had no identifiable geographical or cultural centre, and it had no evident or defensible geographical limits. It was surrounded by hostile and more powerful neighbours, and its survival accordingly depended on a highly organized and highly efficient military establishment. The military were thus vital to the state's existence, and they acquired in consequence enormous prestige and wide-ranging privileges. Their power was limited only by their own willingness to limit it, and by their loyalty to the king. When this Prussia consolidated control over the whole of Germany in 1870-71, these militarist traditions spread through Germany, with major consequences for the character of Germany's political and social structure and processes of policy-making.[23]

Strategic imperatives do not derive only from the primary purpose of defending a state's territory. It may acquire interests which are thought to be vital and for which provision must therefore be made. Britain's wealth and power in the nineteenth century depended on her worldwide empire and her global trading system, and the defence of this system and in particular of its communications came to be seen as a vital interest. British policy therefore had always to take into account the threats that were or might be presented to these communications, and military strategy both made demands on resources to protect them, and counselled against the adoption of policies which might provoke threats that could not be countered. The limits imposed on policies by strategic considerations vary with the threats that can be presented, and so with the extent to which interests are concentrated or dispersed, as well as with location in relation to other centres of power and with the degree of natural defensibility.

Threats form only one side of the equation. The other is resources, economic, demographic, and political. In the twentieth century the kind of war that a state can engage in, and the length of time for which war-making can be sustained, depends on industry, availability of raw materials, technological level, and economic structure. Without large-scale heavy industry and a highly advanced technology, a state cannot itself produce, or produce in sufficient quantity, the complex and powerful weapons systems that have now been developed. Even with such industry and technological skill production of the weapons systems is impossible without a sufficiently large gross national product and with-

[23] Militarism should not of course be equated with aggressiveness. Given Germany's vulnerable situation between two great states, Russia and France, and with poor strategic barriers against them, the majority of Germany's strategists considered it necessary to be swiftly aggressive *if involved in war* in order to minimize the period of time during which war might have to be fought on two fronts: hence the Schlieffen plan for the attack through Belgium in 1914, and the wider-ranging Plan Yellow in 1940. But this very vulnerability caused the weight of military advice normally to be thrown against getting involved in war if it could possibly be avoided, and this was the main reason for military resistance to Hitler, ineffective and half-hearted though it was.

out direct control of, or secure access to, the necessary raw materials. This imposes sharp limits on possible policies. States lacking adequate economic resources, and perceiving threats from a state or states possessing them, cannot pursue policies that contain a substantial probability of military conflict without assurance of support from another state or other states than can supply weapons deficiencies. This has always been so in some degree; but the size of the disparity between the military capacity of the massive economies of the United States and the Soviet Union as compared with the military capacity of other states would virtually destroy the latter's freedom of manoeuvre and independence if it were not for two considerations. The first is that the potential destructiveness of available weapons is now so immense and horrifying that both major powers shrink from confrontations that might lead to their use and so lesser states can pursue their local quarrels with a fair degree of impunity. The second is that even in this situation of super military might, it alone is not decisive in relations between states. If military resources could be used without restraint, North Vietnam could not have resisted the United States for a week.

Economic structure affects war-making capacity, and so foreign policy, in another less obvious way. The more highly developed and integrated an economy, the less can manpower be extracted from it and mobilized for military activity without major disruption. A subsistence economy can engage in war almost, if need be, to the last man. A highly developed economy with a division of labour reflected in a great diversity of interacting skills can release manpower for military purposes only if there are trainable reserves available (for instance of unemployed, or women), or if rapid labour-saving technological advances can be made, or if the political system is able to control demands arising from a falling standard of living. In the case of prolonged war-making these three factors acting together could so fundamentally alter the political, economic and social structure of the state as to destroy permanently the way of life and the values which presumably were being defended. The Soviet Union, the United States, and Britain all displayed in the 1960s traces of such consequences of the wars in which they have respectively engaged since 1914. This in turn affects the character of policy-making; and the possibility of such consequences is, if understood, another control placed by military considerations on policy.

One further particular relationship of economic resources to military strategy should be noted. Developed economies dependent in a high degree on trade can make war only for a very short time unless they swiftly acquire territory which expands their resource base (as did Japan from 1937 onwards), or are sustained by massive credits or gifts from a supporter (as was Britain by the United States after 1940). A high import requirement of food and raw materials means that a high proportion of economic activity must be devoted to production for export. If industry is substantially converted to production of arms for use in war, and production for export is consequently curtailed, essential imports cannot be paid for. Britain's mobilizable overseas assets were virtually exhausted by December 1940, and she would have had to withdraw from the war and accept Hitler's terms within a few months, or accept the total collapse of her economy (which would have come to the same thing) had not the United States under the Lend-Lease Act of 1941 for the next few years supplied Britain at virtually no charge with materials, arms and supplies. Without such a supplier, be it the United States or another, Britain, having in two great wars exhausted her massive mobilizable overseas resources, cannot now make major war for more than a month or two, and knowledge of this fact makes any suggestion of doing so result in speculation against sterling. This happened in 1956, and was undoubtedly a major reason for the British decision to curtail the Suez operation. Thus economic limits on military resources can be a major constraint on foreign policy-making.

Demography likewise has a major impact on military strength. Evidently a large population, other things being equal, can provide manpower for larger armed forces than a small population. But other things are normally not equal. The size of the armed forces required will be affected by the nature of the threats that have to be guarded against, by the quality of the equipment that can be provided, and by the quality of leadership and the morale of the fighting man. Frederick the Great of Prussia in the eighteenth century could not adopt a military strategy which might involve loss of contact with any major body of his troops because the mercenaries whom he hired would simply have surrendered. This had fundamental effects on his strategy, and so on the size of armed forces that he needed. Since the first world war, on the other hand, much strategy is and has been based on the notion of mobile forces, perhaps of brigade-group size, operating independently in the enemy's rear, or without reference to any fixed lines, this strategy being possible because of the degree of commitment of rank and file as well as officers to defence of a cause, with high morale as a result. Morale is thus directly related to the extent to which a cause commands assent or passionate commitment. Hence the importance of propaganda. The hostility of the Ukrainians to the centralized Russian bureaucracy in Moscow was sufficiently strong for many not merely not to resist but actually to welcome the invading Germans in the late summer of 1941, until the brutalities and excesses which the invading armies and still more their following Nazi lackeys were with incredible stupidity encouraged by Hitler to commit caused a violent revulsion of feeling. The Messianic belief of many Japanese in the divine mission of their Emperor and their nation, on the other hand, produced feats of bravery and sacrifice that made the Japanese much more formidable enemies than their numbers alone would have warranted. To this one might add that a people which is by temperament disinclined to see any cause as being sufficiently meritorious to override the primary natural law of self-preservation is not likely to display high morale in wartime. The Italians perhaps exemplify scepticism of this kind.

The effectiveness of a given number of men thus varies with the nature of the issue in dispute and with a nation's character as well as with the quality of leadership and of equipment. The proportion of a population that can be mobilized, however, is affected not only by the nature of the economy, as previously discussed, but by demographic structure. A population with a high birth-rate will have a steady flow of men of most valuable military ages (20-35), while one whose trends show an increasing birth-rate up to say three decades ago, and then a levelling off, will reach a peak of availability of military-age men and thereafter suffer decline. Thus in assessing present and future military strength (and so measuring the military constraint on present and future foreign policies) demographic structure and demographic trends are of great importance. Not least among Hitler's many blunders was the impatience and the awareness that he was himself getting older that drove him to endeavour to create his thousand-year Reich long before the turnround in the German birth-rate had had time to alter the age structure of the German population. As a contrary example, the Fourth Republic and de Gaulle have in this respect bequeathed a handsome legacy to their successors if they are minded to use it.

Finally the military-strategic component of the domestic environment of decision-makers is affected by the nature and quality of the political and administrative systems. The effect on morale of commitment to a cause has already been noted. The extent of this commitment will greatly depend on the degree to which the political and social system is found by its members to be acceptable and satisfying. Mussolini's Fascism was not found to be acceptable and satisfying to the majority of Italians whereas Hitler's Nazism to many Germans was. The ineffectiveness, lack of spirit, and ineptitude in social matters of the French governments of the 1930s was one of the reasons for the support commanded by the French communist party and so for the undermining of the French army and of the French spirit of resistance which played its part in the collapse of 1940.[24] The political system of the Austro-Hungarian empire was seen by the Czechs and Croats and other ethnic groups within the empire as government by aliens, and so was found to be unacceptable. Croatian opposition in particular had much effect on the military strength of the Austro-Hungarians in the early stages of the first world war, until rumours of Anglo-French concessions of Dalmatian coast territory to Italy under the terms of the Treaty of London of 1915 caused many Croations to swing back to Austro-Hungarian allegiance. In the determination of attitudes towards a political system simple administrative efficiency is not without its place, while the importance of administrative skill in mobilizing the maximum potential of a state is too obvious to need more than passing mention. Here also Mussolini's Italy is an example of the effect of quite remarkable administrative incompetence.

The task of strategic advisers to governments, then, consists in identifying the nature of the threats that may be presented to the state, determining the forces and the weapons systems necessary to meet these threats, and measuring the resources as broadly defined in the foregoing paragraphs that are or can be made available for providing these forces and weapons systems. To the military nothing is safe, as to the doctor nothing is healthy, and to the priest nothing is pure, and strategic advisers will always demand more than they can get. It is the task of the government to weigh this advice against competing demands upon limited resources for other purposes of state. But the military themselves will frequently recognize that there are some threats which their state simply cannot counter. In these circumstances three lines of policy are open and may be recommended to decision-makers.

In the first place the advice may be that the threat is of such a nature and such a magnitude that efforts to meet it are not worth making: in this case the advice may be to assume that the threat does not exist and to advise decision-makers to pursue policies that will maximize the chances of the threat not materializing. As a memorandum drafted in the British War Office in February 1920 put it, 'The Army Council are of opinion that:— (a) We cannot afford to regard America as a potential enemy, as the expenditure entailed by adequate preparations to fight her would be so vast as to be out of the question in the present state of the nation's finances, and (b) That it is therefore imperative that our policy should be so directed as to eliminate any possibility of a

---

[24] Of course when Hitler attacked the Soviet Union in June 1941, and the imperialists' war became a people's war against fascism, the French communist party became a leading element in the French resistance against the Nazi occupier —a little late.

rupture between the United States of America and the British Empire.'[25]

Secondly, in the slightly less extreme case, the policy recommended may be to establish forces of such a size and character that although if the threat materialized they would be inadequate to resist for more than a short period, none the less they might be able to cause sufficient damage to the opponent for him to be unwilling to push an issue to the point of armed conflict unless the issue was of very great importance to him. This has been the traditional policy of the Swiss. Clearly unable in military terms to resist a determined assault from either France or Germany, they have none the less been able to preserve their immunity from attack without any particular subservience to French or German pressures, by maintaining forces of such a size that, in conjunction with their mountainous terrain, the losses they could inflict on either of their powerful neighbours have seemed, even in Hitler's time, in-commensurate with the gains that conquest of Switzerland would bring. The calculation is of course always precarious and uncertain.

The third method of dealing with a threat too formidable to be resisted is to compensate for military insufficiency by diplomatic means. This is the most direct and evident effect of military-strategic considerations on foreign policy. Diplomacy may seek to increase capacity to resist by associating the state with other states, or it may seek to lessen the threat by undermining the perceived opponent. The former expedient may involve a whole range of associations from a loose consultative understanding to a binding alliance (which by definition involves a commitment to give military support); each of these in varying degrees increases the likelihood of a state not being alone and thus reduces the chances of the threat materializing unless its weight is in turn increased. The latter method is classically illustrated in the policy of France, whose leaders from the time of Richelieu onwards, perceiving that Germany if united would dispose of greater resources than France, with great diplomatic skill and a variety of different devices kept the German states from coming together. The Franco-Prussian war represented disaster to France not because she was militarily defeated, but because Germany was thereby united. Similarly the Bolsheviks, perceiving at least until 1945 a threat from the capitalists which would be too great for them to meet, have by diplomatic means sought to compensate for their weakness by playing upon differences among the capitalist states.

*   *   *

[25] E. L. Woodward and R. Butler, eds., Documents on British Foreign Policy 1919-1939, first ser. vi (HMSO, 1946), pp. 1054-5.

Much of the discussion in this chapter, and particularly these last paragraphs, have shown that however much it is desirable or necessary for analytical purposes to endeavour to isolate the domestic from the international environment of decision-makers, in fact the two are closely connected and intertwined. In the next chapter the elements of the international environment will first be examined, and then the relationship between the two environments will be more systematically explored.

5

Influences on foreign policy-making
II. The international environment

THE DISCUSSION IN THE previous chapter centred on the limits imposed on foreign policies, and the motivations or impulses imparted to them, by the domestic environment within which decision-makers see themselves to be operating. But foreign policies are not made in a vacuum. They are made in relation to other bodies similarly acting in the global arena. No relations among humans or human groups can be maintained over anything more than a very short period of time without a certain minimum regulation, be it conventional, customary, ethical, legal or institutional. But regulation of whatever kind acts in greater or less degree to limit the freedom of manoeuvre of the units that are regulated, and the success of foreign policy decision-makers in achieving their goals will be affected by the extent to which they reckon accurately with these constraints. This is the first element of the international environment. The second and more important element is the policies and actions of other internationally-acting bodies, of which the other states are the most important. The chances of success of a foreign policy are reduced if insufficient account is taken of what other states or groups have done or are doing, or are likely to do in the future, in response to the particular policy in question or to some other stimulus in a different part of the international arena. How much account must be taken will vary according to the relative capabilities of the states or other bodies involved in a particular question, capabilities being defined to include the priority respectively attached to the question by the participants, and their willingness or unwillingness to mobilize in relation to it the resources of which they potentially dispose. This introduces the concept of power, which will be discussed in the concluding section of this chapter.

Individuals or groups accept regulation of their behaviour because acceptance is thought to be more tolerable than the consequences of resistance (punishment, material loss, foregoing of material gain, psychological ostracism or other penalty), and/or because they think the source of regulation has authority in the sense that he ought to be obeyed, whether by reason of his office or his quality, or because the social system which he regulates is thought to be valuable and might not survive without him. Once regulation has gained acceptance, it has some self-sustaining capacity, because lethargy and the habit of acceptance combine to make resistance more difficult. In international society each of these reasons for acceptance of regulation is weak. There is no authority generally accepted as having the right to make regulations that ought to be obeyed. There is no universal agreement that international society ought to be preserved, at least in its present form. Violation of such regulations or ethical or conventional or legal principles as do exist can attract no greater penalty than the other members of the society are themselves able and willing to impose. The degree of constraint imposed on foreign policies by the norms and institutional structure of international society is thus governed by the losses that decision-makers believe they and their state will suffer by violation or defiance.

The constraint none the less is not negligible. It is greater for some states than others, and in some questions more than other questions. Procedures for facilitating intercourse are widely accepted, and they form a distinctive feature of international society. Within a state a businessman who, seeking to gain control over a rival concern, invited the head of the concern to his office, seized him and locked him up, would be likely soon to find himself arrested by the police and thereafter imprisoned or otherwise punished. As between states, however, if the government of one chooses to arrest the diplomatic agents or the political leaders of another there is no superior authority that can offer redress or impose penalties. None the less, even between states of very unequal power, the inviolability of the political leaders and the properly authorized diplomatic agents of other states is normally observed. Even when two states go to war with each other, it is customary for diplomats and their staffs to be given safe conducts for their departure. The reason for this system of diplomatic immunity is simply that almost all governments recognize the advantage to themselves and to their states of being able to negotiate and make agreements with the governments of other states, and almost all recognize that the smooth working of this process depends on certainty that whatever agents are required to say or do they will not be held personally responsible unless they engage in criminal activity. So even in the extreme case of war between two states this principle is usually upheld, for any violation of it by one of the warring states would destroy the confidence of the governments of other states that their own representatives were safe.

The near-universal acceptance of these principles has in the past two decades been undermined by the Chinese communists' seeming willingness to be ostracized, by the emergence of many new states whose governments have not seen sufficient advantage in the system of diplomatic immunities for them always to regard the persons of diplomatic agents as being inviolable, and by the overriding importance attached by Soviet governments to maintenance of their control over eastern Europe which led to the treacherous seizure and execution of Imre Nagy and Pal Maleter of Hungary in 1956, and to the arrest and reported ill-treatment of Dubček, Černik and Smrkovsky of Czechoslovakia in 1968. The system of diplomatic immunities is none the less the most widely accepted convention of international society. Its importance lies not so much in the constraint it imposes on action as in the facilities it affords for the passing of information and so for the wiser formulation of policies. The less adequate the quantity and quality of information received by decision-makers, the more probable it is that their decisions will not produce their intended results, so the nature of the diplomatic system, and the extent to which states participate in it, forms an important element of their international environment.

The diplomatic system is paralleled, and in some degree supported, by international law, and by nascent international ethical norms. International law is law of a special kind. It does not flow from the enactments of a body with the authority to make law (like a legislative assembly in most states), nor normally from the judgments of a court. It is constituted by agreement among states on the rules, principles and conventions which they will observe in their mutual relations. Such agreement may be formalized in a treaty, bilateral or multilateral, and treaties may be buttressed by legal enactments passed by normal constitutional processes through the legislatures of states. Or agreement may take the form of tacit consent to rules of conduct not formulated in any legal instrument. There is an International Court, first founded in 1920, and reconstituted as the International Court of Justice in 1945, and Article 38 of the Statute of the Court explicitly recognizes the different kinds of agreement that lie behind international law: '1. The Court, whose function is to decide in accordance with international law such disputes as are submitted to it, shall apply: (a) international conventions, whether general or particular, establishing rules expressly recognized by the contesting states; (b) international custom, as evidence of a general practice accepted as law; (c) the general principles of law recognized by civilized nations.'[1]

Tacitly or formally agreed rules and principles of these kinds regulate such matters as diplomatic immunities, freedom of the seas, belligerent rights, rights over territorial waters, freedom in outer space, overflying rights, neutrality in war, compensation for nationalization of foreign property, and many other similar questions. In recent decades attempts have been made to establish legal principles in even more sensitive areas: the renunciation of war as an instrument of national policy by the Kellogg-Briand Pact of 1928, which received the signatures of sixty-five nations; the condemnation of the Nazis and the Japanese leaders at the Nuremberg and Tokyo trials for planning aggressive war; the establishment of the crime of genocide; and the Declaration of Human Rights. This last is in part a reflection of, and in part a stimulus to, the emergent signs of a few international ethical norms, of which the most widely accepted is perhaps that policies based on racial discrimination are wrong. The almost universal condemnation of South Africa's *apartheid* policies illustrates adherence to this principle, although the actions governments of states are willing to take to endeavour to enforce the principle vary very widely.

This is the crux of the matter so far as the constraining effect of law and ethics on foreign policy-making is concerned. Governments of states are themselves the judges of whether they will conform to law and custom and norms or not. Whether or not they do so will depend on the nature and importance of the issue, on the character of their external relations, and on the nature of their internal political system, beliefs, and traditions. If an issue is believed to be of primary and vital importance, the likelihood that a government will yield to a legal or ethical principle to the contrary is minimal unless other and more powerful states are determined to enforce compliance; and this is rare unless substantial political or other reasons march together with the principle in question. But even this generalization needs to be qualified by reference to the state's general external relations, and internal traditions.

[1] As quoted in H. Kelsen, *The Law of the United Nations* (Stevens, 1950), p. 874.

Thus some states are deeply and necessarily interrelated with other states, for economic or strategic or other reasons, while some can to a much greater degree (though none wholly so) pursue their aims independently. Moreover for some the way things are is broadly satisfactory, while for others it is profoundly unsatisfactory. Those who are broadly satisfied powers, and heavily dependent on a network of relationships, will be more inclined to conform to international law and ethics, for these tend to stabilize the system, while those who wish to upset the system altogether (for instance, the Nazis, or the Bolsheviks, or the Chinese communists) are less likely to accept the regulations that help to make it work. Finally the nature of the state's own system enters into the reckoning. The people of a state may believe that their governments have normally acted, and should normally act, in accordance with their obligations and with international law; in the degree to which the political system of this state makes the government responsive to opinion in all its forms, to that extent will the government of such a state be less able to violate the ethics and law of the system. There is no doubt that the constraint placed on United States actions in Vietnam in the late 1960s by the rise of articulate opinion hostile to United States intervention derived partly—though of course only partly—from the judgment that the actions were of questionable international legal validity or morality, and that it was neither right nor in the interests of the United States to weaken still further the already fragile international legal edifice. This is a case, and there are many, where an element of the domestic environment of decision-makers, and an element of their international environment, are organically related, and interact with each other.

Closely related to the diplomatic system, convention, law and ethics are the institutional arrangements which operate in the international arena. Institutions may be quasi-universal in membership, or they may consist only of a limited number of states associated for strategic, economic, geographical-regional, cultural, or historical reasons, or a combination of these. Both types of institution may be general in their purposes, or may exist to facilitate the performance of a particular function. Institutions may also vary very widely in their structure, and in the quality of the constraint that they impose on the freedom of manoeuvre of their members. Probably the loosest of all international institutions is the British Commonwealth, a historical relic of a former great empire. The Commonwealth is a shadowy consultative association, formally linked by general recognition of the British Crown as symbolic head, operating through periodic meetings of Prime Ministers, and Ministers of External Affairs, Finance or Defence, and now serviced by a secretariat. The Commonwealth does not serve any specific or defined purposes, no military or economic agreement exclusively links all Commonwealth members, and many have important extra-Commonwealth ties, like those of Britain and Canada in NATO, or of Australia and New Zealand in the ANZUS pact with the United States. No attempt is made to agree common policies to be followed by all members—though occasionally a consensus emerges from discussions—and some Commonwealth members are deeply divided from each other, the most striking example being India and Pakistan. In what sense then does the Commonwealth exist as an institutional constraint on the policies of its members?

Former Prime Minister Jawaharlal Nehru of India described membership of the Commonwealth as 'independence plus'. The plus elements included participation in the information-sharing activity of the Commonwealth Office in London and the ministerial meetings (many Commonwealth members had not the human or financial resourses to staff a large number of embassies, so access to the information flowing into London very substantially increased their knowledge of what was happening round the world); participation in the imperial preference arrangements, by which members maintained in relation to each reciprocally lower tariffs than against other countries; continued access to legal sources (from which had derived the legal systems of their countries), continued use of familiar commercial customs, codes and practices, continued links with military forms and military supplies upon the basis of which their forces were organized; participation in defence discussions predicated upon the assumption, if not that members would automatically come to one another's aid if any was involved in war, but at least that, with few exceptions, no other member might be an enemy. India's geographical situation as a massive peninsula in one of the world's great oceans, with the world's highest mountain range covering much of her northern frontier, would suggest that her primary strategic concern must be naval: in fact control of the western entry to the Indian Ocean by Britain in Suez and Aden in the Red Sea, of the southern entry by South Africa, and of the eastern entry by Singapore, meant that India's governments after independence felt able to limit their defence efforts essentially to land forces for the defence of the north-eastern frontiers against China and the north-western frontiers against Pakistan. The basis of these assumptions is not of course unchanging, but they had much to do with the early emergence of India as a power to be reckoned with in the years after 1947.

But the more an association is valued, the more it imposes constraints on its members. The degree of influence members of an association can

exert over each other depends upon the relative priorities they attach
to maintenance of the association and of membership in it. Someone
who passionately desires to remain a member of a cricket team will put
up with far more discourtesies and slights than will one who does not
much care whether he stays in the team or not. General de Gaulle was
able so effectively to bend the other members of the European Economic
Community to his will primarily because he persuaded them of his
willingness to disrupt the Community if it was not patterned to his
liking, whereas the other members saw maintenance of the Community
as being far more important than resisting what might be only the
temporary unpleasantness of the General. The other members of the
Commonwealth were unable to cause South Africa to moderate her
apartheid policies because Verwoerd and his colleagues saw membership
of the Commonwealth as being less important than *apartheid*. So membership of an association constrains policies in the degree in which
members respectively see its maintenance, and membership of it, as
being more or less important than other goals. Even so loose an association as the Commonwealth has thus some effect on members' policies,
if only by the fact of its existence, and by consultation. But the effect
is surely becoming less, as the information function in London is reduced, as other regional, cultural, strategic, or economic ties develop, as
the value of imperial preference dwindles, and as the assumption of
defence harmony becomes less universal.

At the other extreme from a loose association like the Commonwealth is a tightly controlled organization like the Warsaw Pact and
its economic counterpart, Comecon. The same principle applies. In the
early years after 1945 the communist governments in the countries of
eastern Europe depended entirely on Soviet support to remain in power.
Tito in Yugoslavia was able in 1948 to defy the Soviets precisely because his leadership of resistance against the Nazis, and his building of
a political and administrative structure in the latter months of the
war, gave him an internal base of support on which he could rely. The
Polish, Bulgarian, Romanian and Hungarian communists came in on
the backs of the Red Army and were regarded with varying degrees of
hostility by their peoples, while the Czech communists gained sole
control of the government by a Soviet-backed *coup d'état* in February
1948: in all cases the governments could not survive without Soviet
support. Economically likewise they needed assistance, and as the cold
war intensified they needed military support also. The Soviet government was thus able to dominate its associates even before the Warsaw
pact was signed. But as gradually the economic situation improved,
and the military danger came to seem less pressing (and as changes

occurred within the Soviet Union itself after the death of Stalin), the overmastering need for Soviet support lessened and the Communist leaders (Gomulka in Poland, Nagy in Hungary, Ceauşescu in Romania, Dubček in Czechoslovakia) felt able at various times and with varying degrees of success, to strike out on their own. But the limits within which they could move clearly remained sharply circumscribed, for control of the association was seen by the Soviets as being so vital that they were prepared to use their overwhelming military force to assert it, even at heavy cost to almost all their other major foreign policy goals. In this case, where initially the very survival of regimes was in question, the constraint imposed by association with the Soviet Union was overwhelming, but it is the military strength of the dominant member which has ensured that the constraint continues, though less stringently. But as the economic recovery of the weaker members has advanced, and as the external military threat has been seen to recede, the Warsaw pact association has increasingly come to be a constraint on foreign policy in Moscow also, for the rulers in the Kremlin do not wish to jeopardize other objectives by the use of their military might if they think they can possibly avoid it.

A third type of international institution with limited membership, offering constraints of a different kind, is that exemplified by the European Communities. The three Communities (European Coal and Steel, Euratom, and European Economic) were designed for the performance of particular functions: integration of the coal and steel industries of the six member countries, integration of activity in relation to the peaceful uses of atomic energy, and integration of tariff systems leading to economic union. Most of those whose initiative led to the foundation of the Communities, however, saw them primarily as steps on the road to a federated western Europe; and each of the Communities accordingly had a supranational element among its institutions, though of different kinds. The High Authority of the ECSC was given powers in strictly delimited spheres to take decisions binding on the member countries. The Treaty of Rome laid down successive stages in the development of the European Economic Community at which different classes of questions would become subject to decision by majority vote in the Council of Ministers, the vote then being binding on all members. It is true that under the pressure of de Gaulle procedures and conventions have developed which have substantially curtailed the effectively supranational element of the Communities, but even so the acceptance by six states of any decisions binding upon them which have not been made solely by their own governments imposes a limit on their freedom of action of a different kind from that imposed by any other association. A Franco-Soviet trade agreement might well help the French very substantially towards their goal of a *détente* with the Soviet Union; but the consequences for France of an attempt to vary her tariff on, for instance, cars imported from the USSR would be of a different kind from those that would follow from a similar action by Great Britain whose freedom of action in this field is limited less sharply by her signature of the General Agreement on Tariffs and Trade.[2]

Other institutions with limited membership can be located along a scale in relation to these three types. The Organization for African Unity and the Arab League lie close to the Commonwealth end of the scale; the Organization of American States, the Central Treaty Organization and the South-East Asia Treaty Organization lie towards the same end but a little closer to the Warsaw pact; while the North Atlantic Treaty Organization in some degree parallels the Warsaw pact with the highly influential position of the United States, and in some respects comes close to the European Communities with the assignment of armed forces by the treaty signatories to a unified command. Finally the Western European Union, which emerged in 1955 from the ruins of the European Defence Community, has the shadow of a supranational element in the British undertaking not to reduce the 1955 level of her forces on the European mainland without a supporting majority vote of the other WEU states; but the escape clauses are wide enough to make such a majority vote probable, for most members would prefer that the escape clauses should not be invoked. The supranational element is thus largely ineffective, and Britain has in fact gained reluctant agreement to the reorganization and reduction of her forces.

Institutional membership by their states forms part of the international environment of decision-makers. The nature of the environment will vary, as has been shown, according to the nature of the institution, and according to the various degrees of commitment to it of the member states as against their other policy goals. But their policies are moderated also by the effect of their institutional membership on the policies of other states towards them. The Federal German Republic's relations with Czechoslovakia are evidently very much affected by the facts that the Federal Republic is a member of NATO and Czechoslovakia is a member of the Warsaw pact. In a less direct, but also im-

---

[2] The ability of members of the EEC to make separate trade treaties was originally intended to end on 1 January 1970; but in October 1969 the Council of Ministers agreed that the right to negotiate bilaterally should continue in exceptional cases until the end of 1973, subject to prior authorization by the Council, to a determination by the Commission and Council of the outline content of the negotiations, and to approval of the agreement by the Council before its signature.

portant sense, the Warsaw pact institution as a whole forms a not insignificant element of the Federal Republic's international environment. So institutions can be important both to members and to non-members, though again the degree and nature of the influence will vary.

Quasi-universal institutions are far more numerous than institutions with limited membership. The United Nations Organization in 1968 had 122 members, excluding only Switzerland, the Chinese People's Republic, North and South Korea, North and South Vietnam, the Federal German Republic and the German Democratic Republic, and the Vatican, among states recognized as such by at least some members of the international community.[3] It had six principal organs, a General Assembly, a Security Council, an Economic and Social Council, a Trusteeship Council, an International Court of Justice, and a Secretariat. By the Charter the Organization has through the Security Council a supranational power in relation to all members except five major states, the Republic of China, France, the USSR, the United Kingdom, and the United States who are permanent members of the Council. By Article 24 the members of the Organization 'confer on the Security Council primary responsibility for the maintenance of international peace and security, and agree that in carrying out its duties under this responsibility the Security Council acts on their behalf';[4] and by Article 25 the members 'agree to accept and carry out the decisions of the Security Council in accordance with the present Charter'. Such decisions by Article 27 (as amended) 'shall be made by an affirmative vote of nine members including the concurring votes of the permanent members'. The effect of these provisions is that in the exercise of its enforcement powers in relation to the maintenance of international peace and security, the Security Council can take decisions which are binding upon all members, and even the Council itself need not be unanimous, a majority vote of nine out of fifteen being sufficient provided that the nine includes the five votes of the permanent members. Only these five therefore retain legal sovereignty as far as enforcement action in relation to peace and security is concerned.

The apparently revolutionary implications of these provisions have been in large part nullified by conflicts among the five permanent members, and particularly between the United States and the Soviet Union. Their growing hostility first prevented the carrying through of the

[3] Some characteristics of statehood, but usually not the capacity to conduct their own foreign policy, were possessed by the following in 1968, also not members of the United Nations: Andorra, Bhutan, Liechtenstein, Monaco, Muscat and Oman, Nauru, San Marino, and West Samoa.

[4] The United Nations Charter is quoted in H. G. Nicholas, *The United Nations as a Political Institution* (Oxford University Press, paperback, 1967), pp. 207-39.

military arrangements provided in the Charter for giving the Security Council military means of enforcing its decisions. Thereafter, as the United States and the Soviet Union increasingly came to see the world as being divided into their friends and their enemies, on very few occasions could effective decisions be reached in cases where peace was threatened or broken, for any decision would have adverse implications for one party which would be seen by either the Soviet Union or the United States as one of its actual or potential friends. Even when decisions have been reached, the means of enforcement have usually not been in existence, and it has been difficult to create them. The Congo in 1960-61 affords one of the few examples of a case in which both the Soviet Union and the United States sufficiently realized the dangers of escalation to a major conflict for them at the outset to agree to give wide discretionary authority to the Secretary-General, Dag Hammarskjöld, who used it to mobilize armed contingents from member states other than the great powers, and to intervene with military force.

The sharp constraint on state action intended by the framers of the Charter for all but the five has thus not materialized. At first sight it might appear that the effect of the Security Council voting provisions might be to make association with one of the five more necessary for other states in order to have assurance that the Security Council might not act against them should they be involved in a dispute. This would increase the influence exerted over them by the power to which they attached themselves. In practice this has happened only in small degree, partly because of the Security Council's lack of means of enforcement, and partly because both major powers have been reluctant to see coercion not merely of even their most loosely associated *protégés*, but also of states which they hoped to attract into their orbit; their reluctance has been due to fear that failure more effectively to defend such states might provoke a move into the other camp. The history of the Levant since 1947 exemplifies both these propositions, where the United Nations has been unable to prevent three wars and has been unable to evolve terms for a settlement; and where Soviet support for the Israelis against British and to a less extent United States imperialist domination and exploitation of the Arabs has swung to Soviet support for the Arabs against Israel, now seen as the tool of United States and British imperialism. The turn of the Arabs to the Soviet Union primarily resulted from the inadequacy as they saw it of United States and British support for their economies and against Israel.

The conclusion of this is not that the existence of the Security Council is a negligible element of decision-makers' international environments—merely that it is a much less important element than was

intended; and that the degree of its importance is to be seen in the judgments made by decision-makers in the calculus of losses and gains in
relation to various goals in which ignoring proceedings of the Council,
or non-compliance with a decision, is one term. Incidentally it should be
observed that it is not perverse uncooperativeness on the part of the
Soviet Union that has stultified the working of the Security Council,
true though it is that the Soviet Union has vetoed[5] almost exactly ten
times as many resolutions as all the other permanent members put together: the stultification is the result of disagreements among the five,
and since at least until recently the Soviet Union was in a permanent
minority in the United Nations the veto power came to play an important role in its endeavour to prevent the Organization being used
by the United States as an instrument of policy against it or its associates.

Frustration in the Security Council led to attempts to use the General
Assembly for purposes that had not originally been intended. The
power of the Assembly to discuss, and to make to the members of the
United Nations or to the Security Council or to both recommendations
about all matters within the scope of the Charter was explicitly limited
by Article 12, by which the Assembly was precluded from making any
recommendations with regard to a dispute or situation with which the
Security Council was in its own judgment dealing. The primacy of the
Security Council in matters relating to international peace and security,
explicitly stated in Article 24 (1), was thus effectively confirmed. In
November 1950, however, when the unprecedented ability of the
Security Council (because of the temporary absence of the Soviet Union)
to authorize military action in support of South Korea against North
Korea's invasion was jeopardized by the return of the Soviet delegate
to the Council, the United States secured in the General Assembly passage of a resolution permitting the emergency summoning of a special
session of the Assembly to act in matters relating to international peace
and security in cases where the Council 'because of lack of unanimity
of the permanent members, fails to exercise its primary responsibility'.[6]
The legality of this so-called 'Uniting for Peace' resolution remained in
dispute, but whether it was legal or not the supranational powers of
the Security Council were not transferred. The Assembly could, it is
true, take decisions by a two-thirds majority, but its decisions could be
in the form only of recommendations, requests or appeals, which mem-

[5] That is, has withheld its concurring vote even though all four other permanent members, and not less than five (or before amendment three) of the
non-permanent members, have voted in favour.
[6] Nicholas, *op. cit.* p. 114.

bers could legally obey or ignore as they chose. The nature of the constraint imposed by the United Nations on the freedom of manoeuvre of state decision-makers is thus not essentially changed. The Security Council has legal authority to take decisions binding on all states members of the United Nations; but its ability to reach such decisions has been virtually nullified by United States–Soviet conflict, and this conflict has also been largely responsible for the failure to create means of enforcement responsible to and under the control of the Council and the Secretary-General. The Assembly has power to make recommendations, but not to give instructions. In both cases therefore the effectiveness of Council resolutions and of Assembly recommendations will depend on the decision-maker's perception of the relative importance of the gains and losses that defiance or compliance will respectively bring. Thus Britain and France after only brief delays accepted the Assembly's cease-fire resolution over Suez in November 1956, while the Soviet Union at almost precisely the same time ignored the Assembly's call for the withdrawal of Soviet invading forces from Hungary.

Of the other principal organs of the United Nations, the International Court of Justice has already been referred to, and the Secretariat is of importance in the foreign policies of states in so far as the Security Council or the General Assembly gives authority for action, and in rather less degree as a channel through which 'world opinion' may find expression or be mobilized. Speeches or reports to other organs by the Secretary-General may not by themselves be likely greatly to influence the behaviour of governments; but to the extent that such speeches or reports reflect the views or command the support of significant members of international society they may serve to strengthen other factors in bringing about a modification of behaviour. Most governments will endeavour to avoid an adverse public statement by the Secretary-General; but equally the Secretary-General must be circumspect in making such statements, both because the effective conduct of his duties may be jeopardized if he provokes the hostility of important members of international society, and because the prestige and so the influence of his office may be impaired if an adverse speech produces no evident consequences. The first Secretary-General, Trygve Lie, incurred the hostility of the Soviet Union over Korea, and thereafter found it increasingly impossible to act, while the authority of U Thant almost certainly suffered from the failure of his public statements about Vietnam to bring any nearer an early end to the conflict.

The Trusteeship Council and the Economic and Social Council, on the other hand, form more important elements of the external environments of decision-makers. The responsibility of the former was to oversee the administration of non-selfgoverning trust territories by states designated as trustees: the territories in question were all, with the exception of Somaliland, formerly administered under mandate from the League of Nations. This was a limited and diminishing responsibility. The importance of the Trusteeship Council derived from the fact that its procedures served as a model for General Assembly action in relation to Article 73 of the Charter which with reference to all non-selfgoverning territories (and not merely former mandates) laid on colonial powers obligations to promote the wellbeing of the inhabitants, to develop self-government, and to transmit to the Secretary-General regular information about economic, social and educational conditions in the territories. 'Anticolonialism' gradually became an international ideology which, as more and more colonies gained independence, could command the reflex emotional support of a steadily increasing number of members of the United Nations.

No state could afford to ignore this ideology. For the USSR it was an asset to be exploited; for the totalitarian nature of the Soviet system enabled its rulers so effectively to control the behaviour of non-self-governing peoples within its borders, and information about them, that the fact that the peoples of Estonia, Latvia, Lithuania, Georgia, Azerbaijan, Armenia, Kazakistan, Uzbekistan, Kirghizia, Tajikistan, and Turkmenia in varying degrees desired self-government virtually escaped notice. For Great Britain, France, and Portugal, on the other hand, the ideology with its institutionalized means of expression in the General Assembly became in the 1950s and 1960s an increasingly pervasive element of their external environments. The United States, which thought itself (on the whole justly) to merit little of the stigma of colonialism, found itself in a position in the Assembly of growing ambivalence, as the ally in NATO of the former great imperial powers, and as the opponent of perceived Soviet expansionism, and so of Soviet sponsored independence movements. So automatic became the assumptions that a British-controlled overseas territory must be being exploited, and that its inhabitants must be desiring to throw off the yoke, that the Assembly twice voted, in 1967 and in 1968, for resolutions requiring Britain to transfer Gibraltar to Spain, despite the fact that a free plebiscite of the inhabitants had shown an overwhelming majority in favour of a continuation of the British tie. The Charter principle of self-determination was thus set aside in favour of assumptions about resented colonial status which the evidence in this case denied. The irony in the situation was sharpened by the fact that transfer was being required to a Spain still governed by a quasi-Fascist regime whose nature had excluded Spain from NATO and from the United Nations itself until 1955, and to which the majority of the anticolonial states had hitherto been antipathetic. The institutionalized principle of trusteeship, with which the idea of self-government and the ideology of anti-colonialism came to be associated, thus became a major element of the external environment of the governments of all states, whether as a constraint upon action, or as an asset to be exploited.

There remains for consideration one further group of institutions which constrain the behaviour of governments of states. These have come into existence because of changes in the nature, scope and range of state relationships, changes which have themselves resulted mainly from the advance of science and technology. A century ago relations between states still consisted largely of diplomatic relations between governments, and in substantial degree of relations between monarchs: it was not until 1874 that letters between individuals or firms or other groups became sufficiently frequent for arrangements to be made, in the Universal Postal Union, for standardizing procedures for handling mail. By the middle of the twentieth century several hundred international organizations of various kinds had been brought into existence, reflecting the web of international relationships not merely among states but among other groups and among individuals. Many of these organizations came under the aegis of the Economic and Social Council of the United Nations. The Council itself established a dozen or so Commissions,[7] and it acted as a coordinating body for such specialized agencies as the Universal Postal Union, the International Labour Organization, the International Telecommunications Union, the International Bank for Reconstruction and Development, the International Monetary Fund, the International Civil Aviation Organization, the Food and Agriculture Organization, the United Nations Educational, Scientific and Cultural Organization, the World Health Organization, the World Meteorological Organization, the International Trade Organization (never formally in existence, but some of its proposed functions performed under the General Agreement on Tariffs and Trade and the United Nations Conference on Trade and Development), the International Atomic Energy Agency, the Intergovernmental Maritime Consultative Organization, and the International Development Association. In addition the Council formed consultative arrangements with some

[7] Economic, Employment and Development Commission; Commission on Human Rights; Commission on Narcotic Drugs; Transport and Communications Commission; Fiscal Commission; Statistical Commission; Social Commission; Commission on Status of Women; Population Commission; Economic Commission for Europe; Economic Commission for Asia and the Far East; Economic Commission for Latin America; Economic Commission for Africa. Some of these existed only for a short time.

two hundred non-governmental organizations such as the World Federation of Trade Unions, the Inter-Parliamentary Union, the International Chamber of Commerce, and the World Federation of United Nations Associations; but there exist an unknown number—probably over a thousand—of other such organizations with which the Council has no formal relationship. 'A large proportion of the people of the world are connected with one or more of these organizations, for they include in their membership nearly all the large churches, trade unions, businessmen's associations, co-operative societies, farmers' groups, and women's organizations, as well as numerous professional, scientific, humanitarian, and social reform organizations. They deal with almost every possible subject from theology to the Olympic games, from child welfare to astronomy, from cancer to the problems of labor, from aviation to women's rights.'[8]

The impetus towards, or restraint upon, action by governments imparted by these numerous organizations clearly varies very widely, both according to the nature of the organization and (as in the case of legal and ethical principles) according to the responsiveness or otherwise of a particular political system to popular or pressure group influences. Some organizations may influence policy questions of first importance, as the International Monetary Fund's directors may have a say in the exchange rates of currencies. Others, such as the International Political Science Associations, are likely to have negligible effects, except to the extent that meetings of opinion-forming professional elites from different countries may produce marginal consequences on opinion in their countries when they return. Here is another, though not significant, example of interaction between the domestic and external environments of decision-makers. But difficult though it may be to measure the influence of this massive network of institutions and organizations upon governmental behaviour, it is clear that the network forms a probably increasingly important element of the external environment within which decision-makers must work.

One peculiar feature of some of these organizations deserves to be noted. The distinction should be emphasized between on the one hand the very large number of non-governmental organizations, and on the other the Economic and Social Council Commissions and specialized agencies, which are composed either of representatives of governments, or of persons evolved by a variety of methods from consultation or dis-

[8] Quoted in N. D. Palmer, and H. C. Perkins, *International Relations*, 3rd ed. (Houghton Mifflin, 1969), p. 321, from L. C. White, 'Peace by pieces—the role of non-governmental organizations', *Annals of the American Academy of Political and Social Science*, cclxiv (July 1949), 88.

cussion or election by governments. In many of these institutions, therefore, governments find themselves in positions similar to those of policy-forming members of groups within states. A shareholder in a company can (at least in theory) share in the decision about the annual rate of dividend, and he will then, as an individual, be in relation with the company as an entity, of which he himself forms a part, when the company's representative sends him the dividend warrant. The head of a university department may participate in the making of decisions about the number of staff in his department, and he will then as an individual similarly be in relation with the university as an entity, when the university administration authorizes him to proceed with the advertisement of vacancies. In both cases, however, if the shareholder or the professor feels sufficiently strongly about the issue, he can withdraw, the shareholder by selling his shares, and the professor by resigning. In the case of international institutions the choice of withdrawal may in effect hardly exist. The government of Norway might be profoundly opposed to a generally supported proposal of the Universal Postal Union to authorize the levying of a surcharge on all parcels from abroad weighing more than two kilograms; but opposition could not realistically be carried to the point of withdrawing from the Union because it is only through membership of the Union that the movement of Norwegian mail can be organized. The shareholder can put his shares in another company. The professor can seek a post in another university. There is only one international postal system. There is similarly only one meteorological system, only one international currency system (although the links between units in the system may be stronger in some cases than in others), and disease knows no frontiers. Membership of these organizations thus enables functions (of varying degrees of importance) to be performed which can be performed in no other way. The option of withdrawal may exist only at the cost of very heavy losses which it is likely to be possible to recoup, if at all, only by rejoining the organization. Equally deadlock on an issue (on proposed action, for instance, to control the smuggling of cocaine) is likely to be disadvantageous to all parties. The effect of this situation is that although in at least some cases state sovereignty is formally maintained in the sense that states cannot be bound by decisions to which their representatives do not agree, in fact the pressures to reach agreement are strong, and parties usually find themselves in bargaining situations where the 'no agreement' option is advantageous to no one.[9]

Non-governmental organizations come into existence, it has been suggested, to advance a particular interest or to promote a particular

[9] See Chapter 6, pp. 127-8.

goal, ethical or other. Not normally included in the category of non-governmental organizations is one further element of states' environments, namely international companies. The extent to which business influences foreign policies either in 'socialist' or in 'capitalist' countries is a disputed matter on which evidence is difficult to obtain, but this is not the point at issue here. As a constraint in the external environment of decision-makers, international companies have effects because of the ties they create between countries. The existence of Unilever is a factor in Anglo-Dutch relations. The collaboration between the British Aircraft Corporation and Sud Aviation in the building of the supersonic airliner Concorde is a factor in Anglo-French relations. Similarly the growing cooperative activity of the central banks of the ten major financial powers is a not negligible feature of the international arena. Finally even individuals can on occasion contribute a tiny element to the external environment of decision-makers, as perhaps did Bertrand Russell when from Penrhyndeudraeth during the Cuba crisis of 1962 he cabled Kennedy and Khrushchev.

But of course the major part of the external environment of decision-makers is formed by the existence and decisions of the governments of other states. States exist to further the interests of their peoples, and governments should act as best they may in accordance with this end. Interests in most cases are so conceived as to cause or require disagreement, competition or conflict with other states. The issue of this disagreement, competition or conflict will depend on a large number of factors. In a simple two-state question the issue of the disagreement will be affected, in the first place, by the extent to which the two governments respectively feel they need the support of the other in other questions. The Israeli attack on the Beirut airport at the end of 1968 in retaliation for an Arab guerrilla attack on an El Al aircraft at Athens was undertaken, despite the near-certainty of United States displeasure, presumably in the calculation that United States support was less necessary than it had been, and would not be wholly withdrawn anyway because of the strength of the Jews in New York, a crucial state in presidential elections, and because the United States could not afford to let the whole of the Levant come under the control of Soviet-oriented Arabs. Thus the United States found great difficulty in restraining Israel, despite the overwhelmingly greater resources at the disposal of the American government.

The result of disagreements will be affected, secondly, by the ways in which the governments of the states in question conceive their roles. The Russian pressure on Iran at the beginning of the twentieth century was regarded by the United States with almost total indifference, while the similar pressure by the Soviets in 1945-6 provoked a United States response which in large part made possible the successful Iranian resistance: United States decision-makers had formed a new conception of Washington's international role.

In the third place, the result of disagreement between two states will be affected by the nature of the question at issue—whether it is a major question for both parties, or only for one; whether it is geographically close for both parties, or only for one; whether its resolution is a matter of urgency for both parties, or one can afford to wait longer than the other. The extent of the concessions that Stalin was able to extract from Ribbentrop in the negotiations for the Nazi-Soviet pact on the evening of 21 August 1939 was crucially affected by the fact that Hitler had to announce an agreement within at most two days if he were to have time to frighten off Britain and France from supporting Poland and still leave time for the destruction of Poland before the autumn campaigning season was over.

But questions are almost never at issue between two states. Even if other states are not directly involved or do not directly interfere, the way a question between two states is settled will have consequences for the relations of each with other states. The way in which the German–Czech crisis of 1938 was settled in the Munich agreement had effects on Czech attitudes towards Britain and France, and towards the Soviet Union; on Soviet attitudes towards Britain and France, and towards Germany; on Germany's attitudes towards Britain and France; on British and French attitudes towards Germany and Italy; on British attitudes towards Japan; on United States attitudes towards Germany, Japan, and Britain and France. Some of these states were more involved in the crisis than others, and some hardly at all. Foreign policies are not made in a vacuum: action taken in relation to one problem, or to one state, will have repercussions round the globe, of which only some will be foreseeable and foreseen, and only some will be perceived. One of the most difficult tasks of decision-makers, frequently ill-performed, is to calculate the consequences in other arenas of action in relation to a particular issue, to assess the extent to which other goals may be jeopardized, and to judge priorities, in the short term and the long term, of one goal against another. Precisely a calculation of this kind needed to be made by the Soviets in deciding whether or not to invade Czechoslovakia in 1968.

Much of the preceding discussion in this and the previous chapter may be summed up by saying that foreign policy depends on power. This is deliberately to give to the concept of power a very wide definition (and it is not the whole story, as will be shown at the end of this chapter).[10] Power may be simply defined as 'the capacity to produce intended effects',[11] or 'the ability to influence the behavior of others in accordance with one's own ends'.[12] The exercise of power by a state is to be observed when the government of one state, because of the actions or existence of another, changes its proposed behaviour : the change may involve an alteration of policy, or the maintenance of a policy which without the exercise of power would have been changed. The ways in which power may be exercised—ranging from the mere existence of a state, through diplomacy and economic pressures to subversion and unlimited military violence—will be discussed in the next chapter; but it is not to be assumed that power is greatest when it is exercised in the most violent form. At first sight it might seem that the ability of a state to impose its will by military victory is the ultimate measure of power; but it may on the contrary be argued that the need to resort to violence demonstrates a state's lack of power. This argument gains force in an age when nuclear weapons contain the threat of total destruction for their users : behaviour would not have been influenced in a desired direction if both states involved in the relationship were destroyed.

The concept of power is therefore more usefully employed if its measurement includes the idea of minimizing loss : on this view the smaller the loss suffered in bringing about a behavioural change, the greater the power of the state; and its power is greatest when its mere existence produces a change in another state's policy, or inhibits the adoption of a policy that would otherwise have been followed. The common sense of this view is demonstrated by the fact that the more resources a state has to commit to bring about a behavioural change in one case, the less it has available to bring about simultaneous changes in other cases; and so looking at a state within the system as a whole, the less it has to commit resources, or suffer loss, over one issue, the more it is able to influence behaviour throughout the system, and so the greater its power. The inability of the United States adequately to modify North Vietnam's behaviour without military violence and the suffering of heavy losses reduced the ability of the United States to influence behaviour in other areas, and seeing what Vietnam did to the United States, other governments will be less likely to yield on issues they consider vital when Washington presses them, in the expectation that no United States administration will want to get into a mess like this again.

It is immediately apparent from the foregoing that power exists only

[10] See pp. 120-1 below.
[11] J. Frankel, *International Relations* (Oxford University Press, 1964), p. 97.
[12] A. F. K. Organski, *World Politics* (Knopf, 1958), p. 96.

in a relationship between or among two or more entities. To speak of the 'power of Great Britain' in isolation is meaningless. Britain has no capacity to influence behaviour which can be assessed in isolation from another entity whose behaviour is to be influenced. The capacity will depend on a large number of elements which have already been discussed —the state's size, location, terrain and climate; its natural resources and their accessibility : its degree of dependence on trade; its level of technology, and the extent to which it is a deficit or surplus country in capital and technical skill; the degree of its economic mobilization and the extent of untapped potential; its economic structure and stability; the size, structure, skills and trends of its population; its political structure and stability, its constitutional system, and the quality of leadership; the character of its people, their morale, and their values and social mores; its military resources influenced by all of the foregoing; the nature of its international environment, ethically, legally, institutionally, diplomatically, and the quality and range of interaction between the government's domestic and international environments—all these will contribute to the capacity of the government of a state to influence the behaviour of another; but the capacity will differ in relation to state B from what it will be in relation to state C, and it will differ when it is being exercised on issue X in relation with state B from what it will be when being exercised on issue Y also in relation with state B.

Even if it were possible simply to quantify all these elements of power (and clearly some, such as the number of tanks of a certain specification, are easier to quantify than others, such as the positive or negative value of location), one could not add them all up and state the answer as the measure of a state's power, because the value of different elements varies according to the relationship and according to the issue in question. In 1947 the Soviet Union was able to dissuade Poland and Czechoslovakia from accepting the invitation to participate in the Marshall Plan discussions, but was not able to prevent the discussions from taking place; the same assembly of elements of power was able to influence the behaviour of the Polish and Czech governments, but not the governments of Britain and France and the other fourteen participating states. In the Cuba crisis of 1962 the power of the United States was almost certainly primarily a function of military-strategic considerations—the local logistic and conventional weapons superiority of the United States as against the Soviet Union, and the consequent inability of the latter to sustain their position against military pressure without escalation to a thermo-nuclear exchange and hence to a degree of unacceptable loss. In the Vietnam conflict, on the other hand, the military strength of the United States was larger than in 1962 and overwhelmingly greater than that of North Vietnam, but its total employment was inhibited by elements of the United States government's domestic and international environments. In this issue therefore these were crucial elements in United States power, or rather lack of it. Chamberlain was able in 1938 to obtain Hitler's signature to a piece of paper stating the desire of the two peoples never to go to war with each other again, but he was not able significantly to moderate Hitler's demands on Czechoslovakia.

These three examples illustrate the complexity of the interaction patterns involved. In the first case the same state was able to influence the behaviour of two states in a particular question, but not sixteen others. In the second case one element of the power of a state was crucial in one question, another element was crucial in another question. In the third case the leader of one state was able to influence the behaviour of the leader of another on one question, but not on another question. The first case thus illustrates the general point already made—that the power of a state can be assessed only in terms of the modification of the behaviour of the government of another state that the first can produce. The second shows that the elements of the power of a state are all interrelated, and that the ranking importance of the various elements will vary from one issue to another and from one bilateral relationship to another. A large population of which a substantial part has received military training will, other things being equal, give to the government greater power in relation to a state at a similar level of technology but with a smaller population than it will in relation to a state with the same smaller population but a higher level of technology. The third example suggests that when two questions are at issue between two states the power of each in relation to the two questions will, other things again being equal, be affected by the relative priority given by the two governments to each of the questions and the size of the effort that each is prepared to devote to the achievement of the different goals. The will to use resources is thus crucial, and this will is in its turn fundamentally affected by the relative importance attached by the governments to the particular question at issue as compared with other goals, both domestic and international.

Moreover each of the elements of power is continually changing, though some (such as geographical location) change relatively slowly, while others (such as quality of leadership) may change relatively rapidly and frequently.[13] The effect of all this is that the power of all

[13] In a geographical sense, location does not of course change at all. But the political significance of location, in the sense of its contribution to the capacity to influence the behaviour of others, does change—as a result, for instance, of changes in technology.

states is constantly in flux: at any one moment of time it varies from issue to issue, and from one relationship to another; and from one moment of time to another power changes as the elements of power alter and as the interaction of the elements is accordingly modified.

But to say that power exists and can be assessed only when a modification of behaviour is brought about and observed is not totally to deny the possibility of describing a hierarchy of states according to their power. It is reasonable to suppose that the government of a state with favourable geographical characteristics, a large, young and skilled population, a large gross national product, plentiful economic resources, a stable political system, well-armed military forces, and with goals reflecting substantial satisfaction with its international environment, is likely to be able to influence the behaviour of governments disposing of less of these attributes to a greater degree than it can be influenced by them. This need not necessarily be so, and will not always be so, as the United States–North Vietnam example suggests, but it is a reasonable working hypothesis, and serves to give some rational foundation for the normal classification of states into great powers (sometimes now subdivided into superpowers and great powers), middle powers, and small powers. It must always be remembered, however, that cases may occur when a small power will be able in conflict with a great power to cause modification of the behaviour of the great power rather than submit to modification of its own.

The terminology 'great power' and 'small power' does, however, imply assessment of power based on inventories of the elements of power, and so tends to blur the essential meaning of the concept. To keep the meaning clear it is perhaps desirable to define a great power within the terms of the power concept as it has been here developed. The commonsense idea of a great power includes the thought of influential action over much or all of the globe, it includes the expectation of influence being sustained over a period of time, and it seems as a great power a state that can act off its own bat. So far as the last criterion is concerned, even the seemingly greatest states in the mid-twentieth century, the United States and the Soviet Union, have thought it desirable or necessary to ally themselves with other states, and the alliances must have been thought to have some value, otherwise they would not have been made. In both cases the two states in question are the nuclear elements of their respective alliances. Their membership of the alliances, that is to say, is on various grounds more important to the other members than it is to them. To the extent that this is so they are able to influence the behaviour of other members of the alliances more than the other members are able to influence theirs. Membership of an alliance always in some degree limits the freedom of manoeuvre of members (though believed to afford them other advantages), so one can describe a state as the nuclear element of an alliance if its freedom of manoeuvre, and so its ability to achieve its purposes, is limited by membership less than is the freedom of manoeuvre of the other members, and so their ability to achieve their purposes. A great power may perhaps accordingly be defined as a state which, operating on a wide geographical range, and over a period of time, is able substantially to influence the behaviour of most other states, and so to achieve many of its purposes, acting either alone, or as member of associations or alliances of states in which it is the nuclear element. It *derives* this ability from its wide command of the elements of power which have been listed; but it is properly *designated* a great power by virtue of this wideranging influence operated relatively independently.

The major influence on foreign policy making thus derives from the fact that it is made with reference to other similarly acting bodies over which the policy-makers of the state in question have no authority or jurisdiction, and that the international arena within which policies are made is in high degree anarchical. Relationships are therefore governed by power, and the national interest is defined in terms of power. Since power is constantly in flux, and its assessment is always uncertain, governments will constantly strive to increase the power of their state, and since all governments will do this state relationships are necessarily conflict relationships. This is the argument of the realist school.[14] The argument is well founded in the sense that governments of states do normally act in this way because they do normally perceive and experience the system in which they operate as being of this kind. It is one thing however to state as a means of interpreting behaviour in the real world the hypothesis that states act to maximize their power; it is quite another thing to see in the hypothesis the elements of a general theory of international relations.

The behaviour of governments of states may be seen in terms of a means–ends continuum. If a broad objective of Britain's policy were, for example, to maintain good relations with France, then an official visit by the British head of state to France might be a means to this end, as for instance the visit of Edward VII to France in 1903; but discussions between foreign ministers might be an important means to the end of bringing about the visit, and a change of foreign minister in one or both states might be an important means to the end of bringing about the discussions. But similarly the broad objective itself of good relations with France would be a means towards still broader ends of,

[14] See, for instance, H. J. Morgenthau, *Politics Among Nations* (Knopf, 1948).

for instance, increasing economic interchange and so perhaps raising the level of economic well-being, or increasing military resources by alliance against a perceived threat, so serving the general end of national security and defence. If the general ends for which states exist are for security, maximal economic wellbeing, and the facilitation of socio-cultural intercourse, then power also is to be seen as a means, and not necessarily the only means, of serving these ends. The arguments presented in Chapter 3, where it was asserted[15] that in certain cases the governments of states ought to act to destroy the state which they represented, suggest that the attempt to maximize power may sometimes detract from, rather than increase, the ability to serve basic purposes; but stopping short of such extreme positions as this, it may well be the case that cooperation in, for instance, international monetary matters may be the most effective means of promoting economic welfare for all, or preventing serious economic recession for all.

Power is thus relevant in an international relationship of conflict, or in an international arena in which the action is dominated by conflict relationships among the performers. The attempt to employ or to increase it is not appropriate where both parties perceive the benefit to their respective purposes to be derived from cooperation. In almost all international relationships both elements are present, and for this reason relationships between states are more accurately described as bargaining relationships than as either conflict or cooperation relationships. Power thus always enters into relationships among states, whether bilateral or multilateral, and it is always an influence, and frequently the most important influence, on the settlement or resolution of a question. It is however not always the only appropriate influence, and it is properly to be seen as a means towards other ends rather than as an end in itself.

There remains one point of crucial importance. Power consists in the capacity to influence behaviour. People act in ways which they believe in the situation as they see it will produce the consequences, whether of making a gain or avoiding a loss, that they desire. This is then a further reason why power cannot be quantified. Whatever the surplus of resources or elements of power available to the decision-makers of one state, they will have no power over the decision-makers of another state unless these latter are aware that the surplus exists, and believe that the decision-makers of the former state have the will to deploy them. Equally the government of one state with a relative deficiency in the elements of power as compared with another will none the less have power if the government of the second state has an exaggerated view of the resources of the first or itself lacks the will to deploy its own.

[15] See pp. 45-7.

Power is thus critically dependent on perception and will. Whether behaviour will or will not be modified depends not on the actual relationship of the resources respectively available to the parties, but on how each perceives the relationship of the resources, on the will each has to use his own resources, and on the judgment each makes of the will of the other to mobilize his.

6

Means of achieving
objectives

IN THE LAST CHAPTER relationships between states were described as
being essentially bargaining relationships, in the sense that almost all
issues contain elements of common interest as well as elements of conflict. In the great majority of cases, however, the elements of conflict
either are, or are thought to be, larger than the elements of common
interest. In these cases the attainment of objectives will be seen as primarily requiring the exercise of power, of endeavouring to cause the
other party or parties, that is to say, to do something (or not to do something) which otherwise they would (or would not) have chosen to do.
The methods used may be those of diplomacy (which may be buttressed
by the offer or granting of rewards or the removal of penalties, and by
the threat of punishments; and for which the ground may be prepared
by propaganda, by economic measures, by subversion, or by force); or
these other methods—propaganda, economic reward or deprivation, subversion, and force—may be used independently of specific diplomatic
activity, and indeed may additionally be employed by agents or groups
other than those formally charged with the conduct of relations between
states.

Analysis of means of achieving objectives must therefore include consideration of ways in which the domestic environment of the decision-
makers of other states may be influenced in a desired direction. The
means available are thus of two kinds—those employed in direct or
formal government to government relationships, and those deriving
from informal access or penetration ('means by which the agents or
instruments of one country gain access to the population (or parts of it)

or processes of another country').[1] The distinction is made for analytical purposes, for of course the two methods interact with each other. To this should perhaps be added the case where relations between two states are such that one of the two will in its behaviour constantly consider whether an action is likely to sharpen the hostility, or stimulate the goodwill, of the other, even though this latter takes no action of any kind to influence the former's behaviour. There can be little doubt that the actions of Walter Ulbricht and his fellows in the German Democratic Republic are dominated in this way by their anticipation of Soviet reactions; but a case such as this should perhaps properly not be considered among means of achieving objectives, since it derives simply from the nature of the relationship and not from any action by the Soviet Union or its nationals.

Diplomacy is in large part an activity of the modern world. It is true that among the ancient Greeks, or in the Roman world, or between the Chinese Middle Kingdom and its tributaries, negotiating missions from time to time departed and returned; but it was not until the fifteenth century, with the Italians in the lead, that permanent missions began, mainly for trading purposes, to be established at foreign courts. By the eighteenth century the practice had spread through Europe and the foundations of the modern diplomatic system had been laid. The development of the system reflected the emergence of powerful, centralized, territorially-delimited states, inescapably impinging on each other, distrustful of each other's ambitions and designs, but recognizing that there was advantage for all in the establishment of procedures for constant communication, discussion of disputed issues, and the making of agreements.

The system could not have continued, nor its customs and immunities have been established, had there not been a general recognition that the interests of all were thereby served. None of the princes was wholly opposed to war, but if ends could be gained by less costly means so much the better. Many of the eighteenth-century diplomats became masters of the art of extracting advantage by intrigue and bribery, so that the definition of a diplomat as a man sent to lie abroad for his country was not without substance. Such methods in the twentieth century,.however, carry greater risks with smaller prospects of success, partly because there are fewer key figures whose favour, if won, may be decisive; partly because decision-makers must in greater or less degree be responsive to, and may be called to account by, a political elite, a

---

[1] A. M. Scott, *The Revolution in Statecraft* (Random House, 1965), p. 4. Professor Scott's book contains the most thorough study of these techniques of exerting influence that has yet been written.

party, or an electorate; and partly because the speed of communication is such that an emissary cannot now easily be disavowed in the event of his being discovered in deceit. A relatively rare recent example of deliberate deception was Soviet Foreign Minister Gromyko's assurances to President Kennedy on 18 October 1962 that Soviet assistance to Cuba was defensive only and the Soviet government would not render offensive assistance, a deception which when publicized seriously discomfited the Soviets and moved world opinion against them.

The diplomat of the eighteenth century and the first half of the nineteenth had large freedom of manoeuvre within the framework of general directives, because detailed instructions could not normally be sought and received sufficiently quickly for action in evolving situations. The invention of the telegraph, the telephone, and radio transformed the diplomat's role, and the development of means of transportation likewise transformed the methods of diplomacy. Occasionally in the nineteenth century, as at Vienna in 1815, at the Congresses in the subsequent years, and at Berlin in 1878, the leading decision-makers themselves met; but travel was a slow and arduous business, and diplomatic activity was normally conducted on a bilateral basis by agents in the various capitals, or sometimes by ambassadorial conferences, like that on Belgium and Luxembourg in 1830-32, attended by the Foreign Minister only of the host country. Traditional bilateral diplomacy of this kind still continues, and the common judgment that the ambassador has become little more than a postman will not bear examination. In the first place the embassy remains the primary source of the information upon which all policy making is based;[2] secondly the skill with which the ambassador carries out his instructions may affect the extent or the speed with which the desired end is achieved; and thirdly the recommendation of the man on the spot may still be decisive. On 9 September 1938 Nevile Henderson in Berlin was instructed to warn Hitler that if he used force against Czechoslovakia France would be bound to intervene and in that case Britain would be unable to stand aside. Henderson having previously asked for a warning of this kind to be given before Hitler's speech at Nuremberg on 12 September, now urgently represented that he had already in effect said this to everyone that mattered and a warning and a threat now would merely drive Hitler over the edge.[3] His advice was accepted. It is clear that Hitler did not believe Britain would fight over Czechoslovakia, and probably did not believe she would fight over Poland in 1939 either. Whether his

[2] See Chapter 7, pp. 165-9 below.
[3] E. L. Woodward and R. Butler, *Documents on British Foreign Policy 1919-1939* third series, ii (HMSO, 1949), pp. 278-85.

policy in Czechoslovakia would have been different had the warning been given, and how much his expectations about Britain's attitude over Poland were affected by her behaviour over Czechoslovakia, it is of course impossible to say; the point at issue here is the decisive influence of an ambassador on a crucial point of policy.

This traditional conduct of diplomacy by authorized agents is now supplemented, and in some degree replaced, by personal diplomacy by Foreign Ministers, by summit diplomacy in which heads of government meet, by conference diplomacy in which issues are discussed multilaterally, and by what may be called parliamentary diplomacy through public debates in United Nations or regional assemblies. The Foreign Ministers of all the major powers now travel extensively, though the amount varies with temperament, circumstances and method, and none has yet equalled the record of John Foster Dulles in the 1950s who covered more than 400,000 miles in six years.[4] The method used for the conduct of diplomacy is often not a matter of free choice, but the method chosen will affect the results achieved.

The purpose of diplomacy is to assist in the achievement of goals. Its success may be seen, but is not necessarily to be seen, in the reaching of agreements. If as between two states one wishes to resist a demand made by the other but the circumstances of the decision-maker making the demand are such that he could not sign any agreement which did not satisfy it, then diplomacy preserving the *status quo* without an agreement would be a success for the state opposing the demand. Khrushchev's threats that he would sign a peace treaty with the German Democratic Republic if an agreement was not made on Berlin were met by western diplomacy which succeeded in avoiding an agreement on Berlin of a kind which alone Khrushchev was able to contemplate, and the peace treaty was none the less not signed. On the other hand occasionally diplomacy is directed towards establishing in the minds of decision-makers of other states a perception of common interest which can be exploited only by joint action and from which the element of conflict is virtually absent. The economic assistance offered by Secretary of State Marshall in June 1947 to the war-shattered states of Europe was contingent upon joint action by the recipient states, and the diplomacy of Bevin of Britain and Bidault of France was successful in creating and mobilizing this perception of common interests among the decision-makers of fourteen other states.

The typical situation in which diplomacy is employed, however, is a bargaining situation in which there are elements of conflict and common interest, or alternatively and in addition complementary interests

[4] K. J. Holsti, *International Politics* (Prentice-Hall, 1967), p. 223.

involving exchanges of different objects.[5] The results of negotiation in this typical situation will be affected by each side's perceptions of the resources of the other, by each side's judgment of the extent of these resources which the other has the intention and the will to commit,. by each side's assessment of the extent of his own resources that he is willing and able to commit, by the relevance of available resources to the bargaining situation, by respective bargaining skills, by reputations both as bargainers and from the point of view of keeping or not keeping agreements, by constraints on each side imposed by such factors as public opinion, and by judgments by both sides of the costs or benefits of agreement or no agreement not merely in relation to the state or the issue in question but in relation to other states and issues in the international system.

The critical variable in this list is the last. At the outset of a negotiation each side will normally present proposals. One or both of these sets of proposals may be known to be unacceptable to the other side, and they may be presented because one or both parties does not intend the negotiation to lead to agreement but intends to use the negotiation to stall an issue, or for propaganda purposes. Disarmament negotiations frequently are of this character. Few states are willing to be the cause of the breaking-off of such negotiations, both because the need to spend money on armaments is universally deplored, and because most people are against war and think large armaments increase the likelihood of war; but defence of their state is seen by decision-makers as a prime goal, and since the different situations of states create different strategic needs it is difficult to discover elements of agreement which will not work in favour of some and against others. Very occasionally sufficient common interest will be discovered to make a limited agreement possible, as in the cases of the treaties banning the atmospheric testing of nuclear weapons, and aiming at control of the proliferation of nuclear weapons; but normally disarmament negotiations are deliberately kept going by both parties, often with the presentation of unacceptable proposals, not with the intention or expectation of reaching agreement, but in order to gain propaganda advantage and not to incur the odium (and indeed the risks) of breaking them off.

In negotiations of this kind, as in all negotiations, the three options will at all times exist of settling on the terms now available, of deciding on no agreement, or of continuing to bargain in the hope of improving on the available terms, or simply to keep the negotiation alive.[6] In the

---

[5] This distinction is drawn by F. C. Iklé on p. 2 of his invaluable study *How Nations Negotiate* (Praeger, 1967), on which this section of the text much relies.

[6] Iklé, *op. cit.* pp. 60₋1.

disarmament case the costs of deciding on no agreement are generally seen to exceed the benefits that might be obtained, and negotiations are normally kept alive even though agreement is usually not expected. In some cases, as in the Berlin example quoted in an earlier paragraph, the no agreement option can represent success if it can be chosen without excessively undesirable consequences. In other cases the no agreement option can be deliberately chosen, even though agreement is desired, either because the terms on which such an agreement seems to be possible are thought to contain disadvantages greater than the fact of agreement could bring, or in order to create or strengthen a reputation for being a tough bargainer. These reasons are not usually exclusive and can both be operative together. The tough bargaining reputation may be desired for a future negotiation with the state or states in question, or for a different and probably more important negotiation with other states, or simply as a general asset in international relations. When France walked out of the EEC at the end of June 1965 the reasons were partly that the costs of proceeding to the next stage of development envisaged in the Rome treaty without agreement on the common agricultural policy were seen to be greater than the benefit of keeping the EEC moving forward, and partly to sustain the reputation of being a tough bargainer (to the point of willingness to disrupt the Communities) from which de Gaulle had already gained so much for France.

In determining whether to select either of the other two options—settle now, or continue to bargain (in the case where agreement is expected and desired)—the full range of the other variables comes into play. A decision by one party to settle will be based on judgments that the benefits of agreement (or the costs of no agreement) exceed the costs that the present terms will impose, that the other side probably recognizes this to be so, and no action or commitment of resources is likely to persuade them otherwise, or that any alteration of terms will make the other side prefer no agreement. The task of negotiators, and the role of diplomacy in the achievement of objectives, is to create this judgment in the minds of the other side at the most favourable possible point of resolution of the issues under discussion.

A variety of techniques may be employed to produce this result. Bargaining reputation affects all of them. Timing, in starting a negotiation, or in introducing a particular proposal, or in reinforcing it by one of the techniques to be described, may be decisive for success or failure, whether the timing is deliberate or fortuitous. An example may be the German proposal on 15 August 1939 that Ribbentrop should visit Moscow, the proposal being made a week after the special British

negotiator, William Strang, had left, and a day after the Anglo–French military mission had been unable to answer Voroshilov's crucial question whether Russian troops would be permitted to pass across Polish territory.

The point at which a decision to settle is reached may be much affected by the type of initial proposal, and by the personal style of negotiators. Some negotiators prefer to begin with extreme proposals in the expectation of making concessions which will be substantial in relation to the starting-point and which may therefore create an impression of reasonableness and extract concessions in return; others prefer to table 'honest' proposals which are close to what is thought to be the minimum acceptable terms; still others start from a rigid position from which they will move only if the likelihood appears great that agreement will immediately be reached. Which of these techniques is more likely to produce favourable results depends on the issue and on the other party to the negotiation: western diplomats tend to use one of the first two techniques, in the expectation that concessions and reasonableness will produce concessions and reasonableness, while the Soviets tend to use the third method, in the belief that concessions will be regarded as weakness and will accordingly suggest an excessive desire for agreement. The Soviets, moreover, have developed to a fine art—if art it can be called—a diplomatic style which consists of long drawn out haggling on minor details and on procedure (in the expectation that impatience or weariness will lead to greater pliancy on subsequent substantial issues), constant repetition of the same points and arguments containing no response to counterarguments, personal discourtesy to disrupt the development of a case, and repeated displays of suspiciousness about the intentions or integrity of the other parties. The impression given is that the 'no agreement' option is constantly at the forefront of Soviet negotiators' minds, and if the other side desires agreement concessions are made to appear more necessary.

The major weapons of persuasion are rewards or promises thereof, warnings, threats, commitments and actions. The loss–gains calculus is crucial when rewards are at issue. The party to whom the reward is offered has simply to decide whether the disadvantages of acceding to the proposed modification of behaviour, or of accepting agreement on the available terms, are less than the advantages contained in the reward. In most cases, for obvious reasons, the reward will not normally be delivered until after the desired action has been taken, and in those cases the party to whom the reward is offered must judge not merely the appropriateness and value of the reward but the good faith of the proposer and his ability to make good his promise. Hitler on more than

one occasion offered, in exchange for some concession, to guarantee
the British Empire, but it was not clear against whom the guarantee
might be needed, except himself, and he had many times revealed that
his promises were not to be trusted. In discussions with the Soviet
Union in November 1940 looking towards a division of the world among
Germany, Italy, the Soviet Union and Japan, Hitler proposed that the
territorial aspirations of the Soviet Union should centre on India and
the Indian Ocean, but Stalin and Molotov did not believe that Hitler
could deliver on these promises because Britain was not yet defeated.
They therefore suggested that their aspirations should be defined as
lying in the area of Batum and Baku and south towards the Persian
Gulf.[7] The offer of reward in exchange for concession is a common
pattern of diplomatic negotiation and some elements of this process are
to be seen in almost every agreement successfully concluded.

Warnings consist in description to the other party of undesirable
consequences that will naturally follow if he persists in a certain course
of action or rejects a proposal, whereas threats involve statements of
the actions that the negotiator himself will take.[8] The withdrawn
instruction to Henderson described in a previous paragraph contained
both a warning and a threat—a warning that France's obligations to
Czechoslovakia must cause her to give assistance if Czechoslovakia were
attacked, and a threat that in that case Britain would have to come
in. The party that is warned or threatened will or will not modify his
behaviour according to his judgment whether the consequences predicted in the warning, or the action promised in the threat, will in fact
take place, and whether the losses that he will thereby suffer will
exceed the disadvantages of altering his proposed course of action.
Verisimilitude can be given to warnings by actions that others may
take (public statements by ministers, proclamation of a state of emergency, mobilization of armed forces). Substance can be given to threats
by commitments that the negotiator may enter into, or actions that he
or his government may take.

The making of, and response to, threats is a delicate business. To
bluff and to have one's bluff called (that is, to threaten but be unpre-
pared to take the action promised in the threat) gravely weakens both
one's position in the issue in question and one's bargaining reputation
for the future. If the threat is in fact bluff, the bluff is more likely to
be called if the threat is not credible in relation to the issue ('If you
do not reduce your tariff on my motor-cars I will drop a thermonuclear

---

[7] *Documents on German Foreign Policy 1918-1945*, ser. D, xi (HMSO, 1961),
p. 715.
[8] This distinction is made in Iklé, *op. cit.* pp. 62-3.

bomb on your capital'), if the threatener is perceived not to have the capability to put his threat into effect ('If you issue a Unilateral Declaration of Independence I will see that the United Nations prevents any state from buying any of your exports'), or if the losses that the threatener himself will suffer if he carries out his threat are thought to exceed the advantages he will gain from the desired course of action (perhaps 'If you do not agree to activate an international monetary system of special drawing rights, I will alter the value of my currency and let it float').

The response of the threatened party to a threat is governed by his perception of the degree of certainty that it will be carried out, his perception resulting from the judgments he makes by the foregoing three criteria. The threatener himself may make the threat without having decided whether he will carry it out if the desired action is not forthcoming. He can however make his threat carry more conviction by undertaking various forms of commitment. He can make his threat public, thus causing himself political loss at home and loss of reputation internationally if he does not carry his threat out. He can declare that he will resign if the desired action is not forthcoming and he is unable or unwilling to carry out his threat. The classical case of commitment is that of the general who threatens that if peace is not made he will fight to the last man, and he then marches his army over a river into hostile territory and destroys every means by which anyone may cross back over the river. Commitments thus involve limitations of one's own ability not to do what one says one will, and so are designed to make one's threats credible. In diplomacy it is difficult to make so unambiguous a commitment as that of the general burning his bridges, and the technique is hazardous in that the other party may always judge that the losses he will suffer by refusal to act as desired will be less than the disadvantages of compliance. Threats are therefore frequently veiled or couched in 'diplomatic' language, and situations are always ones of uncertainty in which perception and judgment are crucial for outcomes.

In many cases, of course, offers of reward, warnings, and threats buttressed by commitments, are used simultaneously as techniques of persuasion. These techniques can be further reinforced by action designed to make agreement more desirable or the costs of no agreement greater, and likely also to persuade the victim that few further concessions are likely from the other side. Such actions may include measures to influence the domestic environment of decision-makers—propaganda, economic steps of one kind or another, contact with opposition groups, encouragement to subversive or revolutionary elements, direct military force—or endeavours to persuade the governments of other states to undertake similar actions. Measures of this kind deserve separate consideration as means by which states endeavour to achieve objectives, but they are occasionally used as direct supplements to diplomacy and so should be mentioned in this context.

The suitability or effectiveness of each or all of these techniques is much affected, as was mentioned previously, by the type of diplomacy being employed. Using traditional methods the technical aspects are normally well or adequately covered, the business can be conducted, if both parties so desire, in almost total secrecy, and the various bargaining techniques can be employed with not necessarily excessively grave consequences if threats or rewards do not materialize. There is always the possibility of their being proposed 'on a personal basis', or of an envoy being found to have exceeded his instructions. When personal or summit diplomacy is being used, however, the stakes are automatically raised, but they are differentially raised according to the political system from which the top level decision-makers come. The fact of personal involvement increases the pressures for results to be obtained, but the pressure is much greater on decision-makers who come from systems in which they can be called to account or voted out of office than on representatives of systems where responsibility is not or cannot be enforced. It was much easier for Molotov to attend and depart from Foreign Ministers' conferences in the years after the second world war without any progress having been made than it was for Bevin or Byrnes to do the same, because Molotov (so long as he was supported by Stalin) could not be removed, whereas the British and United States electorates were liable to become impatient. Bevin and Byrnes found it necessary to explain and justify the failure to make progress, and their explanations were naturally cast in terms of condemnation of the Soviet Union, and so intensified conflict, and made even more difficult the agreements which they desired to reach. Khrushchev did not have so much freedom as Molotov because his home base was less secure than was Stalin's, and so for his failures he always found it necessary to proclaim justification. The shooting-down of the American U2 reconnaissance plane over the Soviet Union in May 1960 provided him with a golden opportunity for wrecking the summit conference with Eisenhower to which he had got himself committed in the expectation of making gains which, as the time drew near, it became apparent he would not obtain. In all these cases it is possible, though not of course certain, that conflicts would have been less exacerbated if traditional diplomatic methods had been used.

Technical questions may well be less effectively handled under the personal or summit format. Conversations may be less well remembered or recorded; records of decisions, or the nature of the decisions themselves, may be less precise. Whether or not this is so will depend on how the meetings are conducted. More important perhaps are the possible ill-effects of personal meetings and judgments by top decision-makers. Much is frequently made of the advantage of 'knowing your opposite number', and of establishing 'personal good relations with the men that count'. But it can well happen that the political leader can make misjudgments as much as the professional diplomat, but if he makes them himself he will be less ready to consider that he may be wrong. Good personal relations may be established, but personal dislike or distrust may equally well result from direct contact, and this is much more serious if the personal dislike is between two heads of government than if it is between an ambassador and a top civil servant in the foreign ministry. Political leaders may also have exaggerated ideas of their own skills. Thus it is almost certain that Khrushchev judged Kennedy at Vienna in 1961 to be a much weaker man than in fact he was, and this may well have been one of the factors leading to the Cuba crisis in 1962; it is certain that Eden and Dulles disliked each other intensely, and this may well have had something to do with the disastrous development of Anglo-United States relations during the Suez crisis in 1956; and there can be little doubt that Roosevelt thought he knew how to handle Uncle Joe, and this must have influenced the extent to which he was prepared to make concessions to Stalin in Europe and the Far East, concessions which may not all have been necessary and some of which were certainly unwise. Ill-consequences of this kind do not of course necessarily follow—Churchill's relations with Roosevelt, or de Gaulle's with Adenauer, certainly aided their countries' interests—but the possibilities exist and thus the method used affects outcomes.

One other variable that is affected by use of the personal or summit method is commitments. The very fact of personal participation by top decision-makers may involve something of a commitment, because of the political losses that may be suffered if no progress is made. But warnings, threats and offers of reward all carry a greater degree of commitment if made personally by those with authority, or thought to have authority, to carry them out. Still more will public statements by negotiating leaders of proposals made, or positions adopted that cannot be abandoned, limit their ability to change their proposals or positions, and thus will make it appear to the other party that the choice is the available proposals or no agreement. Time factors in cases of personal or summit diplomacy will also act to increase pressures: those with greater patience who do not so much mind whether an agreement is reached or not have an additional weapon to force concessions; on the other hand a negotiator who correctly believes that the other party very much desires an agreement may well gain a more favourable point of settlement by fixing a time when he must leave. Some of the concessions made by Stalin at Yalta in February 1945 may have resulted from Roosevelt's use of these tactics, although many have argued that the balance of advantage derived from that summit meeting was very much on the Soviet side.

In conference diplomacy, increasingly found to be necessary as more and more states acquire an interest in more and more questions, other influences come into play. Location is important. If the host country is also a participant in the conference it is customary for that country to provide the chairmanship, or at the very least to share in it. Chairmanship is a position of influence offering considerable scope for moving discussions in particular directions. Moreover the host country has at its immediate disposal the full range of its information-gathering, advisory, and governmental machinery, whereas the others will have the resources only of their delegation and their embassy (if they have one), supplemented when possible by telegrams on specific questions to their own capitals. Conference diplomacy facilitates, and is usually characterized by, the joint action of groups of states on the basis of ties existing before the conference or forged by bargains made during the conference. Thus at San Francisco in 1945 many of the smaller powers, led by Australia, discovered a common interest in opposition to the great powers' concentration of authority in the Security Council, and were able by acting together, with some assistance from the United States, to increase the powers and authority of the General Assembly. Conferences also offer opportunities for parading or seeking recruits for a particular line of policy, or for creating a new image of policy or character: Chou En-lai successfully used the Bandung conference in 1955 to create the impression of a moderate, non-militant communist China. Conferences thus may serve many purposes in addition to those for which they are primarily called; but they may also, sometimes after long and arduous weeks of discussions like those under the General Agreement on Tariffs and Trade, reach agreements that could hardly be reached in any other way. They suffer the disadvantages of cumbrousness, sidetracking, and frequently of premature publicity; but they are a consequence of the increasing extent to which the affairs of states are intermingled with those of many others, and no better method has yet been devised for handling multilateral questions.

Finally there is the new diplomatic method of endeavouring to achieve purposes through the use of international institutional machinery. In many ways the corridors and lobbies in New York add an extra dimension to traditional diplomatic activity: many states have contacts with many or most others only through their diplomatic missions at the United Nations. New York thus acts as a source of information and as a place for diplomatic activity of a range that for many states would otherwise be quite impossible, because of the cost that would be incurred and the trained personnel that would be needed. These activities are facilitated by the permanent members of the United Nations secretariat, and in many issues their behind-the-scenes activity has been of great or critical importance, as in the case of the end of the Berlin blockade in 1949, or the Cuba crisis in 1962. But in addition to acting as a point of contact and a source of information the United Nations acts, through the annual meeting of the General Assembly, as the town meeting of the world. In the general debates most states take the opportunity of addressing themselves to the great current problems, so using the Assembly as a forum for enunciating a new proposal or mobilizing support behind an old one, for creating a particular image (whether pacific or menacing) in the minds of other governments, for indicating alignment with other powers or non-alignment with any, or simply for enjoying an annual hour of glory like representatives of obscure states in party nominating-conventions in the United States. The full range of diplomatic techniques is mobilized, on appropriate scales, to obtain favourable votes on resolutions, and such votes or other intimations of support have some influence on prestige and so on bargaining power. United Nations votes may also serve to add an element of legitimacy to state action. The vote in the Security Council in 1950, in the absence of the Soviet delegate, to aid South Korea against the North Korean attack, in some degree legitimized the military response of the United States and brought military support from other countries. Many of the characteristics of conference diplomacy are likewise to be observed at the United Nations. In a large number of ways therefore the United Nations may be used as an instrument of diplomacy, and as a means of advancing the purposes of states.

One aspect of this activity is that of image or stereotype formation, and mobilization of support through the spoken or written word. This activity, propaganda, is the second major means by which states endeavour to achieve their objectives. It ranges from innocent tours in foreign countries by ballet companies at one extreme to psychological warfare at the other. The sight and sound of the Red Army singers and dancers produces complex reactions of delight, wonder and perhaps unease at such formidable prowess, while the supply of books and journals by the British Council or the United States Information Service can effectively sustain that most powerful means of influence round the world, the English language. Simple cultural activities contribute to image formation, and to the extent that decision-makers are responsive to their environment, or are themselves influenced, so their ability to oppose the state from which the activities originate is in some degree reduced.

The aim of propaganda therefore is primarily, though not wholly, to influence in a desired direction the domestic environments of the decision-makers of other states, to decrease their ability to oppose. The availability of this means of influencing behaviour, as of other methods of influencing domestic environments, is the consequence of increasing popular involvement in politics and of the development of communications technology. In the eighteenth century in Europe, and to a less extent in the nineteenth century, there was little point in trying to influence opinion in other states, even had effective technical means been available, because governments were in the main little subject to popular pressures, and in less degree responsive to them. Since the first world war, however, and even more since the second world war, governments round the world have increasingly been unable to ignore a general movement of opinion, or specific pressure from significant political groups, at the same time as the technical possibilities for other states to stimulate such movements or pressures have been steadily expanding.

The effectiveness of propaganda as a means of advancing purposes thus depends on the susceptibility of the target, and on the availability of appropriate technical means to exploit susceptibility. Availability of means is to be seen from both points of view—whether, that is to say, the state desiring to bring influence to bear has the technical capacity to do so, and whether the target is technically in a condition to be exposed to the influence. There would be no point, for instance, in beaming radio programmes to a country where almost none of the inhabitants possessed radios; nor would such programmes have much effect if the power for their transmission could not cope with jamming by the target country. The technically simplest method of exerting influence, dissemination of the printed word, can be controlled by censorship, and its effectiveness is limited by illiteracy. The Chinese communist regime has peculiar strength in this regard because of the difficulty and cumbrousness of the Chinese written language: illiteracy is being attacked by training in a basic Chinese varying between 800

and 2,000 characters, so that the masses of the Chinese people will be able to absorb the simple sloganized material put out by the government, but will have no access to writings not rendered down into the basic character form. The Chinese government thus has a degree of control over the thought processes of their people that no other regime can match.

Propaganda techniques as a foreign policy tool may include cultural programmes or exchanges, distribution of books and literature, and the use of radio and television. These mass media may serve to disseminate information, to propagate a particular opinion (whether true or false), to advocate particular courses of action, and to stimulate groups in opposition to the target government. The extent to which these techniques can be used will depend on the attitude of the target government, on the degree of literacy, on the availability of receivers able to pick up programmes, and on the range of technical defences that the target government is able or willing to deploy. The technical considerations which affect susceptibility to propaganda are thus themselves subject to political factors. A society whose values require the free circulation of information and opinions is much more open to the propaganda method than one in which control of opinion is the norm. A society of this kind, moreover, is much more likely to be one in which political leadership is responsive to opinion; and propaganda successfully changing attitudes or mobilizing opposition is therefore more likely to achieve its object, which is to bring about a modification in governmental behaviour.

The countervailing limit on effectiveness derives from the extent to which opinion generally, or specific groups, are susceptible to influence. Susceptibility will be affected by the methods of propaganda employed, and by the degree to which a political and social system is felt by its members to be satisfactory and stable, or unsatisfactory and open to change. So far as the first of these is concerned propaganda is likely to be more effective if it has a fair degree of internal consistency and fits with facts or evidence known to the target people; if it agrees generally with that people's experience or expectations; if it is directed towards strengthening existing attitudes rather than creating new ones; if it is repetitive but constantly imports new elements; if it is simple to understand and interesting; if it is relevant to the needs or aspirations of target groups; if it can appeal to emotions as well as or instead of, to reason; if it is directed towards, and so tailored for, particular groups rather than towards opinion generally; if the target groups are young rather than old; if the target groups or people are generally friendly towards and wish to believe the propaganda source, rather than the

other way round. The last of these will be much affected by the kind
of image or stereotype that words and deeds create, an image that may
well not correspond with what the originals believe it to be. Thus the
British probably see themselves as exhibiting qualities of fairness,
moderation, and stability; the French expect their culture to be valued;
the Soviets see themselves as the fatherland of the proletariat of the
world; the self-image of the United States is of purveyors of liberty
and justice. Propaganda based on self-images of this kind which do not
correspond with the images held by the target peoples will not be
effective. Thus Soviet propaganda based on the image of themselves as
the fatherland of the world proletariat would be more likely in 1969
to be acceptable, and so effective, to communists in, say, Spain, than to
communists in Czechoslovakia. In 1938 the images in the two countries,
and so the effectiveness of Soviet propaganda, might well have been the
other way round (the Spanish communists having recently suffered from
being used by the Soviets to try to advance their own influence in the
Spanish civil war, and the Czechs at that time facing the much greater
and more immediate menace of Hitler).

The great exponents of propaganda as a means of achieving objectives
have been the Bolsheviks since 1917, Goebbels and Hitler after 1933 (and
before, in the struggle for power), the United States since the late
1940s, Britain on a smaller scale since 1940, Nasser of Egypt on a much
narrower front since 1952, and Mao Tse-tung and the Chinese mainly
in the last decade. The Bolsheviks achieved substantial, if intermittent,
success in the interwar period, mainly because they appealed consistently
to groups feeling themselves to be underprivileged, and because reaction
to the world economic crisis and fear of Hitler caused many to wish to
believe what the Bolsheviks told them about the Soviet system and
about their enmity to Nazism and Fascism. Credibility and acceptability
have been undermined by seeming inconsistency with behaviour (the
Nazi-Soviet pact, sabre-rattling over Berlin and in Cuba, the crushing of
the Hungarian revolt in 1956, the intervention in Czechoslovakia in
1968), by more information about the Soviet system (Stalinism and the
great purges), and by the counter-blasts of the Chinese.

Goebbels had great success so long as he played upon the injustices of
Versailles, the inadequacies of European governments in the 1930s, and
the Nazis' desires and intentions to bring about necessary changes
peacefully, and by new methods to solve economic problems; but his
effectiveness declined rapidly, and even became counterproductive by
causing ridicule or stimulating hostility, when during the war he repeatedly made claims that were easily demonstrated to be false, and
when he used agents, such as William Joyce broadcasting to Britain, who

provoked laughter, contempt or anger. Nasser's Voice of the Arabs from Cairo continued to carry conviction in the Levant despite his repeated catastrophic failures, partly because its audience, and particularly the young, wished to believe its claims and promises, partly because its strong language appealed to emotion and hatreds which Arabs widely shared and partly because no other agent was seen as possibly able and willing to destroy Israel, the scapegoat for all the Arabs' miseries and sufferings. From Washington United States programmes have achieved varying results—some success in reinforcing pro-American attitudes of political and economic elites in developed countries, but some disasters when programmes extolling democracy or the American way of life have been directed towards poverty-stricken countries of Asia where 'democracy' if it means anything at all means corruption, and the delights of affluence arouse envy or hostility.

Propaganda is thus a delicate instrument to be used with care and discrimination. A good deal depends on luck and on the mutual perception of each other by the peoples of two entities; and even with the assistance of psychologists the techniques that will be effective in producing desired effects are by no means thoroughly understood. But just as revolutions characteristically occur when people are not merely dissatisfied but see some chance or glimmer of improvement, so propaganda will be valueless if the audience is totally apathetic or despairing. Propaganda by the exiled governments of Europe to their peoples during the second world war would have been as hopeless as that of the exiled Spanish government to Spain after March 1939 had not hope been sustained by the continuance of British, and later of Soviet, resistance; while propaganda now to the peoples of the Soviet Union would be unlikely to repay the resources given to it, partly because of the general hostility of most of the audience but more because even those groups that might wish to change the Soviet government or its behaviour would see insufficient prospect of doing so for it to be worth the effort and the risk.

The last observation draws attention to the link between propaganda and subversion. This is an instrument of policy not new in principle, but altogether new in range and scope. The serpent's temptation of Eve to eat the forbidden fruit was an essay in subversion, as was France's support to the exiled Charles II and to the Stuart pretenders after 1688. But subversion now has become an inescapable part of statecraft for major powers, and increasingly for minor ones also. Since all states now have relations at least with some others, internal strife or internal changes may have consequences for other states, whether of a strategic or an economic or some other character. Some states are likely therefore to see advantage in encouragement of such strife or such changes, others in their prevention. Their interest is stimulated not merely by economic or strategic concerns and by perceptions of relations of forces that are being favourably or unfavourably altered, but also by ideological considerations, of a nationalist, communist, democratic, anticolonialist or other kind. Adherence to such universalist ideologies sanctifies action which for other reasons seems necessary. The governments of some states, having won power through subversive tactics, deem it profitable and proper to use such tactics to advance their external interest. Soviet use of such tactics on a global scale has compelled the United States as their chief opponents to use similar tactics in defence.

Subversion, meaning literally the overturning or overthrowing of something, is in the political context concerned with bringing influence to bear by a variety of means on groups within a state (or groups from the state operating from outside) in order to overthrow the government, or to prevent its overthrow, or to cause it to change, or not to change, its behaviour. Within this wide definition propaganda may clearly in come cases be a form of subversion, and even diplomatic statements designed to influence the behaviour of groups might at the extreme be similarly regarded. De Gaulle's 'Vive le Québec libre' in 1967 is perhaps only a more extravagant example than Dulles's promise in 1954 of an 'agonizing reappraisal' of United States policy if the French National Assembly failed to ratify the treaty establishing the European Defence Community.

But the major forms of subversive activity are clandestine rather than public. Techniques may include the spreading of rumours, the infiltration of organizations, the sponsoring of riots, strikes or sabotage, the assisting of disaffected groups in the country or in exile through advisers, money or the sale or gift of weapons, the supporting of militant parties, the creation of political scandals, the organization or supporting of *coups d'état*, the organizing or supporting of guerrilla warfare, and the giving of direct military assistance to insurrectionary groups. The organization of political assassination has not yet come to be regarded as proper (presumably because retaliation might be invited, and growth of the habit might be unhealthy for decision-makers).[9]

All these methods have been used by the Soviet Union: rumours in Britain in 1939 that Chamberlain was intending to do another deal with

[9] *The Times* of 5 August 1969 referred to a story in *Der Spiegel* about an unpublished article written by Lieutenant-General Sir Mason MacFarlane, Military Attaché in Berlin in 1938, recounting that he had advocated the assassination of Hitler, but that Whitehall had vetoed the plan, and he had been informed that such a thing would be 'unsportsmanlike'.

Hitler; infiltration of organizations such as trade unions or left-wing political parties on a grand scale in many countries round the globe; use of communist parties for strikes and sabotage, the best example being perhaps the strikes of late 1947 in Italy and France with the object of breaking the Marshall plan and the nascent Organization for European Economic Cooperation; support to the Nazis in 1932, in the belief that Nazi accession to power would so sharpen the class struggle that a communist takeover would follow; support everywhere to militant communist parties, which since the late 1920s have served as instruments and mouthpieces for Soviet foreign policy;[10] the organization of and support to the *coup d'état* in Czechoslovakia in February 1948; support to the Greek guerrillas after 1946; direct military assistance to insurrectionary groups in Latvia, Estonia and Lithuania in June 1940.

Since the second world war the United States has used similar methods, mainly through the instrumentality of the Central Intelligence Agency. Examples range from rumours of undesirable consequences if the Christian Democrats did not emerge as the largest party in the Italian elections of 1948, through the overthrow of the supposedly pro-communist regime of Arbenz in Guatemala in 1954 and the reduction of assistance to Vietnam in 1963 until the Diem regime was overthrown by army *coup d'état*, to the supply of arms and transport to the Cuban exiles for the abortive Bay of Pigs invasion in 1961. In all these cases, as in the Soviet examples, subversion was being used as a means of advancing United States foreign policy objectives, but these actions have led to the CIA being regarded by radicals the world over as the most glaring illustration of United States imperialism and oppression. The strength of these feelings partly reflects the naïvety of those who believe that in mid-twentieth century any people can live their lives unaffected by the currents and interactions of international relationships; but so far as opposition within the United States is concerned, it does raise a particularly intractable aspect of the problem of democratic control of foreign policy.[11] Much subversive activity must be conducted in secret, or it will fail of its purpose. A power like the United States whose decision-makers in all parties perceive themselves to be menaced by a global threat cannot afford to do without an instrument of policy which the perceived enemy wields with great skill, which is itself the most effective counter to use of the instruments by the enemy, and

[10] Cf. the statements of Thorez and Togliatti in 1949 (previously referred to in Chapter 2, p. 33 above) that if the Red Army entered France or Italy to assist in the overthrow of capitalism, the French and Italian communist parties would welcome them (see *The Times*, 23 February 1949).

[11] See also Chapter 7, pp. 160-1 below.

which serves instead of direct military measures carrying even greater dangers. But if the activity has to be secret, how can it be controlled by the Congress, still less by the people? Is there not danger that these secret agencies will develop policies of their own and by their actions predetermine United States policy? Is it indeed always the case that the President himself is fully apprised and in control of subversive activity? To questions of this kind there is no easy answer, but at bottom the issue is the extent to which the values that democratic regimes exist to serve may be irremediably damaged by the methods that seem necessary to preserve them.

Subversion is the other side of the coin of transnational loyalties. The question was raised in Chapter 3[12] whether the national interest might not in certain perhaps remote circumstances require action leading to the destruction of the state. In this perspective transnational loyalties were seen as desirable. But informal penetration, to use again Professor Scott's term, is possibly effective only because of transnational loyalties, and it links naturally with treason. Whether communist subversion in Cuba or United States subversion in Central America or British subversion in Nazi-occupied Europe receives moral approbation or condemnation depends on the moral values of the observer, and in particular on his attitude towards nationalism and internationalism. If the idea of internationalism is soundly based on the existing nature and range of international interrelationships, then subversion in the absence of a controlling global authority is an inescapable feature of the international system.

Fourth among means available to states for the achievement of their purposes are those that derive from economic considerations. This is to look from another point of view at many of the facets of the economic influence on foreign policy making which was examined in Chapter 4.[13] The extent to which states are able to use economic means for advancing policy ends depends on the level and range of their resources, broadly defined, and the degree to which the costs of diversion of resources are politically acceptable. The extent to which economic methods will be effective in inducing behavioural changes (or even on occasion in contributing to the replacement of a hostile by a more complaisant government) will depend on the nature of the economy of the object state, on its international, particularly its international economic, environment, and on the degree of willingness of the population to accept loss or not to receive advantage rather than alter behaviour.

Economic methods include the offering of inducements or rewards

[12] See pp. 45-7 above.
[13] See pp. 67-72 above.

and the imposition of penalties or deprivations. Both may be used to lend weight to diplomatic persuasion, and both may be used with the intention of affecting the general climate of relations between both the object state and the originator, and the object state and other states. Inducements or rewards may consist of the promise or supply of technical assistance, gifts of consumer goods or capital equipment or armaments, or financial aid on interest-free or low-interest or current interest rate bases, or purchase of the products of the object state in guaranteed quantities and perhaps also at favourable prices. Whether inducements of this kind will be offered will depend on political and economic conditions in the donor state and the relative priority of other purposes against the purposes that economic assistance may serve.

Since 1947 checking the spread of communism has been seen by United States political elites as being of sufficiently overriding importance for billions of dollars to have been devoted to military, economic, technical and financial aid programmes in Europe, in Latin America, in Asia, and to a less extent in Africa. These programmes have not however been motivated by any means entirely by foreign policy considerations. General humanitarian desires to relieve illness or poverty have played some part in making assistance politically more acceptable at home. Aid programmes have generally stimulated United States exports in receiving countries, particularly since aid has frequently been tied to purchases in the United States. More specifically the Department of Agriculture has found in aid programmes means of disposing of embarrassingly large agricultural surpluses created by internal support policies which politically could not be abandoned. So intertwined have economic and foreign policy purposes become that justifications for aid programmes presented by successive administrations to the Congress have varied widely from year to year, and it is clear that the test of value received by the United States is for some as much or more the financial return as for others it is the furthering of foreign policy objectives.[14]

These objectives have had positive and negative aspects. Examples of positive aspects are the restoration of western Europe through Marshall aid, which had vital strategic as well as economic importance for the United States, or the Alliance for Progress in Latin America aimed (not with total success) at reducing the acceptability of communism by assisting economic development. In Africa and to a less extent in Asia aid has had much more the negative aspect of preventing alignment of countries in the 'third world' with the Soviet Union or China if they

[14] For further material on this question see D. A. Baldwin, *Foreign Aid and American Foreign Policy* (Praeger, 1966).

should receive assistance only from those sources. One manifestation of Soviet–Chinese rivalry in recent years has also been the competition between them in making loans to third countries, as for instance during the many months before the repeatedly postponed conference of non-aligned countries in Algeria, eventually scheduled for June 1965, but ultimately cancelled.[15]

Aid-giving countries have often found that the hoped-for foreign policy advantages have not materialized. Gratitude is not a political emotion. Charity as expressing a relationship of inferiority is commonly disliked, the more so if it is deliberately or unconsciously used to create dependence. As between states these emotions are frequently reinforced by insufficient care for local susceptibilities or customs on the part of agents of the aid-giving state who desire in the interests of the receiving state, of the home taxpayer, or simply for efficiency, to see assistance being used to best advantage, and this frequently entails interference at many levels. At lower levels this may stimulate a climate of opinion making more difficult the pursuit of policies by the receiving state favourable to the donor. At higher levels limits on the freedom of manoeuvre of decision-makers themselves is likely to promote resentment and efforts to break the dependence. The chain of events which led to the Suez operation in 1956 began with the refusal of Dulles, and so of Britain, to give assistance for the building of the Aswan dam except on conditions that Nasser found intolerable.

One of the most striking examples in recent history of the use of preferential economic treatment to gain political advantages was the plan developed by Dr Schacht of Germany in the early 1930s. The countries of south-east Europe, Hungary, Romania, Yugoslavia, Greece and Bulgaria were mainly primary-producing countries, and they had suffered acutely in the world economic crisis after 1929 when agricultural and raw material prices fell much more steeply than prices of manufactures—suffered all the more because their production methods could not compete on a cost basis with the great mechanized agriculture of the Americas. Germany needed secure supplies of foodstuffs and raw materials to increase her ability to withstand blockade in war. Schacht's plan was simply to undertake to purchase in bulk, usually at prices well above world prices, all the agricultural surpluses that the Balkan countries had available for export. The bait was irresistible. Payment was to be in marks, not in local currency; but this to countries whose experience of Germany was of a country of great wealth and economic strength seemed no great disadvantage. The Germans, however, allowed the Balkan countries to use their marks for the purchase

[15] See M. I. Goldman, *Soviet Foreign Aid* (Praeger, 1967), pp. 188-90.

only of those German goods that they were willing to sell, not necessarily those that the Balkans wanted; and the Balkan governments found themselves in a stranglehold that they could not break, partly because having sold all their agricultural surpluses to Germany they had little foreign currency to make purchases elsewhere, and partly because their peasants would not allow them to try to break from Germany as it was German purchases, as the Germans carefully told them, that had brought them out of misery into prosperity. It was one of the aspects of Chamberlain's appeasement policies that he was not prepared to offer opportunities to the Balkans to break out of this stranglehold. This economic penetration greatly eased Hitler's political and later military conquest of these countries.

The other facet of the economic instrument, the imposition of penalties or deprivations, includes such actions as currency manipulation, exchange controls, pre-emptive buying of commodities urgently needed or in short supply, dumping (the export of goods in such quantities and at sufficiently low prices to cause heavy losses or total disruption of home production), the imposition of tariffs or quotas or other barriers against exports from another country, or the organization of partial or total boycotts (a ban on imports) or embargoes (a ban on exports) on goods respectively coming from or going to other countries. The degree of effectiveness of such measures is a function of the political and economic situations of the government of each state, and of international attitudes towards them.

From the point of view of the government endeavouring to induce the behavioural change its ability to apply and sustain pressure will depend on the amount and nature of loss that will be suffered by its own people, and the political acceptability of this loss (and this latter variable will of course, as always, be affected by the extent to which the political system is one in which the government has to be responsive to pressures). From the point of view of the country against whom the measures are directed, its ability to resist will be governed by the degree to which the population will accept deprivation, and the extent to which alternative resources can be found either internally, or, if other states are favourably inclined, externally. A developed, integrated economy is more liable to disruption if the supply of certain key commodities is cut off than is a primitive, subsistence economy. An undiversified economy relying heavily on the sale of a single product, particularly if sales are concentrated in one or two markets, is more vulnerable than an economy producing a wide range of goods.

The economic weapon is a common element of diplomatic bargaining. Used delicately, as something to make agreement more enticing, or no agreement more unpalatable, it can be of great effect. But as a primary weapon all the conditions have to be right for it to succeed. One of the few examples of success is the use of currency manipulation by the United States against Britain during the Suez crisis. Ever since 1945 the ratio between Britain's reserves and her short-term liabilities has been such that the collapse of the currency and of the economy could be avoided only if the other major financial centres of the western world (above all the United States) were prepared to give massive support in the event of large-scale selling by holders of sterling. Normally such support is forthcoming and is expected to be forthcoming (so confidence in sterling is sustained), because a collapse of sterling would result in consequences and losses for the world economy of a size and nature that cannot be foreseen. When the Anglo-French attack on Suez was launched, United States opposition suggested that the customary financial support might not be forthcoming, and the consequent flight from sterling swiftly forced Eden and the British government to bring the operation to a halt. The economic weapon was able to work, partly because much of the internal and external opinion significant to Britain was hostile to the government's action, but primarily because no alternative adequate source of financial support was available.

The situation was very different in two other frequently quoted attempts by economic means to bring about alterations in behaviour: the imposition of sanctions on Italy because of the attack on Abyssinia in 1935, and on Rhodesia, because of Ian Smith's Unilateral Declaration of Independence in November 1965. In the Italian case the attempt failed mainly because of the international environment. France was concerned that a possible ally against Germany should not be lost or irrevocably alienated. So, aided and abetted by some leading figures in Britain, the French stubbornly resisted the imposition of measures that might have been effective, particularly an embargo on oil. Germany increased deliveries, particularly of coal. The United States administration (the United States not being a member of the League) endeavoured to encourage a moral embargo on supplies to Italy, but in fact supplies of many commodities, including oil, substantially expanded.

In the Rhodesian case sanctions failed for both internal and external reasons. The response of the white population of Rhodesia to Britain's reaction to UDI was to increase their determination not to yield, and so economic disadvantage was grimly accepted. Much of the pressure was borne by the African population of Rhodesia which had no political ability to influence the government. Measures of diversification of the economy were introduced and the reliance on tobacco exports curtailed. Many firms in such countries as France and the Federal German Republic continued to trade with Rhodesia, and the governments seemed reluctant or unable to act against them. Above all South Africa gave financial support and kept open the channels of supply, and to some extent outlets for exports also, and the British government felt unable to contemplate the heavy losses that Britain would suffer (in addition to those already being suffered from cessation of trade with Rhodesia) if the attempt were made to extend sanctions to South Africa because of her refusal to act in accordance with United Nations decisions. The longer the Rhodesian government survived, the more internal confidence grew, and the more other countries believed that sanctions could not succeed and it was not therefore worth while to incur the losses caused to them by sanctions. The attempt of economic pressures in this case was not merely to change a government's behaviour, but to bring a government down; it failed because those with the political capacity to change the government were stiffened in their determination to sustain it, and because the pressuring government primarily concerned, that of Britain, was not able either itself to incur very heavy losses, or to persuade all other states significant to the Rhodesian economy to act with sufficient singlemindedness to cause deprivations to the politically significant Rhodesians severe enough to make them yield.

From the beginning of the Rhodesian imbroglio Prime Minister Harold Wilson ruled out the use of force, so ignoring Frederick the Great's injunction 'Never ill-treat an enemy by halves'. Force is the fifth means available to states for the achievement of their purposes, and is frequently the last to be used, because the losses that may be incurred by the use of force may be very large. The gains to be antici-pated therefore normally need to be very large also, and the objective accordingly to be of primary importance. On the other hand a well-timed, skilful use of force may produce a quick surgical result when without it an issue festering over the years may lead in the long run to much more serious disadvantage. The loss–gains calculus in rela-tion to the use of force is more difficult to formulate than for any other of the instruments of policy, and the consequences of error are more likely to be fatal.

Some maintain indeed that the use of force as an instrument of policy is no longer rational. So long as the impact of weapons was limited to immediate and identifiable military targets it was perhaps not unreasonable to argue, with Clausewitz, that 'War is nothing but a continuation of political intercourse, with a mixture of other means';[16] but the development of thermonuclear, bacteriological and chemical weapons, each capable of obliterating life on the earth, means that the gains from the use of force may be zero, and the losses infinite. Since war may therefore result in the wiping-out of mankind, and so the ending of political activity, it can no longer be regarded merely as a violent extension of politics subordinate to political ends. In these circumstances states cannot reasonably use force for the achievement of their purposes.

The argument is too simple. In the first place there is no clear line of demarcation between the use of force in war and the use of force in a wide range of forms and situations in conditions nominally of peace. In the second place, so long as conflicts among states exist, and no effective institutions or procedures for their resolution are widely accepted by the politically significant members of the international community, governments will perceive the governments of other states as developing violent means for their coercion or destruction, and will regard it as part of their duty to their own people to develop countermeans which, according to their situation, may need to be offensive or defensive in character. The unusual feature of the current situation is that many weapons are being developed, not with the idea or intention of using them, but with the purpose of deterring the governments of other states from using similar weapons which, without deterrence, would enable them to impose throughout the globe ways of life and patterns of political and social organization that many peoples would find alien or distasteful or intolerable.

The two arguments are linked. The fact that weapons of mass destruction exist does not mean that all use of force must escalate into the use of such weapons. Indeed there has been violence in one form or another in every year since 1945, but nowhere since that year have weapons of mass destruction been employed. This does not of itself give grounds for confidence that they never will be, and the hazards consequently remain appalling; but it does show that force has been used, is likely to continue to be used, and may not necessarily lead to disaster.

The decision to use or not to use force results from the loss–gains calculus, and is critically affected by judgments about the danger of uncontrollable escalation. In the first place the possession of weapons of mass destruction is at present limited to about 5 per cent of the states of the world. Relations between all other states are not complicated by fears of intolerable escalation unless two states in con-

<hr>

[16] As quoted in M. E. Howard, 'War as an instrument of policy', in H. Butterfield and M. Wight, *Diplomatic Investigations* (Allen & Unwin, 1966), p. 194.

flict are so highly valued by opposed states possessing these weapons that great power involvement is probable. Thus Israel and the Arabs have fought three wars since 1948; North Korea attacked South Korea in 1950; communist China sent troops into Tibet in the 1950s and fought a frontier war with India in 1962; Indonesia used military violence in the confrontation with Malaysia between 1963 and 1966; India and Pakistan fought over Kashmir in 1965. In all these cases force was seen as a necessary or advantageous means of seeking a policy goal (in order to survive, as seen by the Israelis; to make a greatly desired gain without serious risk of heavy loss, in the case of North Korea—a miscalculation; to increase prestige and decrease that of an opponent and rival, in the Sino–Indian clash; to divert attention from internal troubles, in the Indonesian case; and to attempt to bring to a successful end an intolerably prolonged situation of acute conflict—Kashmir). In no case except possibly the second Israeli-Arab war, when Britain and France joined in, was there much risk of escalation.

In the second place it does not necessarily follow that even if the two major nuclear powers use force or directly confront each other, escalation to the use of mass destruction weapons necessarily follows. The strategic doctrine of flexible response—envisaging the ability to reply in various ways to various kinds of attack, the reply being adequate but not so excessive as to provoke a heavier assault—rests, however precariously, on the view that even if force is used it may be possible to check the exchange at some point below the thermonuclear. The strategy of NATO, relying on ability to impose a check on any Soviet advance with the use of so-called 'tactical' nuclear weapons, contains something of this idea (although the validity of the distinction between tactical and strategic nuclear weapons, and so the ability to check the escalation process, remains uncertain). Confrontation over Cuba in 1962, and repeatedly over Berlin until 1961, did not lead to military clash; while the use of force by the United States in the Dominican republic in 1965 produced no more response from the Soviet Union than Soviet use of force in Hungary in 1956 and Czechoslovakia in 1968 provoked a response from the United States.

Thirdly, violence being widespread throughout the world, all states including the nuclear states may, and many of them do, exploit this violence for their own purposes. Advances may thus be made, or losses avoided, as it were by proxy. The Korean war was an early example of this. Vietnam has been the most ruthless, where the United States has seen their sustaining of South Vietnam as involving the defence of all the non-communist regimes of south-east Asia which otherwise would fall to the Chinese and Soviet supporters of Ho Chi Minh and his successors. Other cases of exploitation of violence are Soviet support to the communist guerrillas in Greece, Chinese support to the insurrectionists in Malaya, Turkish and Greek support to the warring communities in Cyprus, Moroccan and Tunisian support to the revolutionary war of the Algerians against the French, confused intervention by agents of many powers in the Congo, and de Gaulle's support to Ojukwu of Biafra. So long as causes for conflict exist violence is always liable to be used, and the wide occurrence of civil strife suggests possible truth in the view that 'the dangers to order arising from the coexistence of sovereign governments are less than those involved in the attempt to hold hostile communities in the framework of a single polity'.[17]

Force or the threat of it thus remains a weapon that governments of states will use, usually because they feel they must, to advance or preserve their goals and values. It is none the less true that the level of loss that may be suffered by the user of force dictates greater caution and care than in any previous century. Loss of prestige, goodwill or support at the United Nations as a result of the use of force is not in itself a major restraint, but may not be wholly ignored. For states struggling to achieve modernization and economic development the cost of the armaments necessary to be able to use the instrument of force is not to be lightly incurred. For territories which would be battlegrounds, such as Germany, devastation, particularly if tactical nuclear weapons were used, would be likely to exceed any possible gains that might be won. For states such as these last, as for the major nuclear powers in direct confrontation, force is not a realistic option, and weapons are possessed not for defence in case of attack but to deter a potential attacker by persuading him that his losses if he should attack must be greater than any possible gains that might accrue.

Deterrence thus depends on persuasion, and so on perception and credibility. In a two-state relationship, conditions of maximum stability exist when both sets of decision-makers act rationally, when each state has the capacity to survive a full-scale thermonuclear assault at least in the sense of still being able to inflict an intolerable degree of destruction in retaliation, and when the decision-makers on each side know this to be the case. Elements of instability can be identified in relation to these three conditions. Rationality involves not merely the selection of the course of action best designed to maximize gains

[17] H. Bull, 'Society and anarchy in international relations', in Butterfield and Wight, p. 50.

and minimize losses (which in the conditions described must exclude the nuclear option) but also the existence of procedures to ensure that the choice is always effectively under control. In the United States–Soviet relationship such procedures include fail-safe instructions to aircraft, locking devices preventing the arming of thermonuclear devices without orders from strategic headquarters, and direct communication between Moscow and Washington so that possible misinterpretation of radar information can be checked. A second-strike capacity involves certain survival of enough missile sites (by placing these underground, or making them mobile under the sea in submarines), and survival of agencies capable of giving orders (so airborne command headquarters duplicate those under the ground).

Accurate perception is dependent on communication and the free flow of information, so paradoxically security is greater the more the other side knows about one's own capacity. This is so not merely as regards existing capacity but also as regards new developments: clearly stability would be undermined if either side should achieve such a technological breakthrough as would produce a guaranteed 100 per cent destruction of attacking missiles, for then effective retaliation to a first strike would become impossible; and if Washington suspected that Moscow was making headway towards such a breakthrough then Washington's search for such a breakthrough would become desperate, and the impulse to attempt a pre-emptive strike would become strong, and each of these developments would stimulate Moscow's fears. It is for these reasons that the construction of means of civil defence, and the establishment of anti-ballistic-missile defence systems, each contain the seeds of instability. In all cases the rationality assumption involves calculation of probabilities and since in all cases miscalculation might bring utter disaster, the deterring of a state does not require *certainty* of intolerable retaliation, but only a sufficient probability. For deterrence to be effective, therefore, perfect credibility is not necessary, and therefore steps which have some destabilizing implications are not necessarily fatal.

These then are conditions which limit the use of ultimate force by states which have the means at their disposal. The limits operate not merely on direct relations between the two major powers but on questions in which each conceives the other to have a vital interest. Soviet leaders consider it possible that United States decision-makers see western Europe as an area of vital interest in this sense (but not eastern Europe), while United States leaders have for similar, and other, reasons not been prepared to use ultimate weapons to kill the Vietnamese cancer. In some senses therefore these weapons of vast power have made their possessors more impotent, less able to use force as an instrument of policy, than other states which do not have them. But unfortunately possession is not limited just to two powers, and despite the costs and disadvantages more states may seek to have them.

The desire arises because of the roles of states in the international system as decision-makers see them. Britain's possession of nuclear weapons derives from the wartime partnership with the United States, in which the British contribution to the research that led to the explosion of the first atomic bomb was not less important than the American, coupled with the belief continuing after the war that Britain had worldwide interests and a worldwide role to play. France's decision to develop nuclear weapons was the result of the judgment that Europe could not indefinitely rely on United States willingness to shield her against the Soviet Union, and that even if United States support was secure the position of *protégé* was not appropriate for the cradle of the world's civilization. Chinese leaders saw the possession of nuclear weapons as the badge of a great power, and in strategic terms felt both that without the weapons they could not effectively stand against the United States (and later against the Soviet Union), and that with them their position would be less vulnerable than any other of the major powers because of the size of their population and its rural dispersal. Of other states with the potential to develop nuclear weapons but which have not yet begun to do so India is under greatest pressure, because of Chinese progress, the perception of Chinese hostility, and uncertainty about United States support; Indian development would certainly provoke Pakistan to do the same; Israel, because of continued Soviet build-up of arms to the Arabs, must be sorely tempted to exploit her capacity, and Egypt would then feel compelled to try to follow (although Egypt is currently far from having the necessary capacity); both in Sweden and Switzerland there has been much discussion about whether nuclear weapons would strengthen their traditional armed neutrality; South Africa's isolation may encourage the view that nuclear weapons are a necessary safeguard. Japan's memories of Hiroshima and Nagasaki, on the other hand, have hitherto restrained her leaders from thinking that as one of the world's top half dozen powers she should possess her own weapons; almost all German political groups realize that any attempt to go back on their 1955 undertaking and develop their nuclear potential would provoke reactions, particularly from the Soviet Union, that would increase rather than lessen the hazards of their central position; none of Canada, Belgium, Italy or the Netherlands have yet seen sufficient advantage for them to exploit their capacity, and the Soviets have doubtless been unwilling to allow the Czechs to develop theirs.

Various constraints and impulses thus operate to dissuade or en-courage states to develop these particular means of violence. The dangers of proliferation are that the sophisticated strategic under-standing that has now been developed in Moscow and Washington may not be shared by all decision-makers that may come to possess these weapons; that there may be unwillingness or inability to develop the highly costly safeguard procedures which the Soviets and the Americans operate, procedures which anyway become immensely more complicated the more states are involved; that as decisions and development are bound to take place, if at all, successively rather than simultaneously, there will be grave temptations to states ahead in the process to take pre-emptive action against perceived enemies. Such pre-emptive action against China has more than once been thought about in Washington, and doubtless has been considered in Moscow also.

The use of force as an instrument of policy, and the development of means of applying force, has thus become a matter of immense gravity, delicacy and danger. Whether or not to employ force always involved a most difficult balancing of the gains that would probably be achieved against the losses that might be suffered, but when the losses have now become possibly infinite the calculation suggests that the method should not be applied. But the decision-makers in all states perceive others as being possibly willing to use the method, and not all states possess the ultimate means of violence. In these circum-stances force is bound to remain an instrument of policy, to be used, and whose use will be threatened; and the increasingly close links be-tween internal and international conflict guarantee that opportunities will not be lacking. Just as the dangers are greater than ever before, however, so are the constraints, and there is no necessity that cata-strophic exchanges must occur, though the fragile nature of the cur-rent stability is evident. This is however to view the matter solely from the perspective of the states: viewed from the perspective of the international system other elements of the problem emerge. These will be dealt with in Part III of this book.

In the present context one further point needs to be made. States are likely to be able more effectively to achieve their purposes if they can select means that are appropriate to the purpose, or if they can use all means simultaneously—diplomacy, propaganda, subversion, economic pressures, the threat or use of force—and if they can be used harmoniously. Unfortunately means cannot always be combined so as mutually to support one another: frequently the use of one means will reduce or destroy the effectiveness of another. Moreover the use of one means in relation to one issue will have repercussions for other issues. Thus in relation to Czechoslovakia in 1938 Hitler used diplomacy (persuasion of Britain, and so of France, that Czech control of the Sudeten Germans violated the principle of self-determination), propaganda (that this was his last territorial demand in Europe), subversion (instructions and assistance to Henlein in his negotiations with the Czechs and subsequently in his revolt), and force (the threat to destroy the Czechs and the subsequent dispatch of troops). Only economic pressures were hardly used, but economics played little part in Hitler's methods—though in Schacht's hands they did much to create the conditions in which Hitler's methods could succeed.

On the other hand the attempt to combine diplomacy with economic pressures by Britain and France in the Abyssinian crisis in the latter half of 1935 effectively destroyed the efficiency of both; the desire to keep talking encouraged Mussolini, and other League members, to think that sanctions that would hurt would not be imposed, while the imposition of irritant but not vital sanctions annoyed Mussolini but, after an initial fright, did not make him more inclined to end his war. The internal and international consequences of the use of force by the United States in Vietnam, to take the third case, have undoubtedly limited the ability of the United States to use force in other issues where it might otherwise be appropriate. Moreover force has not made diplomacy any easier. Similarly the Bolsheviks' use of subversion in the interwar period did not aid their diplomatic efforts after 1934 to reach agreements with the western powers that would have increased their security against Nazi Germany and against Japan.

There is interaction, that is to say, between means and ends. The selection of means may affect or determine the end that can be achieved. The selection of means in one issue may make more difficult the selection of the same means in another issue, and so may affect the end that can be achieved in the second case. Optimal policies require therefore a very precise understanding of the ends that it is desired to achieve, and a nice appreciation of the relevance of particular means to the end in question and of the extent to which the use of other means may thereby be precluded or in other questions imposed. Understanding of this kind can never be more than partial, and this introduces another element of uncertainty in the making of policy choices. This uncertainty is compounded by the fact that, as is shown in the next chapter, the ends to which policy is ostensibly directed are by no means always clear.

7

The processes of
policy-making

IN THE PRECEDING CHAPTERS foreign policy has been analysed in terms
of the goals which the actions composing it are intended to achieve,
of the means which are or are thought to be available and most suit-
able for the attainment of these goals, and of the influences external
and internal by which the selection of means and the determination
of actions are constrained. Means, goals and influences interact with
and modify each other. There is a fourth variable which interacts
with all the other three. This variable may be described as the processes by which decisions are reached and policy choices are made. Included in this variable 'processes' are the constitutional arrangements,
written or unwritten, of the state in question, its institutional structure,
the actual as opposed to the formal working of its political system,
the procedures or lack of them by which decision-makers are selected
or identified, and the ways in which decisions are evolved or emerge
and are put into effect.

If a decision has to be taken whether a group of buildings is to be
demolished and new ones put in their place the people concerned are
those who live and trade in the locality, and it is therefore appropriate
that decisions of this kind should be taken by locally evolved authorities (except to the extent that the buildings may have some special
architectural or historical quality and are thus part of the 'national
heritage'). Only part of the population within the state is affected.
But foreign policy decisions are taken on behalf of the collectivity as a

whole, and all its members are affected (though evidently in varying degrees over different issues). The constitutional power to take foreign policy decisions is therefore always vested in authorities representing the collectivity as a whole. In Britain, for example, the Crown is this authority. The conduct of foreign policy is a Crown prerogative and Parliament has no legal right to be consulted in advance when in the conduct of foreign policy the Foreign and Commonwealth Secretary is exercising this prerogative. The formal location of authority is illustrated by the fact that many formal acts by which the state is legally committed are taken by the Crown. The declaration of war is a Crown prerogative, and the ratification of treaties is likewise an act of the Crown: in neither case is the assent of either of the Houses of Parliament legally required (though by convention and for political reasons it is now usually sought and obtained).

In the United States the sovereignty of the people is represented by the constitution to which, with the flag, primary loyalty is given. The states composing the union are prohibited from entering any treaty, alliance or confederation, laying any imposts or duties on imports or exports, keeping troops (other than militia) or ships of war, entering any agreement or compact with another state or with a foreign power, or engaging in war unless actually invaded. Beyond these negative provisions, however, the power to make foreign policy is undetermined except for certain specified acts (provide for the common defence, regulate commerce, control exchange rates, define and punish offences against the law of nations, declare war, raise and support armies and a navy—assigned to Congress; act as commander-in-chief of the armed forces, make treaties by and with the advice and consent of the Senate subject to the concurrence of a two-thirds majority of it, appoint ambassadors by and with the advice and consent of the Senate, recommend measures to Congress, be vested with the executive power— assigned to the President). In the Soviet Union all power is formally vested in the Supreme Soviet, but the power to conduct foreign policy is delegated to the Council of Ministers. In Japan the sole source of all legitimacy was the Emperor, who had divine authority, and as soon as a decision had been sanctioned by the Emperor it could no longer be questioned.

In all these cases, with the partial exception of the United States, the actual processes through which decisions were made included but were much wider than their formal origins, but the formal position was not to be ignored. Mussolini on more than one occasion enviously compared Hitler's lot with his own, Hitler being formally head of the German state, while he had always to take into account a king who was sometimes obstinate and whom he thought stupid. (Of course Mussolini on occasions used the king as an excuse for inefficiency or inaction, but this is precisely one of the ways in which the existence of a formal source of authority may enter into the evolution of policy.)

But the identification of the formal or constitutional authority for the making of foreign policy decisions does not take us very far. Everyone knows that it was not the Queen of the United Kingdom who decided whether to accept Ian Smith's Unilateral Declaration of Independence in Rhodesia, or whether to apply for membership of the European Economic Community, or whether to sign the nuclear non-proliferation treaty. Who did in fact take these decisions is not so easy to determine. But if the evolution of policy is to be understood it is essential to know who are the people who participate in the taking of particular decisions, and this is a first step in the analysis of any foreign policy.

The institutional and individual components of the foreign policy decision-making process will vary according to formal procedures, according to informal but politically accepted or conventionally recognized procedures, according to the nature of the political system, according to the nature and magnitude of the issue in question, and according to the urgency or otherwise with which decisions have to be made. The decision whether an ambassador should or should not entertain to dinner a prominent member of a political group in opposition to the government would be likely to be taken by the ambassador on the spot. The decision might have significant consequences for policy both by implying something (whether erroneously or not) about the attitude of the ambassador's government to the opposition group and so to the government in power, and by extending the ambassador's understanding of the situation and so modifying his reports to his home government. The more important these consequences might be thought to be, the less likely is it that the ambassador would wish or would be permitted to decide the question himself (though of course the consequences of the decision would not always be fully anticipated either by the ambassador or by his government). On the other hand the reaching of the decision by the United States in 1948 to enter negotiations for the conclusion of a peacetime alliance was shared by a wide range of persons in the administration, in the public service and in the Congress. In general the less important a decision is thought to be, the more probably will it be taken by an individual relatively low in the administrative hierarchy; but a large number of small decisions may well cumulatively have a substantial influence on policy, both through their effect on climates of opinion, and through the extent to which they may constrain future decisions. For this reason and for others to be described below no clear distinction can be drawn between persons in the decision-making process who advise on policy, and persons who are decision-makers: all participants in the process participate in the decision, although at different levels, and in different ways.

A substantial number of decisions thought to be of low importance will therefore be taken by single individuals in any political system. But the extent to which this happens will be affected by the nature of the system. The more decentralized the system is designed to be, the more institutionalized the procedures for policy formulation, and the less individuals fear personal consequences to themselves of decisions that they may take, the greater the number of decisions likely to be taken by individuals throughout the system.

The nature of the system affects both the recruitment and the mode of operation of decision-making elites, political and official, and so the decision-making process. As far as officials are concerned, they may be homogeneous or heterogeneous in their social origins; they may or may not be highly educated in a formal sense and vocationally trained in the expertise appropriate to their profession; they may gain their positions through nepotism or purchase, through political service, or through open competition; they may, once appointed, be secure during good behaviour, or they may be subject to sudden dismissal. In the case of Britain officials have traditionally been drawn from a narrow upper social segment, and although the proportion of those educated in state schools has been rising, the proportion that has not been through Oxford or Cambridge remains very small. In 1970 the view was still widely held that specialized training in the nature and conduct of international relations before recruitment was unnecessary and even undesirable; selection has for decades been by open competition, though the form of the competition has weighted the scales in favour of candidates with a particular kind of education and social background; once appointed, an official has had virtually total security of tenure. Favourable consequences of these conditions have been a high degree of *esprit de corps*, an ease of working together, and a freedom in criticism, comment, report, and recommendation of great value in the evolution of policies. Less favourable consequences have been some limitation in the range of contacts made by representatives abroad, with some effect on the breadth of understanding and so on the flow of information; and more significantly a relative decline in expertise in face of the increasingly complex and technical nature of international relations, relative both to former skills in an earlier simpler and more gentlemanly world and to the improving skills of practitioners from other states. This must be counted among the many factors that have produced the very high proportion of disastrous failures in British foreign policies—interspersed with a few short-term and a very few long-term successes—over the sixty years since before the first world war.

A contrast with some of these conditions is to be seen in the United States. The social range from which recruits are drawn is somewhat wider, the formal training is more extensive, acquaintance with the social sciences is normally required, and, while the mode of selection is not dissimilar, the security of tenure is for two reasons less. In the first place, many of the most senior officials in the State Department are replaced when an administration changes. Secondly, all members of the executive branch are open to investigation by the Congress, and from time to time (the Joseph McCarthy period in the early 1950s being the most recent) Congressional investigating committees probe the behaviour and performance of federal officials. United States officers thus lack the high degree of certainty of their British counterparts that their opinions and judgments will remain secret, and that they will not be dismissed or have their loyalty questioned because of changes in the direction of political winds. The freedom with which they write, report and recommend is thus in some degree inhibited. This raises the question of accountability in a professedly democratic system. The question will be referred to again below.

Official recruitment and procedures thus affect the quality of information, judgment and recommendation, and the smoothness of working of the machine. Each of these influences policy. But the role played by officers in shaping major decisions will depend primarily on the political context. The greater the security of the political sections of governments, the longer their tenure, and the less their accountability, the less are officials likely to have a decisive influence on the taking of major decisions. Thus in the United States, where the President is irremovable (except in the unlikely event of impeachment), and his chief aides are his own appointees and dependent on him, officials exercise only so much influence as the President chooses. In the France of the Third and Fourth Republics, on the other hand, where governments changed with great frequency, the continuity of policy rested much more in the hands of the Quai d'Orsay, and official influence was greater for this reason. In Britain the influence of the office will vary both with the political security of the government and with the degree of influence commanded in Cabinet by the Foreign Secretary (thus the influence of the office was strong with an insecure

Labour government and Arthur Henderson as Foreign Secretary between 1929 and 1931, but weak with Neville Chamberlain as Prime Minister in undisputed control of party and parliament between 1937 and 1940). In the Soviet Union official advice is subject to the whims of a leadership responsible to none but itself, and so able much more easily to behave inconsistently.

At the political level methods of recruitment likewise affect the formulation of policy. The contrast is marked between the typically long party, parliamentary, and junior office apprenticeship of the British leading decision-makers, with in the United States the catapulting of the chief executive, sometimes from the Congress, more frequently from a state Governor's mansion, but rarely from offices giving experience of administration and still less of foreign policy-making at the federal level. The new President then surrounds himself with aides, cronies of himself or his cronies, selected with due regard to party services, to regional affiliations, and to ethnic and religious balances, but with little more regard to federal governmental experience than in his own case. It by no means follows that the former method is superior. Party and parliamentary skills do not necessarily coincide with administrative skills or with the wisdom and judgment that foreign policy-making requires, party considerations are not totally absent in the British case either, and the choice of the Prime Minister is effectively limited to the members of his party in the two Houses. If the quality of members is poor, the quality of governments is likely to be poor also. The Soviet case is perhaps nearer to the British, in that top decision-making roles are all filled by members of the communist party; but membership of the party being the only road to major responsibility and power its ability to attract talent into its ranks may be higher than in Britain where satisfying non-political roles can be played outside either of the two main political parties. It certainly would appear to be the case that in the post-1950 period in Britain, as in the post-1930 period, disenchantment with politicians and the activity of politics unfavourably affected both the quality of recruitment of political elites, and the degree to which they were called to account for their ineptitudes.

But in foreign policy, to return to a point touched on in a previous paragraph, responsibility and democratic control are peculiarly difficult to enforce. Whether or not an executive is responsible, believes itself to be responsible, or believes it ought to be responsible, will crucially affect its behaviour. In the United States the opinion is widely held that the people ought to know what is going on; and the constitution is so drafted that President and Congress are driven in their mutual rivalry constantly to appeal to public opinion for support. Thus public debate on foreign policies occurs more frequently and more openly in the United States than in any other country. This creates difficulties. Much of the matter of international relations must remain secret while issues are being resolved, because the outcome of a negotiation can be severely impaired if a negotiating position is prematurely revealed, and because a negotiation may not be possible at all, or others in the future may be prejudiced, if the other parties to it do not have confidence that what they say or propose will remain undisclosed. Opinion generally is therefore not merely ill-informed because of lack of understanding or interest, but to some extent must be ill-informed because of the requirement of secrecy. Moreover most foreign affairs by their nature are in several senses distant—distant frequently in a geographical sense, in that they relate to matters on the other side of the globe; distant in a psychological sense, in that they are exceedingly complex and are difficult to understand for this reason and because their concern is with alien and unfamiliar cultures; distant in a temporal sense, in that policy has frequently to be sustained over long periods of time, and the end results are difficult to anticipate and to foresee. The less immediately people feel themselves to be affected, the less positively they respond, and the less willing they are to make sacrifices. For these reasons, the more the values of a community require that the government shall act according to the people's will and shall be publicly accountable for its behaviour, the more the conduct of foreign policy is affected. Summit conferences offer a particular example: at such conferences an irresponsible decision-maker has a built-in advantage, as was shown in the previous chapter;[1] for if nobody can call him to account it matters little to him if the conference produces no result, but the decision-maker who has a party or a public longing for progress can return empty-handed only at substantial political disadvantage to himself and his party. The pressure is accordingly on him to make concessions to produce some seeming advance. The general democratic problem of the accountability and responsiveness of the ruling elites to the ill-informed, the emotional, and the shortsighted, is thus more acute in the field of foreign policy, and the consequences of error are frequently more serious.

It does not, however, follow from this that foreign policy-making is always more effective in systems where the decision-makers are not responsible. Decision-makers in such systems may be irresponsible also

---

[1] See p. 132 above.

in the colloquial sense of being fickle or erratic, and the procedures may be erratic also. Hitler in the 1930s was surrounded by a variety of cronies and agencies, and he maintained his position partly through his unpredictable and so terrifying personality and his public magnetism, and partly through playing agencies and rivals off against each other. Among leading individuals and groups that played roles in foreign policy-making were von Neurath and the Foreign Ministry, Goering the commander of the air force and the chief economic planner, the Army Command, the *Auslandsorganisation* responsible for liaison with and the mobilization of Germans abroad, Ribbentrop and his private office with the right to see Foreign Ministry telegrams, Rosenberg the party ideologist thought to be a particular expert on eastern and Russian affairs, and Hess, Hitler's deputy and responsible for party affairs. The policy that emerged in relation to a particular problem was much affected by which of these agencies happened to be involved and to be an information channel, what was the state of relationships among them, and which happened to be in well with Hitler and to advocate courses of action to which his intuition responded. Thus over the Spanish civil war in 1936-37 Goering wanted to intervene to gain control of Spanish minerals for his economic planning, and later to give his bombing squadrons battle practice; the *Auslands-organisation* hoped through successful intervention to increase its influence and prestige; the Foreign Ministry and the Army opposed intervention because they feared the reaction of France and possibly Britain and possibly the USSR, and could not see sufficient possible gains to set against very large risks; Ribbentrop and the party exploited the differences in order further to undermine von Neurath and the Foreign Ministry, and succeeded in getting the ambassador replaced by a party official. Out of these rivalries emerged a policy of cautious intervention, to be ended if serious danger of conflict with France and Britain developed. Intervention followed by withdrawal would have got the worst of all worlds—a hostile Spain, a strengthened Britain and France, an embittered and resentful Mussolini. That this did not happen was due in this case not to Hitler's skill and courage (which were decisive in some other issues such as that of the Rhineland in 1936) but to the luck of French and British mistaken judgments.

The point at issue is that where several rival agencies may be involved, where they jockey for influence with a key decision-maker, where there are no established procedures for the circulation of information and the coordination of action, where the information flow to top decision-makers is much affected by chance—where in other words the policy-making process is not institutionalized—the likeli-hood is much greater that policies will be decided on the basis of a very partial view of the situation. That the Nazi weasel was able to achieve such successes for so long was due to the extent to which he petrified the democratic rabbits, but when the fascination was broken the blunders then committed brought Germany to catastrophe. The correlation between institutionalization and democracy by no means always holds, for the process in the United States may in this regard be as close to that of the Soviet Union as to that of Britain; but among the interrelated variables which affect the process of policy-making and so affect the policies themselves, the degree of responsibility and account-ability of the decision-makers, and the extent to which the process is institutionalized, are some of the most important.

Decisions will therefore be taken, and policies formulated, by per-sons who have come to fill certain roles, and the roles will be played in the context of certain values, customs and procedures of a greater or less degree of flexibility. Policies will be much affected by the ways in which persons are recruited to these roles, and by the nature of the system in which the roles are played. These factors will also affect the extent to which decisions are taken by individuals, although in all systems some decisions thought not to be important will be taken by individuals low in the hierarchy. At the other end of the scale highly important decisions may in some systems be taken by one or two individuals, and time pressures may also sharply reduce the num-ber of persons or interests who may be brought into the taking of particular decisions.

But the normal condition is that decisions will be made by a group, and the degree of importance assigned to the decisions will affect the composition of the group. Groups taking decisions may contain repre-sentatives of the executive, of the legislature, of the bureaucracy, and of interests outside the governmental machine; and membership of groups will vary widely, not merely as between one state and another but as between one issue and another within the same state. Again the degree of variation will be affected by the nature of the system. Where functions are constitutionally assigned, part of the composi-tion of the group is fixed if a decision is to be legal : thus, as has been mentioned, a United States President cannot formally sign and so commit the United States to a treaty without the approval of the Senate signified by a concurring vote of two-thirds of the Senators present at the time, and the members of the Senate have on occasion used this power both to amend and reject treaties, and to cause some of their number to participate in the treaty-negotiating process. Where procedures are highly institutionalized it is likely that in relation to certain questions an individual will automatically be part of a group by virtue of the office he holds: thus in the United Kingdom it would be unusual for a decision concerning, say, the opening of diplomatic relations with communist China to be taken without the participation of the head of the Far Eastern Department of the Foreign Office, whereas in Nazi Germany, as has been shown, or in Stalin's USSR, participation in a decision by virtue of office or function' was by no means so automatic. Where issues are very complex and are in many of their aspects interrelated with others, the automatic functional assignment becomes difficult even in institutionalized systems—indeed adequate intercommunication and liaison may break down in such systems also, and the process of reaching decisions (and so possibly their effectiveness) may be much slowed down by the attempt to ensure that all interested parties are properly consulted.

Chance may enter into the formation of groups. Should a particular item of information come into the hands of a particular member of a government he is likely to participate in decision-taking on this question, even though he would not otherwise normally have done so. A known special interest in a particular question may lead to inclusion in a group. The chance of who happens to be in town when an issue blows up may be decisive: thus it was Eden's temporary absence from London on holiday in January 1938 which facilitated Neville Chamberlain's pouring cold water on Roosevelt's idea for an international conference to draw up a code of international behaviour, a decision by Chamberlain which had much to do with Eden's resignation a month later and was deeply discouraging to the Anglophiles and the anti-Nazis in Washington. The chance of timing may also affect availability: on the first day of the Cuban missile crisis in 1962 Charles Bohlen was included in the United States decision-making group as the leading expert on Soviet affairs; but since he was due to leave as ambassador to France, and it was important that the fact of top-level meetings being held should be kept secret until decisions had been arrived at, he was replaced by Llewellyn Thompson, and Thompson proved to be one of the major influences leading to the choice of blockade rather than airstrike.[2]

Finally the structure of a government, and the outlook and political position of members of it, will affect the composition of decision-making groups. Sometimes arduous negotiations among entrenched interests will be necessary even before a group can be formed. Some United States Presidents, like Eisenhower or Hoover, will choose to

[2] R. F. Kennedy, *13 Days* (Pan, 1969), pp. 35 and 114.

participate only in limited degree in foreign policy-making, while others, like Kennedy or Johnson, will take a direct and extensive part. Formally constituted groups, like the National Security Council in Washington, or interdepartmental committees in London, may exist to deal with assigned questions; but the extent to which they are used may vary with different political leaders. The mere existence of a group formed for one purpose may lead to its gradually increasing its role for other purposes. This was certainly one of the ways, among many others, by which the secretariat of the communist party of the Soviet Union under Stalin gradually extended the range of its participation in, and finally dominated, decision-making. Chamberlain's inner cabinet of Halifax, Simon, Hoare and himself similarly acquired an expanding role.

Thus decision-making groups within the elites are constantly changing. Who is in, who out, may be vital. But decisions can only be taken, judgments made, policies formed, on the basis of information received by those who are to decide. No human in any situation, nor any later observer, ever has perfect information, in the sense of being wholly aware of all the elements of a situation and having total understanding of all the consequences of any course of action which may be decided upon. In the field of foreign policy the information problem is particularly difficult, because much information is deliberately kept secret, because dealings are with representatives of other, alien, cultures, and because questions are so complexly interrelated that many consequences of action cannot possibly be foreseen.

The appropriateness of a policy to the situation with which it is designed to deal will therefore be heavily influenced by the quality and quantity of the information upon which it is based. Information will flow to decision-makers from a wide variety of sources—from their own ambassadors, diplomatic representatives, consular officials, military, commercial and cultural attachés, from ambassadors and other representatives of other states, from other departments or organs of their own government, and from press, radio, television and private sources. The primary source is of course the first of these. But the quality and quantity of information obtained by diplomatic representatives will again vary widely. It will be affected in the first place by the range of diplomatic representation: many of the new smaller states of the world have not the trained persons or the financial resources to maintain more than a few embassies, and they have to rely therefore on information received from agents of other states. The British Commonwealth, as was mentioned earlier, in part continues to exist because it facilitates the flow of information among states with only small diplomatic representation,[3] and one of the important aspects of the United Nations (particularly for smaller powers) is the opportunity it affords for diplomatic contact to be made between almost any two states in the world.

The quality and quantity of information obtained by a diplomatic agent will vary, secondly, according to his own predilections, training and personality. The Bolshevik Joffe in Berlin in 1918 made his contacts as much among the Spartakists as with the government, and his understanding of the situation in Germany was affected thereby; while Britain's Nevile Henderson, also in Berlin after 1937, found himself at home mainly with hunting, shooting and fishing landowners, Junkers, minor aristocrats, and army officers—representatives of an older Germany who warmly approved of Hitler's achievements and who tried to close their eyes (and so Henderson's) to the nature of the man and his methods, and to the extent of his ultimate ambitions. The elegant and cultured French ambassador, François-Poncet, was less to his taste than the Italian Count Attolico or the Belgian Davignon, and their information compounded his misconceptions.

Thirdly, the information a representative obtains will be much affected by the relations between his own government and that to which he is accredited, and by his own personal feelings and acceptability. It is evident that Lord Halifax in Washington during the second world war had an intimate understanding of the American scene, both because Britain and the United States were deeply involved in a common enterprise and so their interests were closely interwoven, and because Halifax personally was much respected in the United States capital. On the other hand relations between the Soviet Union and most of the non-communist world have normally been such that the flow of trustworthy information obtained by diplomatic representatives has been sharply limited. The mutual personal regard of Malcolm MacDonald and Jawaharlal Nehru greatly enhanced MacDonald's understanding of and reporting about the Indian situation during his period of office as High Commissioner in Delhi in the late 1950s, while at the other extreme the overwhelming abhorrence for the Nazis felt by the United States Berlin Ambassador William E. Dodd, so that he could hardly bear to shake them by the hand, did

---

[3] Whether this function can continue to be performed depends on the extent of implementation of the Duncan report on Britain's foreign activities. See *Report of the Review Committee on Overseas Representation 1968-69* (Cmnd 4107, HMSO, 1969).

not contribute to the free flow of information into the United States embassy and on to Washington.

Information floods in to an embassy from all directions. It cannot and should not all be transmitted back to the home capital, because the communication channels would become clogged, and because such a heavy flow from all embassies simultaneously would be unassimilable in the government offices at home. Selection therefore has to be made. In the process of selection some vital piece of information may be omitted. The likelihood of this happening will depend on the extent to which an ambassador is himself informed (and this in turn will be affected by the degree to which he commands the confidence of his home government) and on the way in which he conceives his mission. An ambassador whose instructions or whose own judgment lead him to set as his prime goal the development of trade between his own country and that to which he is accredited will single out and select certain kinds of information as being significant, while one who sees his purpose as being to prevent war breaking out (as did Henderson in Berlin) will consciously or unconsciously see information that contributes to the achievement of this purpose as important information.

Of even greater consequence for the selection and transmission of information is the ability of a representative to comprehend what he is told or what he sees. An ambassador in Moscow with no knowledge of Marxism-Leninism is likely more frequently to be baffled or to misunderstand than one who has such knowledge, while a Soviet ambassador whose pattern of thought has been determined by Marxism-Leninism can interpret what he sees only within this philosophical framework. Of course it is the case that all diplomatic representatives are conditioned, and their understanding is limited, by the culture within which they have been brought up, and this is a main part of the information problem in the field of foreign relations; but the effect of this conditioning is likely to be less if the society is an open one in which cultural norms permit or encourage the questioning of fundamental assumptions, than if the cultural norms (like those of the Soviet Union) impose a pattern of thought out of which only the most original and gifted can possibly break. It may with a measure of truth be asserted that the USSR has never had a steady flow of good information about the outside world—in the early days because its diplomatic representation was limited and those representatives who were in post saw themselves at least as much as the link with and inspiration of local communist revolutionary parties as the representative of one government to another (and thus hardly endeared themselves to the governments to which they were accredited); in slightly later years because embassies abroad were sometimes used as means of getting opposition leaders out of Moscow (as Kollontai was sent to Stockholm, Rakovsky to Paris and London, Kamenev was offered Tokyo but refused, and much later Molotov was despatched to Ulan Bator); and in the Stalinist period because ambassadors had to be carefully selected and rigorously trained and conditioned so that they would not step outside the party line or be contaminated by their contacts with capitalists. The blinkers of ideological conditioning have much to do with such blunders as Tukhachevsky's invasion of Poland in 1920, the refusal to participate in the Marshall Plan in 1947 (for participation would surely have led to Congress's refusal to appropriate the funds), or the invasion of Czechoslovakia in 1968 and the creation of an internal resistance and hostility which was surely not anticipated.

An ambassador's personal opinions or preference, as distinct from his cultural conditioning, may bias his selection of information. It is less likely that he will select and report particular information in order to advance some project of his own. This latter procedure is however normal when ambassadors of other states proffer information. It is never done without a purpose. The purpose may be the relatively innocuous one of gaining goodwill, it may be intended to produce consequences desired by a friend or an ally, it may be accurate or not accurate, and in both cases it may be accepted as being accurate or inaccurate. Prime Minister Wilson's information to Chancellor Kiesinger in February 1969 about the conversation between President de Gaulle and the British ambassador in Paris, Christopher Soames, was clearly intended not merely to forestall a possible future use of the conversations by de Gaulle, but to increase Kiesinger's leanings towards Britain and disenchantment with the French. During the two sets of negotiations conducted by the Soviet Union in 1939, with Britain and France as was publicly known, and with Nazi Germany in strict secrecy, all parties, but particularly Germany and the USSR, used diplomats of other states, junior and senior, to pass on hints of their intentions and thus influence the course of the negotiations. Sir Stafford Cripps, when British ambassador in Moscow, on instructions passed on to Stalin information received in London about Hitler's impending attack on the Soviet Union in June 1941, but Stalin chose to treat the information as being without foundation, or at least so to act as to remove any possible excuse for Hitler to launch such an attack, which included making no preparations to meet it.

Information received from other departments or organs of government may also on occasion be given in order to produce a desired consequence, for ministers have rival projects and different conceptions of what the national interest requires. The degree to which circulation of information within a governmental machine is affected by motives such as these will vary according to the nature of the system. The information flow is completed by regular and systematic surveys of the mass media by diplomatic representatives abroad and by the external affairs ministries at home, for often journalists will not merely give life and colour to reports but will come upon and reveal occurrences which official sources are anxious to cover up and which may be important for the formation of policy. It appeared in the early months of 1969 as if the British government was not well informed about Federal Nigerian air raids on Biafra, and that reports by journalists conveyed more information to Whitehall than had the High Commission in Lagos. Certainly these reports produced disquiet among members of Parliament of all parties, and contributed substantially to the government's difficulties in sustaining their policy of support to the federal government.

The gathering of information, the making of low-level decisions on the basis of it, the selection by various criteria of relevance of information to be passed on, is only the first stage of the process. The information has to be communicated. All social relations depend on communication, as does the greater part of learning, and motivation of behaviour. But the reproduction in one mind of the perception of another can rarely be an exact or precise process. When the medium of communication is the written or spoken word, some element of misperception is likely, because language is an imprecise instrument. Moreover the memories, expectations and value system of the person to whom the information is communicated will create predispositions to accept or reject information as credible or not credible, and such predispositions will affect the degree of confidence placed in the originator of the information now and in the future. The degree of 'openmindedness' clearly varies from one individual to another, but no one can be completely openminded.

Some misunderstanding is therefore always probable in human relationships, but most of it may be insignificant. In international relations the likelihood of misunderstanding is high. In the first place, language translation is often involved, and this may marginally increase the chances of misperception even between two bilingual persons. In the second place, much information in international relations is concerned with highly complex or technical questions in economics or defence or science, and communication from the expert to the less expert offers greater scope for misunderstanding. Thirdly, misunderstanding is less likely between persons brought up in the same cultural environment.[4] This is not merely the case with abstractions like 'democracy' (which clearly conjures up quite different images, and provokes quite different reactions of favour, disfavour or indifference, for an American, a South African, and a Chinese), but with physical tangibles: there are evidently special associational matrices of words like 'snow' for a Russian, or 'water' to a Bedouin Arab, or 'beef' to a Hindu, which only with great difficulty can be apprehended by people from other cultures. It is characteristic of most international transactions that they take place between people of different cultures: indeed in so far as two states are more than merely legal and administrative entities, communication between their representatives is almost sure to be less effective than between either representative and most of the members of his own state. Finally, the likelihood of misunderstanding is increased when the subject of communication is intangible or abstract—aspirations, intention, purpose, motivation. None of these is by any means necessarily clear to the source of the information, so the chances of misconstruction by the receptor are great. But many decisions in international relations are based on beliefs about the aspirations or purposes or motives of the decision-makers of other states.

Misperception of a different kind may result from the psychological phenomenon known as cognitive dissonance. The beliefs people have about the conditions of their existence, the values they cherish, and the wants they seek to satisfy, create in their minds certain expectations and desires about information concerning their environment. Information which conflicts with these expectations or desires creates cognitive dissonance, which may be resolved by rejection of the information, by irrational responses, or by a review of expectations and desires. A man believing himself to be happily married, with a loving wife and family, on being told that his wife is having an affair with another man may simply disbelieve what he is told, may strike his informant on the nose, may become suspicious of or hostile to his wife, may carefully think over his situation from this new possible perspective, or may openly discuss the information with his wife. Which of these possible courses he selects will depend on a large number of factors, including his own psychological make-up and the degree to which he feels himself committed to, or his happiness dependent on, the expectations and values with which the information conflicts. Decision-makers in foreign policy

[4] I refer again to Deutsch's suggestion that the limits of an autonomous political or social organization may be described 'in terms of a *communication differential*: among members or parts of an organization there should be more rapid and effective communication than with outsiders' (see Chapter 3, p. 39 n. 3 above).

may likewise react with disbelief, or irrationally, when information creates cognitive dissonance. The previously mentioned seeming refusal of Stalin to accept Cripps's warnings about the imminent German invasion in 1941 may be an example of this, but documented instances have been cited by Professor R. C. North in his study of the 1914 crisis.[5]

The transmission and circulation of information is further affected by technical factors, and by requirements of secrecy. Information channels may become overloaded because the capacity of telephone cables, wireless frequencies or cipher rooms may be insufficient to cope with the quantity of incoming messages : this is particularly likely to be the case during times of crisis, and the consequent transmission delays will sharply, and possibly fatally, increase the time pressures for rapid decisions which anyway are central features of crisis situations. Overload may occur also in the minds of decision-makers, not merely in terms of the quantity of information to be assimilated, but in terms of its content—an immensely complex question, in which the stakes are high, will tend to crowd out other questions from the decision-maker's mind, possibly with critical consequences for them. Overload of a slightly different kind may also result from an inadequate information circulation system, so that information received somewhere in the governmental machine is unable to reach the appropriate persons, or unable to reach them in time. Complexity again is relevant here, because the appropriate persons may not always be obvious to the operator routing the information, and excessive duplication is not merely costly but will increase the danger of overload. Finally, secrecy may cut the circulation of information, and it may well happen that the significance of a piece of information received at a particular point in the system may not be appreciated because secrecy has prevented circulation of the information necessary to its accurate evaluation. Communication failure can lead to disaster, as instanced by Pearl Harbour in December 1941.[6]

---

[5] R. C. North, *Fact and Value in the 1914 Crisis* (Stanford Studies in International Conflict and Integration, 1961).

[6] The United States had broken the Japanese codes, so it was known in Washington that negotiations were about to be broken off, that the Japanese embassy had been instructed to destroy its codes and secret files, and accordingly that some offensive action was imminent. That the United States fleet at Pearl Harbour was none the less caught so completely by surprise by the Japanese was due partly to a mild form of cognitive dissonance (firmly held convictions in Washington that the Japanese attack would be towards south-east Asia and the Indies), and partly to transmission delays in a cable of general, though not specific, warning from the Chief of Staff, General Marshall, causing it to reach Hawaii only after the attack was over. See D. F. Drummond, *The Passing of American Neutrality* (University of Michigan Press, 1955), pp. 361-8.

The information upon which a decision-maker bases his policies is thus in all cases incomplete and in varying degrees inaccurate. He acts on the basis of the situation as he believes it to be and not on the basis of the situation as it is. None of the 'influences' on policy which have been discussed in earlier chapters have any effect whatsoever in themselves: they have effect only in so far as they are perceived by the decision-maker. The fact (if it were so) that the river Rhine could be bridged or crossed in boats would be irrelevant to the formation of French policy towards Germany if the French decision-maker believed it could not be. The fact (if it were so) that the British coal mines could produce all the fuel and power necessary for the British economy would be irrelevant to the formation of British policy towards the Levant if the British decision-maker believed that the British economy had to be supplied with oil imported from that area. The fact that the President of the United States has no power to declare war and (if it were so) that in no circumstances would Congress do so would be irrelevant to the policy of an enemy towards the United States if the decision-maker in the enemy's capital did not know this.

The distinction must therefore be drawn between what may be termed the psychological environment of the decision-maker, and his operational environment.[7] The psychological environment is how the decision-maker sees the situation, the operational environment is how the situation in fact is. His decisions result from the way he sees the situation. His view of it derives from the information that reaches him, subject to the hazards of information-gathering, of communication and of perception that have been analysed. International relations are thus not relations between states, or directly between governments composed of decision-makers, but in some senses are relations between beliefs, beliefs about the nature and component elements of situations, and about the effects in these situations of the adoption of various courses of action.[8] Among these beliefs are beliefs about the beliefs of other decision-makers. One may postulate therefore the following schema: the operational environment, which is reality (all the elements of a

[7] The terminology is that used by J. Frankel in *The Making of Foreign Policy* (Oxford University Press, 1963).

[8] 'I think, looking back on Cuba, what is of concern is the fact that both governments were so far out of contact, really. I don't think that we expected that he [Khrushchev] would put the missiles in Cuba, because it would have seemed such an imprudent action for him to take, as it was later proved. Now, he obviously must have thought that he could do it in secret and that the United States would accept it. So that he did not judge our intentions accurately ... you see the Soviet Union and the United States, so far separated in their beliefs ...'— President John F. Kennedy speaking on television on 17 December 1962, and quoted in E. Abel, *The Missiles of October* (MacGibbon & Kee, 1966), p. 198.

situation, and all the consequences of all possible courses of action in the situation, as an omniscient observer would see them), reality being not perceived or perceivable; the view of this reality held by the decision-maker in state A; the view of reality held by the decision-maker in state B; the view held by decision-maker A of decision-maker B's view of reality; the view held by decision-maker B of decision-maker A's view of reality; the view held by decision-maker A of decision-maker B's view of decision-maker A's view of reality, and so on *ad infinitum*. This is not purely fanciful. Crucial elements of the operational environment of France and Germany in March 1936 were the overwhelming superiority of the French armed forces over the German in numbers and equipment, the German army's opposition, in the face of this disparity, to Hitler's plan to march troops into the demilitarized zones of the Rhineland, and the instructions consequently given to the German troops to withdraw if the French army moved. Hitler none the less gave the order for the remilitarization to be carried out, and the move was successful, because he correctly judged that the French judged their environment to be such that they could not move. Perception is thus the determinant not merely of power, as was seen in Chapter 5, but of all decisions taken by persons acting on behalf of states in the pursuit of goals.

The matter is further complicated by the fact that the psychological environments of different members of a decision-making group will vary. Experience and heredity predispose some to think well, and others to think ill, of human behaviour, and perceptions of information, and judgment of appropriate responses, will vary accordingly. In finely balanced questions personal friendships or antipathies among members of groups may influence judgment. The result of consideration in a particular group will be affected by who happens to be the most senior or the most influential, and by whether the competences of members of the group are or are not clearly defined. The attitude and judgment of members will likewise be affected by their functional or institutional affiliations, whether within or outside the governmental sector.

It is not of course suggested that in every decision all these considerations come into play, but some of them may. In a minor issue, for example, with a political and commercial component, if the competent Board of Trade official happened to be senior to the competent Foreign Office official, and particularly if the Board of Trade officer chanced to have been a school head of house when the Foreign Office official arrived as a new boy, there can be little doubt that the way the matter was resolved would be influenced, and the probability is that the commercial element of the problem would be emphasized. In great questions, however, the full range of group dynamics may operate, with different psychologies interacting, different judgments made of political or personal advantage to be won or lost, different views held of the national interest, and so different perceptions formed of incoming information and different opinions reached about the action that should be taken. A recent account of such interplay is Robert F. Kennedy's posthumously published recollections of decision-making in the 1962 Cuba crisis.[9]

Decisions emerge from this process: the receipt of information; selection and communication of some of this information; action upon it by an individual by virtue of his office, or circulation of it among members of a group, formally or informally constituted, consulting in writing or verbally or possibly in conference. The decision that emerges is in greater or less degree conditioned by what has happened at each stage of this process, so that the choice eventually made may not be from among all possible courses of action but may be among those remaining few that appear feasible or are conceived. On occasion it may be difficult even for participants to determine how the choice came to be made. For these reasons decision-making is properly to be thought of in processual terms.[10]

But just as the ways in which decisions are reached are by no means always identifiable and precise, so is the effectiveness of their execution subject to human and technical constraints. The decision may be for immediate action, for delayed or future action, or for no action. The action or inaction may be made contingent upon other developments occurring, or not occurring, in the evolution of the question at issue, or in some other related area. The person instructed to act may be left wide discretion in his method, or no discretion at all. The decision may be precise and clear, or it may be imprecise or ambiguous, deliberately or unintentionally. The consequences of decisions will be affected by their nature, by the communication system, and by the quality of the executive agents.

Action is likely most closely to coincide with intention if the decision is precise, for immediate action, and to be carried out personally by a skilled member of the decision-making group. The more ambiguous the decision, the greater the delay, the larger the number of communication channels through which the decision must pass, and of course the less

[9] R. F. Kennedy, *13 days*.

[10] For an extended and subtle discussion of this question, which includes (p. 66) the phrase 'the decision-maker is not a man or a group of men, but a process' see J. W. Burton, *Systems, States, Diplomacy and Rules* (Cambridge University Press, 1968), Chapter 4.

efficient the agent, the greater the likelihood that action will not coincide with intention.

Numerous examples of these general statements could be given. Ambiguity of decision may bedevil policy. After Mussolini and Hitler met at their first summit conference in June 1934 neither of the two foreign ministries was able to discover what they had decided about Austria, the key question that divided them, and it was not until Hitler eventually took the plunge, in March 1938, that he, the ministries, and probably Mussolini also, knew what Italy would do in the event of an *Anschluss* between Germany and Austria. Sometimes ambiguity may be deliberate, as being the only way to prevent a breakdown in discussions, or to reach an agreement, when both parties prefer that discussions should continue, or an agreement be reached, rather than a breach should be caused. In that case resolution of the issue is postponed until circumstances are judged by one or both parties to have changed—and the reaching of the agreement will itself produce some change. Many disarmament agreements have been of this kind.[11]

If implementation of a decision is delayed, or if its operation is made contingent upon some future occurrence, the more likely it is that conditions will have so altered as to make the decision less appropriate. Every decision to participate in an alliance contains this difficulty, particularly if the alliance is for a long period of time, and frequently the originally intended range of the decision is altered to meet changed circumstances. Thus the North Atlantic Treaty Organization has on the one hand seen Gaullist France endeavouring to moderate the effect of its original decision to join the alliance, in the judgment that the conditions making the decision appropriate had altered; while on the other hand extensive discussions have been held within NATO as to whether it should operate in any way outside the geographical area covered by its participating countries.

The intention of a decision may be falsified by the way in which it is carried out, by technical communications failure, or by communications failure in the sense of misperception of the decision by the agent who is to execute it, or by the receptor to whom it is notified. The British ambassador in Berlin between 1937 and 1939, Nevile Henderson, offers an example of the quality of an agent affecting the consequences of a decision. At a British and French meeting in April 1938 the governments agreed that if the situation should in the future warrant it, Henderson should warn the German government that in the event of a German attack on Czechoslovakia France would be bound in accordance with her alliance with the Czechs to come to their assistance, and

[11] See Chapter 6, pp. 127-8 above.

Britain could not guarantee that she would not be forced to become involved also. Henderson was told not to give this warning unless and until instructed to do so. In fact he dropped the warning casually more than once in conversation with German officials and ministers, so that when on 21 May he was instructed finally to give the warning (because of reports of German troop movements) he was unable to give it with any force and it made little impression on German Foreign Minister Ribbentrop.[12] This ineptitude did not in itself have momentous consequences, for the reported troop movements did not in fact conceal German preparation for an immediate attack, but the series of such ineptitudes committed by Henderson may well have contributed to the impression in Berlin that Britain would never fight whatever the Nazis decided to do.

Technical failure may be illustrated from a case early in 1932. Japan's invasion of Manchuria had led to a spate of ineffective diplomatic action by the League of Nations and by the United States. Anglo-American cooperation was vital. In February 1932 the United States Secretary of State Stimson produced the idea that a joint *démarche* should be made within the framework of the nine power pact of 1922, and British Foreign Secretary Sir John Simon spoke to him about it on the trans-atlantic telephone. Simon's intention was to say that he did not want to take up this idea until he had got the League to accept Stimson's earlier proposal for a declaration of non-recognition of territorial changes brought about by war; but apparently Stimson gathered the impression that Simon did not want a joint *démarche* at all. Stimson accordingly acted unilaterally by writing and publishing a letter to the Chairman of the Senate's Foreign Relations Committee, setting out the administration's position. This action in turn angered London. The *contretemps* was the result of the failure of telephonic communications, but it had lasting consequences in contributing to the myth (which still exists in the United States) that Japanese aggression could have been stopped in time if Britain had been willing to act jointly with the United States.[13]

This leads on to the final point about the effectiveness of actions

[12] Compare E. L. Woodward and R. Butler, eds. *Documents on British Foreign Policy 1919-1939*, third ser., i (HMSO, 1949), pp. 260, 264 and 335, with *Documents on German Foreign Policy 1918-1945*, ser. D, ii (HMSO, 1950), p. 317.

[13] H. L. Stimson, *The Far Eastern Crisis* (Harper, 1936), pp. 161-5. Sir John Pratt (*War and Politics in China* (Cape, 1943), pp. 228 and 281-2) points out that a week before the letter to Borah Simon confirmed in writing his expectation of being able to take up the nine power pact proposal after the League had accepted the non-recognition doctrine; but Stimson's initial misunderstanding on the telephone, evidently contributed to, as well as serving as an excuse for, his decision to write to Borah.

resulting from decisions. The effect they produce depends on how they are perceived and communicated by those to whom they relate. Thus in the Henderson example given above it could be the case that the British warning was in fact given with great force and conviction, but that it was perceived by Ribbentrop as being of little significance. Or it could also be the case that in reporting the interview for Hitler, and for other members of the German Foreign Office and government) Ribbentrop judged it desirable to give the impression that he rebutted the warning with great vigour, that he attached little importance to it, and that Henderson in reality attached little importance either. Whichever of these explanations is the correct one (and they could all offer part of the truth) it is clear that the effect of the London decision to give the warning was in substantial degree lessened by Henderson's method of handling it, or by Ribbentrop's perception of it, or by Ribbentrop's method of communicating it to the top decision-maker, Hitler, or by some combination of all these factors.

These examples illustrate the point already made that while in the processes of policy-making decisions result from the way in which the facts of the situation are seen by the decision-makers, the actions that flow from the decisions take place in the world as it in fact is. The consequences of decisions will therefore be affected not only by their nature, by the communications system and by the quality of the executive agents, but by the operational environment within which they take effect. One component of this operational environment, as far as decisions made on behalf of a particular state are concerned, is of course the psychological environment of the decision-makers of other states, as has just been illustrated. Thus in analysing the effect on policies of the processes by which the policies are evolved, it is crucially important always to bear in mind the distinction between the purposes which decisions are intended to achieve, and the results which they are able to achieve. In the language used in an earlier part of this chapter, the perfect information required for the best decisions to be taken (which only an omniscient observer could know) is total information about the situation as it is, which includes information about the consequences of every possible course of action that might be taken.

One final comment needs to be made. The decision-making process has been formally analysed—receipt of information, communication of it, circulation through the communication net, possible constitution of a decision-making group, interplay among members of the group, emergence of a decision which may be one of many kinds, communication of the decision to agents of varying qualities, perception of it and communication by first receptor, consequence and response as determined by the operational environment. This formal analysis bears little relation to reality. It implies a succession of single staccato decisions. Nothing of the kind takes place. In reality, at least in a major capital, questions are simultaneously pouring in from all sides for answers, and decisions taken on one question will affect, and their effectiveness will be affected by, the decisions being simultaneously taken on other questions. This is another and no less important aspect of internal information—the extent to which information about decisions being taken in one field passes, and in time, to people taking decisions in other related fields. Again the effectiveness with which this is done is likely to be in considerable degree a function of institutionalization. At low levels, where many less important decisions are taken, coordination is likely to be less essential. At higher levels, and on major issues, if established procedures exist and are regularly used, coordination of decision-taking in related areas is more likely to be achieved. But whatever the system, failure in this respect can cause the total failure of policies.

Two outstanding examples suggest themselves. French military strategists, building on the experience of the first world war, advised in the late 1920s that with the rising power of Germany and the failure of other methods of containing her, France could be secured by the construction of a defensive fortification so powerful that no forces would be able to break through it. The advice was accepted, the Maginot line constructed, and the French army organized and its logistics planned to sustain an unbreakable defence. While this was being done, French diplomats, led by Louis Barthou, sought to recreate the former alliance with the Russians to the east, and to strengthen their ties with the Little Entente, and particularly Czechoslovakia. The strategy made nonsense of the diplomacy. Hitler and Stalin demonstrated their recognition of this, the former in Czechoslovakia in 1938, the latter in the Nazi-Soviet pact in 1939, and in 1940 France found herself without either allies on the mainland, or security.

The United States, to take the second example, by rejection of the Versailles treaty, and so of the League Covenant, turned her back on the squabbling world and endeavoured to withdraw into the western hemisphere. When in the 1930s the squabbles grew more threatening, the Congress abandoned the traditional American principle of freedom of the seas for neutrals in war and attempted by legislation in the Neutrality Acts to insulate the States from the dangers evidently mounting in Europe. But at the same time as politically the United States was striving to cut herself off from the rest of the world, so economically in the 1920s her trade and her investments in other countries expanded: the extent of her economic involvement was dramatically demonstrated in the crisis and slump of 1929-33. Strategically fortress America made a little more sense than its French counterpart, but it married with economic policy no better than did Maginot France with French diplomacy. So (though this is not the only reason) isolationism ended in, and contributed to, disaster.

The foregoing chapters have, it is hoped, demonstrated the complexity of the relationships from which foreign policies evolve. Goals are set by the decision-makers' interpretation of the values of the sociopolitical environment in which they live, and by the priorities which they think should be given (whether or not under internal political constraints) to some of these values as against others. A variety of means are available which may be used to advance towards or to achieve these goals, but all means are not always mutually compatible, and some are appropriate to some goals but not to others. Thus the nature of goals will influence the choice of means, but the choice of means may make some goals unattainable. In selecting means decision-makers make judgments in the light of their perception of a wide range of influences or elements in their environment, elements that derive from within the state, or from the conditions of existence of the state, or from its role in the international arena. These perceived influences or capabilities likewise affect the choice of goals and the determination of priorities among them, and in turn the means and the goals react back upon the perception of the influences. The various elements of the environment, moreover, are perceived to interact with each other. A fourth dimension of interaction is added in the form of the process by which policies are evolved, the process itself affecting and being affected by the choice of goals and the degree of their attainment, the choice of means and their efficacy, and the perception of influences. A separate analysis can be made of each of these segments of foreign policy making, and understanding can be advanced thereby; but such understanding can be only partial, and must lack explanatory power. A comprehensive theory of foreign policy requires a complex model incorporating the four major interacting elements.

PART III

Macro-international relations

8

International systems

THIS BOOK BEGAN BY stating that knowledge is a unity, but that understanding can be advanced only by breaking up the universe of knowledge into intellectually manageable parts. That part which might be called international relations was described as being 'concerned with study of the nature, conduct of, and influences upon, relations among individuals or groups operating in a particular arena within a framework of anarchy, and with the nature of, and the change factors affecting, the interactions among them'.[1] Examination of this segment called international relations was then further broken down into study of the behaviour of, and interactions among, certain particularly significant groups in international relations, the groups known as states. This behaviour was shown as being affected, among other influences, by the relationships or interactions between the state under study and other bodies similarly acting on the international stage; but the interactions were seen as being significant in relation to the state in question and were not themselves the primary focus of interest. An alternative way of looking at international relations is to regard the interactions, their nature, how they change and why, as being central; and this will suggest questions, and possible answers, of quite a different kind from those that have been considered so far.

The word 'interactions' leads straight to the word 'system'. A system, in the simplest definition, is a set of interacting parts. The parts may be

[1] See Chapter 1, p. 10 above.

material or immaterial, may that is to say have an existence accessible to the senses (as the interactions of electricity, petrol vapour mixed with air, compression chambers and pistons form with other components the system known as an internal combustion engine, which can be seen, heard, smelt, felt and, if you like, tasted), or existence only in an abstract sense (like the interacting quantities in a set of equations). The essential point is that change in any of the components, or in the interactions among them, produces changes throughout the system, or its break-down. Thus to increase the amount of air mixed with the petrol vapour will cause the engine to operate more or less smoothly, and with greater or less power; while to increase the flow of an unchanged mixture of petrol and air will cause the engine to operate more rapidly (provided that the electrical supply and the other components are capable of adequately responding). Too much air will cause the engine to stop altogether.

Thus the optimal working of a system in terms of whatever its purpose may be (that of the engine, for instance, to produce maximum power at minimum cost) depends on the condition of the units being optimal and the interactions among them being optimal also, and what is the optimal condition of the units will be affected by the nature of the interactions and *vice versa*. In the case of the engine the optimal amount of air in the petrol mixture varies according to the temperature of the whole system; and the automatic choke in an engine is a device enabling the system automatically to respond to the rising temperature of the engine by increasing the amount of air in the petrol-air mixture until normal operating temperature is reached. The system in its parts and in the interactions among them must be seen as a whole.

This presents two very difficult problems, related but different. One is a problem of conceptualization, the other of intellectual manage-ability. The difficulty in the first derives from the fact that our charac-teristic way of looking at things is to analyse them, to break them down into components and to examine these, as in the previous chapter the decision-making process was broken down into information, communi-cation, formation of decision-making groups and so on, and each was then discussed. The characteristic scientific method is to hypothesize a relationship among a limited number of variables and then to create an experimental environment in which the other variables are held constant and in that environment to test whether the hypothesized relationship holds. It was this method of attack that produced the re-markable scientific advances of the period between the seventeenth century and the middle of the twentieth, and a great deal of scientific progress will doubtless continue to flow from it. The systemic method of thinking on the contrary would ideally require that all the variables and their interactions are to be seen simultaneously and as a whole.

One may talk, that is to say, of the cost of a hogshead of German hock, and explain this in terms of the value of the land on which the vines are grown, the cost of the vines and their ultimate replacement, the cost of fertilizers and pesticides, the cost of labour in keeping the ground and the vines in condition, in picking the grapes, and in making the wine, the cost of the yeast and sugar and wine-making equipment, the cost of the hogshead, the cost of transporting, bottling and marketing it, and the cost of various levies, charges or profits on the way. But one could also talk about the cost of not digging up the iron (if there were any) in the ground underneath the vines, or the cost of many humans living in isolated communities away from centres of culture or learning, or the cost of insufficient labour for much more lucrative activities which could increase the wealth of the community, or the cost of discontent at low wages and hard conditions making possible (if it were so) Hitler's rise to power—and the cost of this last might make the hock expensive indeed. Similarly one might assess the merits of a television tube in terms of the price that has to be paid, the clarity of definition and stability of the picture, the ease of replacement, the durability and reliability of the tube, and so on; but reliability refers to the degree of probability that the tube will perform its function, and this can be affected by a failure within the tube itself, or by a failure in the tube caused by stress from outside it as for instance by a short circuit and a fuse blowing, or by a failure somewhere else in the television set, or by a failure in the electrical supply, or by a lightning strike from a storm.

One can, that is to say, look at the cost of something in terms of whatever has contributed to its price, or in terms of other things caused, or not done, because this item has been produced; and one can assess the suitability of an article in terms of a limited set of immediately observable attributes, or in terms of a wider context into which it fits. If one pursued the theme remorselessly one could probably demonstrate that everything interacts with everything else, and thus by a different route one returns to the starting-point, that knowledge is a unity.

From this arises the problem of intellectual manageability. The foregoing suggests that the universe is a system consisting of units and interactions of wholly unimaginable complexity. The human mind is totally incapable of conceiving such a system. It must be simplified. But as soon as any simplification is attempted, then reality is distorted, and the simplification is an abstraction from reality. Any system less than totality is then a mental construct, and the boundaries proposed for the system are in some senses arbitrary and involve the exclusion and ignoring of some interactions.

Once it is accepted that any system less than totality is a mental construct, a way of looking at things, then one can start at the other end and say that everything can be conceived of as a system, and everything can be conceived of as a subsystem of some other system, except the universe itself. A blood corpuscle can be conceived of as a chemical system, or as a subsystem of a blood system, which in turn can be conceived of as a subsystem of an animal organism, which in turn can be conceived of as a subsystem of an animal society, which in turn may be viewed as a subsystem of an ecology including plants and water and other animals, which in turn may be thought of as a sub-system of the physical system of the earth and its meteorological environment, which in turn may be conceived of as a subsystem of the solar system, itself a subsystem of the universe. Thus the chemical system as the blood corpuscle is conceived is in a sense also a subsystem of the universe, but the attempt to identify, observe and interpret inter-action between the gravitational pull of Jupiter and this chemical system would be unlikely to be possible, or if possible to be profitable in the sense of yielding significant understanding.[2]

This is the criterion by which to judge whether a particular con-ceptualization of a system is or is not a good one—whether or not it yields significant understanding, in the same way as in the previous part of this book it was decided to concentrate on the activity of states, as the activity of other actors was less likely to be of 'much international consequence'.[3] Whether a particular conceptualization will or will not

[2] A definitional point should perhaps be touched on here. Some use the word 'system' to apply to any case where a link between unit A and unit B may be postulated such that B is affected by A but A is not necessarily affected by B. Others prefer to use the word only in those cases where there is interaction and feedback between the units. As the argument is being presented here, this disagreement dissolves: effect of the chemical system of the blood corpuscle on the gravitational pull of Jupiter is theoretically no more impossible (though even more difficult to imagine) than the other way round. To take a less extreme case, social interactions among humans on the earth are clearly affected by interactions in a meteorological system (by whether, for instance, it is raining or the sun is shining), and a system could have been conceived in which the units were the meteorological system and the social system, the former seemingly affected the latter but the latter could not affect the former. But theoretically effects in both directions were always possible, and in practice they have recently become so with weather experiments, cloud seeding and so on. Theoretically no interaction is inconceivable. In practice only a very small proportion of conceivable interactions are observable and worth analysing.

[3] See Chapter 2, p. 33 above.

yield significant understanding will depend on the appropriateness for the enquiry that is to be undertaken of the identification of the units, and the interactions among them, and the boundaries round the system; on the precision with which the units and the interactions and the boundaries can be defined; and on the clarity with which the processes of the system can be delineated, and the factors determined which enable the system to persist or cause it to change or break down.

Thus it is known that an essential of good health in a human being is the circulation round the body of blood within certain pressure limits and containing a certain balance of red and white corpuscles, a certain quantity of oxygen, and certain amounts of other substances— not too much and not too little—such as sugar. A person wishing to become an expert in the treatment of blood disorders may conceive of the blood as a system and may view the process of oxygenization of the blood by the lungs as an input into his system. He will be critically concerned with the effect on the blood of variations in the oxygenization process, and by his intimate knowledge of blood may be able to conceive of units and interactions among them which will enable him to suggest ways of dealing with the consequences of inadequate oxygenization. He will not, in his role as blood specialist, be concerned with why the oxygenization process is inadequate.

The general physician, on the other hand, is concerned with the health of the organism as a whole. He will conceive his system as the units and the interactions among them of the whole organism, and will therefore be critically concerned with the working of, and the relation between, the lungs and the blood. If the organism contracts tuberculosis or pleurisy or some other illness which prevents the lungs performing their oxygenization function properly, he will be critically concerned to try to maintain this function but he will not be primarily concerned with the effect on the blood itself of inadequate oxygenization. Understanding of how to keep a human alive has been advanced by understanding of the relationship between the lungs and the blood; but understanding of how to keep a human alive might also be advanced by understanding of how to treat the blood to compensate for the lungs–blood relationship not working properly. There is no reason in principle why the same person should not have a profound knowledge of both these systems—the organism as a whole with its brain, nerves, blood, heart, lungs, digestion, glandular and waste disposal components (or subsystems), and the blood system with its various component units and the physical, chemical and biological processes which it contains. But both these systems are exceedingly complicated, the amount of knowledge about each of them is large, and treatment is likely to be better, and understanding to be advanced, if one individual concentrates on one only of the systems.

The need for intellectual manageability dictates this concentration. The full range of knowledge about the human organism is now so great that no one person can possibly be master of all of it. The various component parts are now sufficiently well identified for it to be possible for them to be conceptually isolated and examined in great depth and detail; but when analysis is used to suggest action it is critically important that a piecemeal approach is not used alone. Some must retain the concept of the system as a whole. Thalidomide babies illustrate the possible consequences of failure to do this, or, more exactly, failure appropriately to identify the boundaries of the system in question. The system that thalidomide was thought to be influencing was the nervous system of the parent organism, but in fact the system which it influenced included the growth system of the embryo also. The underlying reason for the use of thalidomide was to promote the wellbeing of mother and child; and although the nervous system of parents may well have been beneficially affected, the underlying purpose was frustrated because the system boundaries were inappropriately conceived.

By what is appropriateness determined? If the system under consideration were the relationship between rates of application of heat and conversion of water into steam the boundaries of the system would probably be inappropriately conceived if they excluded the variable of air pressure, possibly also if in the daytime they excluded the variable of sunshine or cloud, but possibly not if at night they excluded the variable of moonlight or cloud. I say probably and possibly, because ultimately the matter depends on the degree of accuracy with which the system needs to be observed. Total understanding is impossible; sufficient understanding for most purposes could be obtained without taking moonshine into account; only very imprecise understanding could be obtained without measuring the rate of application of heat.

A system thus is a conceived separating out from reality of defined units and interactions among them, the purpose being to create a manageable field for study, and the separation to be effective containing within the conception all the important interactions, and ignoring only those interactions whose exclusion will not affect the results of the enquiry so significantly as to destroy its value. The difficulties of the method, as far as the social sciences are concerned, are immediately revealed. There is tension between the purpose of creating a manageable field, and the requirement to ignore only those interactions which are relatively insignificant. Any social situation contains an immensely complex set of interactions, and it is extremely difficult to determine which interactions are significant and which are insignificant—even if the variables can be precisely defined. Conceiving a system with the purpose of manageability primarily in mind is therefore likely to lead to the exclusion of some significant interactions, or the inappropriate grouping of different interactions as if they were similar, the results being either gross error (as in the thalidomide case), or simple, platitudinous and banal results (the mark of much systems analysis in the social sciences so far). The endeavour on the other hand not to oversimplify in either of the above senses (erroneous exclusion, or inappropriate grouping) may lead to a conceptualization so complex as to be unmanageable. As far as international relations is concerned attempts to grapple with this intractable problem have as yet made little headway.

It is perhaps necessary however to explain rather more precisely how the complexity arises. The idea of a system involves *interaction*, not just *reaction*. As between two entities A and B, conceived as being in a systemic relationship, an occurrence originating from A acts as a stimulus to B and produces a response from B. The response from B in turn acts as a stimulus to A and in turn produces a response. If the entities in question are living organisms, the occurrence in A produces a modification in B's behaviour, and this response from B in turn modifies A's behaviour. The process by which A's behaviour is modified as a result of a change in B's behaviour brought about by an original stimulus from A is known as feedback. Feedback can be positive or negative; that is to say the response from B may stimulate A to continue or intensify its former behaviour (positive feedback), or it may cause A to change or cease its former behaviour (negative feedback). Positive feedback is exemplified in the case of state A building up its armaments because of the perceived hostility of state B, state B in response building up its own armaments because of A's programme, and state A consequently intensifying its programme. Negative feedback is to be seen if the armaments programme of A causes the decision-makers of B so to alter their behaviour as to persuade the decision-makers of A that the threat no longer exists, and therefore the armaments programme is moderated or abandoned.

The example immediately suggests the two main causes of complexity. In the first place, and obviously, state A is not simply in a systemic relationship with state B, but also with states C, D, E, and so on. As soon as just one further entity is introduced, state C, the matter becomes immensely more complicated. In deciding upon their armaments programme the decision-makers in A must consider the responses both of B and C; the decision-makers of B and C must each consider whether A's programme is directed against them, or against the other, or against both, and in determining their responses must consider the effect not merely on A but on each other; the decision-makers in A must now in turn consider the responses, and it could well be that the response of B encourages a scaling-down of the programme (negative feedback) while the response of C encourages its intensification (positive feedback). The introduction of each additional unit similarly multiplies the number and so the complexity of the interactions.

But, secondly, the interactions are not simply of one kind. The relations between states A and B are not composed solely of the interactions of their armaments programmes. They include interactions resulting from economic activity, from diplomatic activity, from political activity, from propaganda or subversion, from the movement of individuals or groups about the world as emigrants or as travellers, from an earthquake in Japan or a failure of the monsoon in India, from a flight to the moon, from the life or death of a Mohammed, and so on. State A's armaments programme, B's response to it, and the feedback effect of B's response on A, have to be seen therefore not simply in armaments terms, but in the context of all the other interactions of which the relationship is composed. Thus the response of B to A's armaments might be to develop subversive activity within A's territory, which might cause A to prohibit the entry of B's nationals. When to the complexity of many interacting units is added the complexity of a wide variety of different kinds of interactions, the nature of the problem clearly emerges.

All this is obvious enough. It is set out in this form in order to illustrate the difficulty of conceiving a parsimonious international system, a system that is to say that includes only those units and interactions which are necessary if understanding is to be advanced. This last phrase suggests a first step in an approach to the problem. Different conceptualization will be appropriate, different exclusions may satisfactorily be made, different boundaries that is to say may be drawn, according to the questions to which answers are sought. Such questions might relate to the effect of their systemic environment on the decision-makers of states, to the different characteristics of different kinds of state systems, to the factors that affect the stability or breakdown of different kinds of system, or to the effect of various interactions on the nature, number, or behaviour of units.

A basic difference in the method of conceptualization appropriate to these various questions arises from the choice of starting-point. In endeavouring to conceive a system which will parsimoniously represent that part of reality which one is interested in studying, one may start by endeavouring to identify and define the significant units and then proceed to try to identify the significant interactions that take place among these units. Most analysts who have applied systems analysis to the study of international relations have gone about the matter this way. States have been assumed to be the significant units, and analysis has been of interacting state systems. The pioneering application of systems analysis, that of Morton Kaplan in *System and Process in International Politics*, stemmed essentially from this point of view. Kaplan conceived six international systems—a balance of power system, a loose bipolar and a tight bipolar system, a universal system, a hierarchical system in directive and non-directive forms, and a unit veto system[4]—and although some of the systems contained units other than states, in most the role of states (called 'national actors') had a central place. Similarly Karl W. Deutsch's brilliant adaptation of cybernetic concepts[5] centres on state interaction, or more precisely the interactions within which state decision-making is constrained and to which it contributes. Indeed many students of international relations speak and write of 'the international system' or even 'the international political system' without considering whether there might be any other international system than a system of states. They mean by 'international system' a state system, and they assume that there is no other.

But since any system is a mental construct, this is to say that there is no other way of looking at international relations than as a system of states. This, if true, would be surprising indeed. It may on the contrary be suggested that there is a totally different way of conceiving international systems. This involves starting from the interactions and not from the units. One might for instance observe that across state boundaries many interacting transactions take place which relate to or arise from the production and distribution of wealth. One might call such transactions economic. One could then say that one was interested in all international economic transactions. An international economic system could be conceived, the defining feature of which would be the economic nature of the interactions. The starting-point for definition of the system would be a definition of a particular kind of interaction, not identification of particular units which interact in various ways. The abstraction from reality that would be being made would be of a particular kind of behaviour, and it is obvious that in an international system so conceived many different kinds of unit would be members. In an international economic system, for instance, members might include the Economic and Social Council of the United Nations, many of the specialized agencies

[4] For elaboration of these models see M. A. Kaplan, *System and Process in International Politics* (Wiley, 1957), pp. 22 ff.
[5] *The Nerves of Government* (Free Press, 1963), and *The Analysis of International Relations* (Prentice-Hall, 1968).

(the International Monetary Fund, the International Bank for Reconstruction and Development, the Food and Agriculture Organization, and so on), groupings such as Benelux, the European Economic Community, and the East African Common Services Organization, states, banks, industries or firms, trade unions, individual producers or commercial operators, tourists. Thus when representatives of the central banks of the major financial states meet to take decisions about international monetary matters they are operating on the international stage, their decisions incidentally affect the behaviour of state decision-makers, but from the present point of view their actions are significant within interacting economic transactions. Similarly, on a smaller scale, when a British tourist converts £50 sterling into French francs, he is acting as a unit in the international economic system, though perhaps not as a very important one.

Or not exactly so. It is not the tourist as an individual human being who is acting as a unit in the system. It is the economic behaviour originating from him that participates in the system. Members of the system, that is to say, are not the individuals or the corporate entities in themselves, but only in respect of the economic aspects of their behaviour. The system in question is a system of action or a behavioural system—the abstraction from reality that is being made is of all manifestations of a particular kind of behaviour in a particular arena, whatever their origin. It is, that is to say, in David Easton's language, an analytic system, the abstracted interactions of which it is composed having been 'factored out of the total web of behaviour of which they are part'.[6] In the case of a conceived state system one can look at the real world and observe decision-makers acting on behalf of states and perhaps be able to say that something very close to one's conception is to be seen in reality at some particular historical period. In the case of a behavioural system one cannot look at the real world and concretely identify the economic aspects of behaviour of interacting individuals or groups.

But since the concern is with the economic aspects of behaviour, the groups (or individuals) to be taken into account are not only those whose activity is primarily economic. Of course the International Monetary Fund must in respect of its economic activity be a unit in an international economic system, because most of its actions have an economic aspect; but the actions of UNESCO may on occasion also have an economic aspect, as may those of the organizers of the Olympic Games.

[6] For an extended discussion of this notion and of the analytic character of all social systems, see D. Easton, A Framework for Political Analysis (Prentice-Hall, 1965), pp. 35-45.

But the actions of the organizers of the Olympic Games may also on occasion have political or cultural or ideological aspects, as may those of the International Monetary Fund. So a range of different behavioural systems can be conceived, each consisting of the interactions of individuals or groups in respect of different aspects of their behaviour, membership of individuals or groups in the system being determined by whether or not they behave in the manner under analysis, not by their title or their seemingly primary function.

Behavioural systems of this kind are relevant to quite different questions from those to which conceptions of state systems may be helpful in providing answers. Conceptualizations of state systems—systems identified by the units and the interactions among them—are likely to aid in understanding the relationship between the system and the subsystems (or the influence of the external environment on state decisionmakers, and *vice versa*), in defining different kinds of state system, and in identifying elements of stability tending towards system maintenance or of instability tending towards change of the system into another kind. Conceptualization of behavioural systems on the other hand should reveal more about the operation of international processes, and about the roles of different units, the states among them.

To restate and recapitulate. There is only one reality, the interactions of the universe.[7] Comprehension or even conceiving of this reality is impossible, but the excising of any segment of it is an abstraction from reality and involves some distortion. Useful abstractions are those in which in relation to the questions to which answers are sought the distortion is minimally significant. One method of abstracting is to conceive or build models of interactions, called systems. If 'international' is taken to mean 'crossing state boundaries' then 'the international system' would be the totality of all boundary-crossing interactions of whatever kind among whatever units. This would still be a conception far too complex to manage or comprehend. Further abstractions from this first abstraction, called the international system, may be made in two main ways. Particular units may be identified, such as states, and all the interactions among these units may be analysed, different types of state systems may be defined, and so on. Alternatively a particular kind of interaction may be identified, and the system would then consist of all interactions of this kind among whatever units. The different conceptualizations are relevant to different questions. The next three chapters will contain, in the first a consideration of the most familiar state system,

---

[7] I have not thought it necessary to go into the metaphysical question of whether or not there is a reality 'out there'. For the purpose of my argument it is convenient to assume that there is.

that of the balance of power, followed by a discussion of game theory and bargaining theory; in the second an elaboration of three behavioural systems; and in the third an examination of the problem of systems change and of transformation influences in international systems.

9

State systems

THE MOST COMMON WAY of conceptualizing international systems is in terms of the supposedly significant units, the states. It is postulated that since state decision-makers are the source and the target of most significant international actions, a system conceived as consisting of states as units and the interactions among them will, if skilfully defined and analysed, assist in understanding the greater part of international occurrences. The system being usually seen as having no authoritative directing or controlling centre, the nature of the interactions will vary primarily according to the number, behaviour, and goals of the significant units or subsystems. Different types of state system may accordingly be conceptualized with two, five, fifteen or fifty significant units, the controllers of which may have various kinds of goals, and will have at their disposal varying capabilities of advancing towards or achieving these goals in relation to each other. The number of units, the nature of goals, and capabilities, interact and are affected by each other: thus X resources (broadly defined) at the disposal of state A clearly provide different capabilities if only state B also disposes of approximately X resources, as compared with the situation where states B, C, D ... N each disposes of approximately X resources, and interactions in the two systems would be very different; similarly the goals that the decision-makers in state A could rationally seek to achieve would be different in the two systems; thirdly, if available resources drastically changed, or if inappropriate goals were sought, the number of units would be likely to be affected.

With these considerations in mind, attempts may be made to construct models of different types of state systems. A preliminary point must however first be made. Most systems have clearly identifiable purposes. The internal combustion engine, to take the example from the last chapter, is designed by its makers to produce motive power, and the design will be different according to whether the amount of power produced is the sole consideration, or whether the object is to produce the greatest amount of power within certain limits of size, weight and cost of construction or maintenance or replacement or running. The biological system of the human organism has as its purpose the survival of the organism, and the units and the interactions among them which compose this biological system have developed over hundreds of thousands of years in response to the environment in which the organism has existed (and which it now itself in various ways modifies). To postulate purposes in this way for state systems will be to distort reality excessively, and will weaken or destroy the value of a model. State systems may not themselves helpfully be conceived as goal-seeking or goal-oriented, although the goals of the subsystems, the states, are central to the concept. This is almost a matter of definition: the less the real world international system is distorted by being conceived as a state system (i.e. the more accurately it is seen as a system in which the only significant units are states), the more is the behaviour of state decision-makers, and so their goals, likely to be critical for the working of the system. This is one aspect of the view of Kaplan that the international system conceived as a state system is subsystem dominant. He sees a system as being dominant over its subsystems when 'the essential rules of the ... system act as parametric "givens" for any single subsystem. A subsystem becomes dominant to the extent that the essential rules of the system cannot be treated as parametric givens for that subsystem'.[1]

If the international system may helpfully be conceived as a state system it is thus likely also to be seen as subsystem dominant. The more it is subsystem dominant the less it can itself have goals, and the goals of the subsystems become one of the critical variables in the model. Misunderstanding on this score has more than once led to grave analytical error and to disastrous misconception of the real world. Analysts in states which set the maintenance of peace as a supreme goal have conceived of state systems as having the purpose of peace maintenance: their models are inappropriate representations of real worlds that contain a Hitler or a Sukarno or a Nasser. Other analysts have constructed

[1] M. A. Kaplan, *System and Process in International Politics* (Wiley, 1957), p 16.

systems of which the purpose is self-maintenance: these models also are inappropriate representations of worlds that contain a Lenin or a Tojo or a Mao Tse-tung. Different types of state systems must therefore be defined in terms of state decision-makers' or subsystem goals as well as in terms of the number of state units and their respective capabilities.

The task of analysts is accordingly to attempt to construct models which display the differing modes of interaction which characterize systems with varying numbers of state units, with varying unit capabilities, and with varying unit goals. The aim would be to describe patterns of interaction, and so to identify courses of behaviour by the units, which are optimal for the persistence of the system in question. To the extent that the patterns were aptly described, and to the extent that the conceived system were isomorphic with a real world situation, the elaboration of the model would assist decision-makers to determine action appropriate to the achievement of their goals, whether of system maintenance, system change, or system destruction. Each of these three problems, however, is highly intractable. The identification and description of interaction patterns is hard enough; the assessment of the degree of isomorphism is even more difficult; and even if both these tasks were excellently performed, the model would be able to prescribe to decision-makers only categories of action, and it might be immensely difficult to judge in the detail of a particular situation whether a proposed course did or did not fit the prescribed category. For these reasons the construction of system models is to be seen as having a heuristic rather than a prescriptive value, of serving that is to say to uncover and to aid understanding of how international processes may work, rather than to suggest courses of action to decision-makers wishing to get certain results in the real world.

This book is intended as an introduction to the study of international relations, and this is not therefore the place for a systematic exploration of the very many types of state system that may be conceived. For an initial attempt at such an exploration the reader should go to the book by Morton Kaplan to which reference has already been made. An example of the method should however be helpful and for this purpose I propose to look in a fairly elementary way at a balance of power system. This example is deliberately chosen because, like the national interest, the balance of power is a concept which recurs with great frequency throughout the literature, but is used to mean different things by different people, or by the same people at different times.[2]

---

[2] The analysis of different usages which follows draws heavily on E. B. Haas, 'The balance of power', World Politics, v, pp. 442-77, and on I. L. Claude, Power and International Relations (Random House, 1962), pp. 11-24.

In the interests of precision, and so of effective communication and avoidance of misunderstanding, it is desirable to confine the use of the word system to one only of the three main ways in which the concept 'the balance of power' is used. In addition to the systemic usage, the term is however sometimes employed to describe a situation. The word 'balance' may evoke the image of a pair of scales with weights in either pan of such amounts that the scales are poised in equilibrium. The 'balance of power' in this sense is then intended to describe a situation in which two states, or two groups of states, or all the states of the world grouped around two centres, are conceived to dispose of roughly the same amounts of power. Many commentators have referred to the post-world-war-two situation as a balance of power (or sometimes since Albert Wohlstetter's article in January 1959, as a balance of terror[3]), meaning by this that the power of the United States (and its allies) was roughly equivalent to the power of the Soviet Union (and its allies).

The language should be seen as the language of imagery only. As will be recalled from the previous discussion,[4] power is not quantifiable. It refers to the ability of one entity to modify in a desired direction the behaviour of another entity. Whether the second entity will or will not modify its behaviour depends on the perception of those able to take decisions on its behalf of the relative capabilities of the two entities, the will of the first to mobilize its capabilities on this issue, and the relative losses that will be suffered from compliance or non-compliance. To refer to the United States–Soviet Union situation as a balance of power means then that the decision-makers both in Washington and in Moscow judge that they cannot modify the behaviour of the other and need not modify their own response to pressure from the other. As soon as the matter is phrased this way, the very general nature of the language is revealed. Of course the United States and the Soviet Union are each able in many circumstances to modify the behaviour of the other, and feel constrained to modify their own. Their respective behaviour will be different in different situations, as capabilities vary, as willingness to commit resources varies, and as perceptions vary. The phrase therefore means no more than that neither the United States nor the Soviet Union is able to destroy the other without unacceptable losses, is able with a degree of consistency to modify the behaviour of the other and not to change its own, or is able to cause the other significantly to modify its behaviour in a question which it judges to involve a vital interest.

[3] A. Wohlstetter, 'The delicate balance of terror', Foreign Affairs, xxxvii (1959), pp. 211-34.
[4] See Chapter 5, pp. 117-20 above.

In addition to this the phrase carries some connotation of a stable equilibrium. The concept of stable equilibrium refers to the case where if a relationship between the entities is disturbed, the relationship tends to return to its previous condition. In an unstable equilibrium, the disturbance results in the establishment of a new equilibrium in the relationship at a different point. The balance of power used to describe a situation in which the power of two states or groups of states is roughly equal carries the implication that, at least over some period of time, if the equality is disturbed, action will be taken to restore it (for of course the 'equality' must fluctuate). It carries an implication, that is to say, of stable equilibrium.

The balance of power concept is unfortunately also used sometimes to describe a situation of unbalance. This is confusing in the extreme. To have a balance at the bank means to have a credit balance in the customer's favour. Politicians have been known to say that 'the balance of power must be in our favour'. This is the bank balance usage, implying the need for superiority; but it is misleading as well as confusing because it implies that power can be counted up and measured like money, and the usage is virtually meaningless if it is put into the context of will and perception.

In the third place the concept is occasionally used to refer to the existing distribution of power in a situation. The phrase 'this caused a change in the balance of power' implies that the occurrence in question (such as for example the equipping of the Prussian army with needle-guns between 1853 and 1858) changed the distribution of power. It does not say anything about alterations in any bilateral relationship, or about one state gaining a superiority; it merely refers to a change in power distribution as among several states in a situation. It is again an unfortunate usage, as it too suggests (though less directly than in the previous case) that power can be measured and so the amount of power possessed by each state quantified.

The balance of power concept is thus used in three quite different and wholly inconsistent ways to refer to the distribution of power in various kinds of situations. It is used, secondly, with a totally different meaning to refer to a policy. A 'balance of power policy' may also have three different guises. It may refer to an attempt to establish or maintain an equilibrium between two states or groups of states, or to an effort to establish or maintain an unbalance in one's own favour, or to a decision to enter the balance of power game.

The example of the first of these to which reference is always made is the policy of Britain in the nineteenth century. The germ of the policy is to be found in Castlereagh's endeavour at Vienna in 1815 to create a 'just equilibrium', in the belief that the safety of Britain could be threatened only if one mainland state held a position of excessive predominance.[5] He believed that Britain should participate in the Concert of powers designed to uphold the 1815 settlements (though not by intervening in other countries' internal affairs), but his successors took the view that his purpose could better be served if Britain stood apart from the mainland, intervening as and when necessary to prevent any power or group of powers from gaining ascendancy. This role of a 'balancer' outside the mainland relationships—pursuing a balance of power policy —was by no means always consistently performed (in the 1850s, for instance, France, widely considered the strongest state in Europe, was joined by Britain in the Crimean war against Russia), but the conception of the role none the less underlay much of British policy, particularly when the fate of the Low Countries was in question.

A balance of power policy is in practice difficult to conduct successfully. The balancer normally needs relatively large capabilities and a substantial degree of strategic security, for a policy involving shifting friendships is liable to promote distrust ('perfidious Albion') and general enmity. Moreover it is impossible for decision-makers in any state ever to know exactly what the condition of the balance is, partly because they will have incomplete information about the resources of other states (and indeed about their own), and partly because they will never be able to make sure judgments about others' will and perception. But to perform the role with full effectiveness it is necessary also to assess accurately not merely the existing condition of the balance but the underlying trends and the way it is changing, and this is even more difficult. Certainly British decision-makers misjudged the underlying realities of the power relationship between France and Germany during most of the interwar period. Finally many other factors, such as ideological ties or aversions, or attitudes of political opinion, may in practice make the pursuit of a balance of power policy difficult.

Precisely because of the difficulty of assessing the balance and the way it is changing, states existing within a closely-knit set of relationships and wishing to pursue a balance of power policy will normally endeavour to gain a balance in the bank balance sense—will, that is to say, endeavour to ensure that their capabilities are perceived to exceed rather than merely equate with the capabilities of the other states with which they are in contact. A balance of power policy by an external balancer is thus normally aimed at rectifying any disequilibrium which the decision-makers of the balancer perceive to be emerging; but a

[5] See C. K. Webster, *The Foreign Policy of Castlereagh 1815-1822* (Bell, 1925), p. 52.

balance of power policy by a state within an interrelated group is normally aimed at creating a perception of surplus in the minds of at least some of the other members. Once again therefore confusion arises from the use of the concept in two different and quite inconsistent senses.

The other usage of the concept as referring to policy is rare and need not detain us. Contrasts have occasionally been drawn—as for instance by Woodrow Wilson—between an immoral balance of power policy (aimed at continually increasing power and so inevitably ending in war) and a moral policy resting on assumptions about the inherent virtue of human nature and the possibility of cooperating in the pursuit of the common interests of all mankind. This is to use a balance of power policy as a way of describing a mode of behaviour, and one could talk about participating and not participating in this mode. Moreover it could be said with some small grain of truth that Woodrow Wilson endeavoured to use United States strength to establish a League of Nations system that would destroy balance of power policies, but that the United States has now become a leading practitioner of a balance of power policy in the sense of adopting this mode of behaviour.

This exploration of the various usages of the balance of power concept before entering on an analysis of a balance of power system has been necessary in order to avoid confusion. Not only do different writers about international relations use the concept differently in any of the six senses set out above, but the same writer within the same book, and sometimes within the same paragraph, may unconsciously shift from one meaning to another. The coherence of the argument is thereby frequently destroyed, or the moral opprobrium which has been attached by some to the balance of power as a mode of behaviour is transferred to an otherwise value-free study of an equilibrium situation. Shifts of meaning are to be found even in so careful a scholar as Trygve Mathisen, who within the same covers writes of 'changes in the pattern of power or balance of power', 'independent groups of a region ... might live in a prolonged state of rivalry, developing systems of alliances and balances of power', 'basic strategic interest, notably for the great powers, is to work for a favourable balance of power', 'the bi-polarization of power entails that there is really no third party strong enough to keep the balance'.[6] The first of these phrases refers to the distribution of power, the second to policies aimed at creating equilibrium, the third to the credit balance notion, and the fourth to the idea that equilibrium needs a balancer.

[6] T. Mathisen, *Methodology in the Study of International Relations* (Macmillan, N.Y. 1959), pp. 80, 97-8, 126, 144.

To complicate matters further, the phrase 'a balance of power system' is used indiscriminately by some writers with reference to any of the senses distinguished above. Confusion can be avoided only if the phrase is used to convey a single meaning and I propose to define it in a particular way. A balance of power system, like all systems, is a mental construct. It may be conceived as a group of states, all interacting, the interactions taking place in an anarchical arena (without, that is to say, any controlling or directing authority operating in the system), the units and the interactions among them being of such a kind that the system as a whole is in equilibrium. The equilibrium in question is not between states or groups of states in the system, but of the system itself; so that a disturbance in the system will be countered by compensating changes in the nature of and interactions among the units. Such disturbance might be caused, for instance, by an increase in the capabilities of one of the units, or a change from a policy of peaceful trading to one of military threat by the decision-makers of one or more states in relation with one or more others. The equilibrium will be stable when the changes in the units and/or in the interactions among them in response to a disturbance are such as to restore the system to its previous condition. The equilibrium will be unstable when changes in response to a disturbance lead to a new equilibrium with the system in a different condition. The system is to be regarded as being in the same condition when the number of essential actors remains unchanged, when similar interactions among them continue, and when decision-makers' basic long-term goals are not varied. Change in any of these elements may alter the condition of the system but allow it to find a new equilibrium, but large change in any or all of them may cause the system to break down or transform into a different system.

A theoretical point of perfect equilibrium would be when the decision-makers of all states perceived the state of the system as being optimal for the achievement of their purposes; but such perfect equilibrium would clearly only be momentary, and equilibrium can be stable without being perfect. In perfect equilibrium all states would not of course be able to get everything that they wanted: it would exist when the decision-makers of all states perceived that any change would make them less able to get as much of what they wanted than they could get if the system stayed as it was.

The variables then are number of units, interactions, and goals of decision-makers. The purpose of analysis of the system is to determine what condition of the variables and what relationship among them will probably result in stable equilibrium, unstable equilibrium, or system breakdown or transformation. No value judgment is implied—that equilibrium of either kind, or system maintenance, is desirable: the enquiry is analytical only.

First as to numbers: the system is likely to break down if the number of states is less than five. Let us see precisely why. If there are just two states in the system (remembering that by definition there is no authority superior to the states) the probability is high that they will endeavour to destroy each other. The states exist as separate entities because the members of the governments, or the populations, or both, believe that they derive some benefit from independence (such as not being run by 'foreigners'). The fact of separation symbolizes and reinforces the feeling that the people of the other state are different or alien or unknown, and the alien or unknown is usually feared or disliked. The other state can serve as a scapegoat for internal disappointments or failures (as the communist menace is seen as the reason why the United States is forced to devote large resources to 'the defence of freedom' round the world and thus cannot solve the problem of poverty or the Negro question at home). Resources are not unlimited, and man's insatiable appetite for wealth or knowledge or power leads to struggle over the possession of resources. For these and many other reasons there are inbuilt elements of conflict (as there may be inbuilt elements of cooperation also). The decision-makers in each state cannot be certain about the goals or the motivation of the decision-makers in the other, and they have good reason for feeling that they must have the means of defending their community—preserving its 'independence'—even if they do not themselves for whatever reason have motivation to expand or conquer.

But even if neither has the desire to expand or conquer, uncertainty is likely to lead to conflict. Uncertainty about the intentions of the other, and uncertainty about his capabilities. Perfect information about capabilities is impossible, so each is tempted to try to establish a margin of capabilities over the other in case, by miscalculation or ignorance, capabilities in fact are less. Assume some point at which both sets of decision-makers perceive capabilities as being roughly equal. Decision-makers in state A perceive some change in the capabilities of B (whether it has in fact occurred is irrelevant—perception of a change is all that is necessary). A's decision-makers, fearing the emergence of a superiority in B's capabilities which might lead or be used to curtail or destroy A's independence, feel it necessary to take some action to increase their own capabilities. This, when observed by B's decision-makers, causes a compensating action, which in turn causes a further compensating action by A. There is thus a built-in escalation, the costs of which will gradually come to seem intolerable. The escalation is likely also mutually to reinforce fear and hostility. In these circumstances there is likely to come a point where the costs of further escalation seem to exceed the costs of open conflict, and as soon as one side thinks that it has a temporary superiority, battle will be joined and thus the two-state system will be destroyed.

The two-state system thus contains an inherent tendency to destroy itself. There has in fact never been such a pure two-state system, although approximations to it have been seen by some in the Rome–Carthage relationship, and in the United States–Soviet relationship between the late 1940s and the late 1950s. The approximation in the latter case was thought to be sufficiently close for the fear to be widespread that escalation for the foregoing reasons was unavoidable. That the system has not hitherto broken down into open conflict does not refute the analysis: there may not yet have been enough time; the system may not accurately have been described as a two-state system; other variables may affect the analysis; and in any case it demonstrates probability, not certainty.

By a similar process of reasoning the three-state system can be shown to have an inherent probability of self-destruction. The reasons for fear, the elements of conflict, and the desire to preserve 'independence' will not be different. The decision-makers in state A, observing states B and C, will perceive a development suggesting an increase in B's capabilities, or an apparent improvement in relations between B and C (for example the signature of a new trade agreement). It is again irrelevant whether either of these perceived occurrences has in fact taken place. In the first case A's decision-makers, fearing that B may use his increased capabilities against A, will make an approach to C pointing out the danger. B's decision-makers, learning of this approach, will fear that A and C are planning to use their combined power to destroy and divide B up between themselves. The decision-makers in B will accordingly make urgent approaches to A and C suggesting to each joint action against the third state, and both A and C will realize that if they reject B's approaches B will join with the other unless they themselves, A and C, join against B. Which pairing emerges from the various approaches will depend on bargaining skills and on the ways in which the rewards and costs of each course of action are perceived by the decision-makers in each state; but the result of the exchange is that one of the three states is destroyed by the combined action of the other two (see Fig. 1). The second case, the perception by A's decision-makers of an improvement in relations between B and C, triggers off the same process. The three-state system is therefore like the two-state system in having a built-in

1. A perceives an increase in B's capabilities, so

2. A approaches C calling attention to B's increase

3. B perceives A-C approach, fears joint action by A + C, so

4. B approaches A and C to suggest to each action against the other.

5. A and C approach each other to test relative advantages of joining against B or of joining B against the other.

6. Two combine to destroy the third according to perceived relative gains and losses and to prevent own destruction.

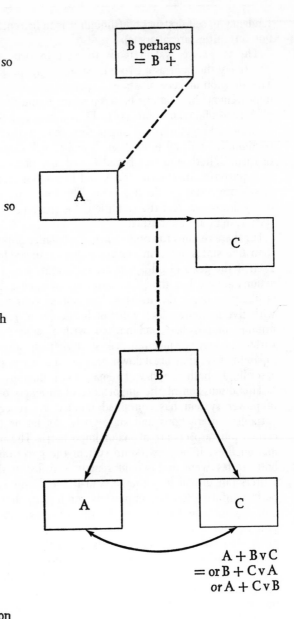

- - - - → perception
———→ approach

Fig. 1.   The breakdown of a 3-state system

tendency to self-destruction (though it is to be repeated that probabilities not certainties are at issue).

The four-state system tends to set into two pairs, which then are effectively the same as a two-state system. The process may be as follows. The decision-makers of state A perceive a development implying an improvement in relations between states B and C. The natural response of A is to make an approach to D, pointing out the evidence of B and C drawing together, and suggesting that if they, A and D, do not combine for mutual protection, B and C will destroy them one by one in turn. Whether in fact B and C had any plans of combining for any such purpose, the evidence of A and D coming together will force them in self-protection to do the same. The four-state system is thus effectively destroyed, and the conditions for the built-in escalation of a two-state system are established.

For these reasons the probability of a balance of power system with less than five states achieving either stable or unstable equilibrium is low. Even if the goals of all actors are conservative and defensive, the interactions among less than five states are of such a kind that the system is likely to break down. This does not of course mean that a system with five or more states will not break down, merely that the greater number of possible combinations with five or more states permits a variety of ways of meeting perceived incipient alignments or increasing capabilities, so that breakdown becomes much less probable. The system accordingly both is and will remain more flexible.

This discussion of the importance of numbers of units for a balance of power system has contained implicit references to the other two variables, interactions and state goals. As far as interactions are concerned four aspects are of major importance. The first of these is information flow. If in a two-state system the governments and peoples of both states were and would remain satisfied with their existing resources (an unreal hypothesis), and if the decision-makers in each had perfect information (an impossible condition), then the conflict escalation process would not occur. At the other extreme if in, say, a seven-state system, state A was able so to increase its capabilities that all the other six combined could not resist it without unacceptable losses, and if A succeeded in doing this without decision-makers in any of the other six knowing anything about it, then the system would be destroyed and would become a system of another kind in which one unit dominated all the rest. Thus perfect information would permit the survival of a form of the system which would otherwise probably break down, while total absence of information would almost certainly lead to the destruction of a system which otherwise might have good prospects of survival. Between these two limiting cases (the first being in practice impossible, and the second unlikely) information flow can be seen as a variable affecting the stability of the system. If the goals of all units are conservative, the better the information flow and the more exact the knowledge of all decision-makers, the greater the likelihood that the system will remain in equilibrium; for decision-makers will then be better able to take adequate but not excessive action in response to disturbances in the system. Poor information flow on the other hand will increase uncertainty and will therefore strengthen the tendency to take possibly exaggerated action in case the disturbance is greater than has been perceived.

Reasoning of this kind has lain behind the establishment of 'hot lines', for instance between Moscow and Washington, and the release of fuller information about weapons developments. One purpose of the hot line is to enable a direct enquiry to be made if some inexplicable trace appears on a radar screen when without that check immediate release of thermo-nuclear strategic strike forces might seem to be necessary. Similarly information for instance about the 'hardening' of rocket sites (making them still operable after a nuclear attack) is comforting rather than the reverse, for it implies that the owner of the hard sites will be less tempted to launch a pre-emptive strike if he knows, and knows that his opponent knows, that he can strike back even if he has been struck first.

If other variables are favourable to the maintenance of the balance of power system it is unlikely that poor information flow will itself lead to system breakdown, for all decision-makers are aware of the imperfection of their information and will endeavour to be no more precipitate or extreme in their action than they judge to be unavoidable. The probability is therefore that where other conditions are favourable to system maintenance, good information flow will lead to stable equilibrium, but poor information flow will lead to unstable equilibrium.

A second aspect of the interaction variable derives from the relative capabilities of the units. The more nearly equal these are thought to be, the more smoothly can the systemic processes operate. If one state in, say, a five-state system is generally perceived to have substantially greater capabilities than any of the others, the dangers will always exist that the other four may feel it necessary to join against the one, or that if the powerful state and one other are perceived to be drawing together, the other three will feel they must form a tightly knit group. Either development carries the possibility of emergence of an effective two-state system; while any alignment with the powerful state not merely causes the others to fear, but may lead to such dominance of the weaker by the more powerful in the partnership as effectively to remove the weaker state from the system as an independent unit. When a system consists of five or more units of roughly equal strength, the less will alignments create fear, the less will freedom of manoeuvre be restricted by an alignment, and the more limited and cautious are compensatory movements in the system likely to be. Put in another way, the greater the disparity in capabilities among the units, the more likely is it that occurrences in the system will encourage fears, promote exaggerated responses, and so lead to positive feedback and disruption of the system.

A corollary of this is that any very large sudden change in the capabilities of one of the units may be excessively disturbing—excessively in the sense that it may lead to system breakdown. Evidently a technological leap giving one state the capability totally to destroy all the others at small loss to itself would destroy a balance of power system, and such a development has become rather less implausible in the twentieth century than it would have been in any earlier period. Thus while relatively slow and small changes in capabilities can be accommodated— it is indeed precisely in the accommodation of such changes that the systemic processes operate—the larger and the more rapid they become, the more the survival of the system is threatened.

This leads on to the third element of the interaction variable, and possibly the one that most critically affects the maintenance of the system. The greater the range of different kinds of action open to decision-makers and the more freely alignments of any two or more actors may be made or broken—the greater the autonomy of the actors that is to say and the greater the flexibility of the system—the more likely is it to be able to survive.

Autonomy and so flexibility may be limited in a large number of ways. Formal treaty commitments over long periods of time may not in themselves seriously limit autonomy, but steps taken to make treaties effective are more likely to do so. Staff talks, involving mutual *exposés* of weapons strengths and strategic thinking and plans, make more hazardous the rupture of the treaty and alignment with the ally's enemy. If the staff talks have been followed by weapons rationalization, so that each is in some degree dependent on the other for certain types of weapons and for the supply of spares to keep these weapons operational, breaking away from the alignment becomes even more difficult. At a different level, a trade treaty involving extensive mutually profitable exchanges of goods increases the costs of any realignment which would involve a reduction in these exchanges. Moreover the more dependent the welfare and wealth of the people of a state are on external economic relations, the less available is the economic range of action to decision-makers.

Autonomy may therefore be limited by external ties that may be contracted, but the degree of limitation will be affected by the nature of the state subsystem. The freedom of manoeuvre for decision-makers in states where they are internally responsible and can be removed from office is less than that of decision-makers who are irresponsible. In the latter case economic deprivation for the people can more readily be contemplated, although constraint in the former case is less to the extent that goals are of such a kind as to make sacrifice acceptable. Sacrifice can be made more acceptable if goals are sanctified and glorified, and if fears and hatreds are stimulated. But the more fears and hatreds are stimulated, the more difficult do realignments become. There is then positive feedback between the desire of responsible decision-makers to mobilize internal support, and the direction and thrust thus given to decision-makers' action by popular opinion. The process can most easily be seen in wartime—the appalling losses suffered in 1915 and 1916, the necessity to mobilize ever larger segments of the nations, the consequent depicting of the enemy as dehumanized brutes committing unheard-of atrocities, had as a result the infliction of terms on the defeated that many at the time, and more subsequently, believed to be unwise.

Attachment to goals, and fears and hatreds, thus reinforce each other. Similarly ideologies reduce flexibility in a system. These are more likely to operate negatively than positively. Similarity of ideological outlook may make some alignments easier to achieve, but strong ideological antipathy may make some alignments impossible. To the extent that either exists, the capacity of the system to respond adequately to disturbances is likely to be reduced.

Flexibility can thus be limited in three main ways—from the state subsystem in the form of varying degrees of constraint imposed from the domestic environment on decision-makers; by military or strategic or economic or ideological ties which can be ruptured only at some cost, and by ideological antipathies, which may be shared by decision-makers, and may be flouted only at considerable political risk; and by the possible unavailability of some courses of action, some means of achieving ends, because of the nature of a state's situation. The less the flexibility of the system, the more likely is it to break down.

Finally brief mention should be made of the costs–gains calculus. It is evident that one of the reasons why the post-1947 system, which seems to have had many of the characteristics of a two-state system, has not yet broken down in open conflict is because both parties have believed that the costs of such conflict are likely to be unacceptable in relation to any possible gain that might be achieved. In a balance of power system, to the extent that actions carry the possibility of leading to consequences involving unacceptable losses, flexibility in the system is again reduced. The extreme limiting case is that in which the loss in question is annihilation, and perception of this possibility would lead to a sharp constraint on the adoption of courses of action that might have this result. Short of this extreme, costs will seem greater or less according to the gains that are sought, and this leads on to consideration of the third main variable in a balance of power system, decision-makers' goals.

The point can be made very simply. The more limited the aims of decision-makers, the more likely is it that the system will persist. In particular, maintenance of the system must be seen by all essential actors as more important than any other goal. Action will of course be taken to improve or prevent a deterioration in one's own position, to exploit opportunities, and to advance one's aims as far as possible; but if the advancement of aims is not limited by the superior goal of not destroying the system, then the system's chances of survival are evidently less. This means that all decision-makers must prefer the existing system to continue. This is not to require perfect equilibrium, which it will be recalled was defined as the condition in which all decision-makers perceived the state of the system as being optimal for the achievement of their purposes: it is to require that while changes in the state of the system may be seen to be desirable and may be made, they shall not be pushed to the point where the system itself is destroyed. Many influences may operate in the real world to encourage limitation of aims in this way: the hold of decision-makers on power may be weakened if the system is disrupted; breakdown of the system may cause (and be caused by) revolutionary changes in the internal affairs of the sub-systems, or states; the process of change in the course of breakdown is uncertain and unforeseeable, and consequences may be very different from those desired; it is usually easier to continue with known practices than to break out into totally new ones. On the other hand if the system is perceived intolerably to constrict aspirations or values (as was the case with Hitler), or as being in some sense immoral (as with the Bolsheviks)—and these two attitudes are basically similar—then action may deliberately be directed at destroying it.

The nearest to a real-world example of a balance of power system conceived in this way is perhaps western Europe in the eighteenth century. There were five essential actors, France, Austria, Prussia, Russia and Britain. Information flow, from official sources and through officially-sponsored intrigue, was relatively full, if only because the range of relevant behaviour about which information was necessary was very restricted. The capabilities of the five states were broadly similar and the rate of technological change was slow. Flexibility of alignment was high (as demonstrated, for instance, in the diplomatic revolution of 1756): there was no ideological antipathy making any particular alignment unthinkable (though some were easier to contemplate than others); the military resources of none were dependent on the support or supply of another (the expedient of using mercenaries from other states was common); economic exchanges in no case imposed severe constrictions; leaderships were irresponsible, so domestic constraints or impulses operated only in small degree; ideologies were broadly similar. In each state the decision-makers saw benefits in the operation of the system, and were prepared to be satisfied with small gains or to accept small losses rather than push aims to the point of threatening the existence of the system. Breakdown came when one member, France, as a result of the revolution of 1789, ceased to give priority to the maintenance of the system but sought to replace it with a new one, and simultaneously dramatically increased its capabilities by the conscription method of Carnot's *levée en masse* of 1793, made possible and fired by the revolutionary enthusiasm of the masses. This eighteenth-century example illustrates the point that was being made previously, that a balance of power system is not one in which peace is necessarily maintained, nor is this its object: on the contrary, as in the eighteenth century, war—but limited war—may be one of the essential mechanisms by which the system operates.

Although eighteenth-century Europe may be thought to illustrate many of the features of a balance of power system, the analysis of the system in previous paragraphs was intended to be purely theoretical and not a description of any past or present set of relationships in world history. Some may question the value of such theoretical exercises. Their value I think is clear. It has been repeatedly stated that the policies of states, and so the interactions among them, are critically affected by decision-makers' perceptions of the situation. Their perceptions will be more accurate, their ability to select courses of action that will lead to intended consequences greater, if they are aware of critical systemic variables and understand the operation of essential systemic processes. This will be true whether their object is to preserve or destroy a particular system. Most historians would agree, for instance, that one of the causes of the first world war was the rigidity of the two opposed state groupings—Germany and Austria–Hungary on one side, Russia and France on the other—so that an action by Austria-Hungary inescapably led to an action by Russia which increasingly led to an action by Germany which inescapably involved France and, with the strategy that Germany had no choice but to adopt, had to involve Britain. It is probably true that none of the major decision-makers wanted a war among the great powers, and it is certainly true that none of them wanted the disaster of 1914-18 in which all alike shared. It is possible that understanding of the crucial processes of a balance of power system, and the inherent instability of a polarized system, might have affected the behaviour of decision-makers at a much earlier stage before the polarization became rigid. It is possible, but of course not certain. The value of a theoretical analysis for a real world situation is also affected by the extent of isomorphism between them. But analysis of critical processes in various kinds of state systems, and identification of functional or dysfunctional influences, may be among the most vital contributions that can be made to the better judgment by decision-makers of the consequences of actions.

The foregoing analysis may be described as the construction of a simple verbal model. The technique is a central one in the social sciences. The revolutionary advances in the natural sciences in the past few centuries have been brought about by the application of a particular method—observation of occurrences or data, determination and definition of variables interacting with each other, hypothesizing a specific relationship between or among two or more variables, constructing an experimental framework in which all variables are held constant except those whose hypothesized relationship is to be tested, replicating the experiment many times and thus verifying or disconfirming the hypothesized relationship. Thus observation of the way a spot of sunlight reflected from a knife dances about the wall as the knife is moved may suggest the hypothesis that the angle at which light is reflected from a reflecting surface may vary with the angle at which it strikes the surface. It is easy to construct experimental conditions in which other variables are held constant (for instance the reflected 'ray' is not passed through water before its angle of reflection is measured), and repeated experiment under controlled conditions will confirm that under these conditions the angle of incidence of the 'ray' of light equals the angle of reflection. The hypothesis is confirmed—it is not 'proved'. No number of past demonstrations that a relationship holds can establish that the relationship must hold in the future: the greater the number of times that a hypothesized relationship has held in the past, the greater the probability that it will hold in the future, and the overwhelming majority of our actions are based on expectations derived from demonstrated probabilities. There is however no certainty. On the other hand a single case where the angle of incidence being 50° and the angle of reflection came out at 49.9° would falsify the hypothesis (if the experimental conditions were properly constructed and controlled). One experiment can therefore falsify a hypothesis: many can confirm or verify a hypothesis, but no number can prove one.

The attempt to apply in the social sciences this method which has brought such immense results in the natural sciences clearly faces many difficulties. Perhaps the greatest of these is identification and definition of significant variables. In the physical case quoted above the task was relatively simple. Of the variables that might be involved—the conception of light as a 'ray', the angle of the ray of light, the nature of the reflecting surface, the media through which the rays passed, the temperature and pressure of the media, the time-scale, and so on—the first four stand out as being decisive for all but the most minutely exact measurements. In social questions, on the other hand, the number of interacting variables is very much greater, and to determine which of these are the crucially significant ones in relation to a particular enquiry is a matter of the gravest difficulty.

But even if significant variables are successfully identified, and a relationship between them hypothesized, the specification of this relationship in precise and verifiable terms may be impossible because of the absence of methods of measurement or quantification. In some cases—as for instance that of the hypothesis that the level of voting participation varies directly with the degree of urbanization of a constituency—two variables can be defined and quantified; but for such a proposition as 'in a two-state system the government of each will endeavour to exceed the power of the other' no adequate means of measurement have yet been devised.

A third major difficulty in the attempt to apply scientific method as defined above is the impossibility in almost all cases of creating a controlled experimental framework and replicating an experiment. One cannot take human beings and put them into a laboratory and cause them to interact in certain ways and not in others and repeat the experiment many times to see if a hypothesized behavioural relationship holds—or at least it can be done only in certain conditions which are not the same as those of the real world to which the hypothesis is supposed to relate. The extent to which any hypothesis can be verified is thus open to question.

Finally there is the problem of the relationship between the observer–experimenter and the phenomena he is observing. The rays of light and the mirror are not likely to be affected in their behaviour by the activities of the physicist; but societies may well be affected by the activity of the social scientist. The most familiar example is that of elections. If a psephologist samples voting intentions in a single-member constituency and on the basis of his sample predicts that party candidate A will gain 42 per cent of the votes, party candidate B 40 per cent of the votes and party candidate C 18 per cent of the votes, the fact of publishing the prediction may well cause the prediction to prove wrong. Suppose for instance that candidate A represented the government, and candidate B the major opposition party, and that there was widespread discontent with the government but little confidence in the opposition and so candidate C attracted a sizeable number of protest votes, then as suggested in the figures above the government candidate might be returned; but publication of the forecast would suggest that candidate C could not possibly win, and if many of those proposing to vote for C disliked the government even more than they distrusted the opposition, then enough of the 18 per cent might join the 40 per cent to cause candidate A to be defeated. The fact of making the prediction would have falsified it. In other circumstances the fact of making a prediction may cause it to come true. Even in less clear cases than these of self-fulfilling or self-defeating predictions, the effect the social scientist's analysis may have on the situation he is analysing greatly increases the difficulty of verifying a hypothesis.

It is to the third of these difficulties that the construction of models relates. The aerodynamic design engineer pursues a similar method. From his observation and knowledge he supposes that a certain new structure in certain conditions will produce a certain flying performance. Before constructing a plane and sending a pilot up to 'test' his complexly related hypotheses, he develops mathematical models of his interrelated variables which he processes through a computer, and he builds physical models of his design which he places in various simulated conditions of the plane's operation, as for instance in a wind-tunnel. With these experiments on abstract and physical models successfully completed the test pilot can with a high degree of confidence take the first full-scale prototype of the machine into the air. He cannot be wholly certain that all will be well, for it may be that some variable that will be significant in actual flying conditions has not been thought of in the construction or testing of the models; but the science of aerodynamics is now sufficiently understood for this to be unlikely. But it should be noted that however many prototypes are tested and however many production craft fly as predicted, there is still no more than a probability that they will continue to do so: the metal fatigue that caused the disintegration of the first Comets after a relatively small number of flying hours was a variable that the designers had not taken account of and only the passage of time could reveal.

The balance of power system analysed in an earlier part of this chapter was described as a simple verbal model. The situation under analysis was that of interacting states in an anarchical arena, the variables proposed were number of units, nature of interactions, and goals of units, and a variety of hypothesized relationships among these variables were suggested and preliminarily explored. This was merely the first stage of the first set of experiments of the aerodynamic engineer. The variables were not quantified—and indeed in the form in which they were presented it would in most cases have been impossible to do so—so the analysis consisted merely in the description of the model and no attempt was made to 'experiment' with it.

The problem of experimentation may be approached from two different angles—from the manipulation of highly simplified abstract models from which confirmed results may be obtained but only within the limits of the initial assumptions, to computer or human simulation of social situations which may be complexly designed but from which it is much more difficult to claim hypothesis confirmation. Game theory exemplifies the first of these.

Game theory is a method for determining optimal courses of action in situations the outcome of which depends on the actions of all the participants. It thus focuses on interaction among the participants and so is analysis of systems conceived and defined in particular and precise ways, and operating within the framework of certain assumptions. It is assumed that among various possible outcomes from a particular situation, participants will be able to determine which they prefer, which they rank second, which third, and so on, and that the outcomes can be ranked on a utility scale: thus outcome one may be seen as twice as good as outcome two, five times as good as outcome three, and ten times as good as outcome four. The outcomes could then be ranked 10, 5, 2 and 1 respectively (or 5, 2½, 1 and ½). Some outcomes may clearly be more accurately represented in negative terms. There is no need for an absolute value to be assigned for each outcome, but merely that an ordinal ranking of utilities is established. It is also assumed that participants will act rationally, that is to say will strive to achieve their preferred outcome.[7]

The simplest form of a game is that in which there are two players only, in which each player has the choice between just two moves, and in which the gain of one is precisely equal to the loss of the other.

[7] Note that a 'preferred outcome' does not necessarily mean 'win': if a mother playing snap with her small daughter wishes her daughter to win then she would play rationally in game theory terms if she played in order to lose. Values can therefore in principle be built into games.

There are then four possible pairs of moves, A_1 and B_1, A_1 and B_2, A_2 and B_1, and A_2 and B_2. If the game is to cover all possible outcomes, and is to be fair—that is, has no built-in advantage to one player—then one of these pairs should mean a win for A, one pair a win for B, and the other two pairs draws. Assuming that both players prefer to win, then a win can be assigned value 1, a loss value 0, and a draw value ½ (as in chess) —or any other ordinal ranking you may choose. The game can then be represented in a simple matrix, as in Fig. 2.

Figure 2.

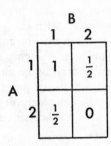

The values shown in the matrix are those for A (since the game is symmetrical the values for B would simply be the reverse of A's, and there is therefore no need to show them). In this game if A makes move 1 and B makes move 1, A wins; if A makes move 1 and B move 2 the game is drawn, as it is also if A moves 2 and B moves 1; if A makes move 2 and B move 2 then B wins.

Simple inspection of the matrix reveals that, if both play rationally, the game will always be drawn, with A playing move 1 and B playing move 2, irrespective of the play of the other participant, or of knowledge by either of the play of the other. Thus A inspecting the matrix will see that if he plays move 1 he may win (if B plays 1), but at worst can only draw (if B plays 2); whereas if he plays 2 the best he can do is draw (if B plays 1) but he may lose (if B plays 2). He will therefore always play 1. Similarly B inspecting the matrix will see that if he plays 1 he may lose (if A plays 1) and the best he can do is draw (if A plays 2); whereas if he plays 2 he may win (if A plays 2), but at worst will draw (if A plays one). He will thus always play 2. Neither can *better* his outcome by changing this move, and any change by either may produce a worse outcome. Games in which the gain of one equals the loss of the other are called zero-sum games; any point in such a game to move from which cannot improve, and may worsen, the outcome for all players is called a saddlepoint. The saddlepoint in the game in Fig. 2 is thus at A move 1, B move 2.

Zero-sum games with saddlepoints can also be constructed for two persons with more than two possible moves, or for more than two persons with only two moves, or for more than two persons with more than two possible moves, although the complication of these games is much increased. In these cases however, in contrast with the game in Fig. 2, each player must take into account the likely action of his opponent, and so the interaction process becomes critical. In Fig. 3 A inspecting the matrix will see that move 2 is better, whatever B does, than move 1, but that if he makes move 3 he would gain 8, if B played his move 1. However he will see that B will never play move 1, because B's move 3 with a possible gain of 6 and possible losses of only 2 or 4 must be better than 1, with maximum gain of 4 and possible losses of 3 or 8. But if B played 3 when A played 3, A would lose 6, so A decides that move 2 is best. Similarly B, assuming that A will reason this way, will play his move 2 because this is the least loss he can suffer against A's move 2. Thus the game has a saddlepoint at $A_2 B_2$: and each will lose if he changes his move so long as the other player does not simultaneously change his also. The saddlepoint has been achieved by the minimax strategy—the acceptance by A of the smallest of the gains (the minimum of the maxima) and by B of the smallest of the losses (the maximum of the minima) which are available. In zero-sum games there will always be a saddlepoint if the minimum of a row coincides with the maximum of a column. The game is zero-sum, but is not fair, because it will always result in a gain of 1 for A.

Figure 3.

	B 1	2	3
A 1	-4	0	2
A 2	3	1	4
A 3	8	-2	-6

Consider however Figure 4. This is apparently a fair game, because of the nine pairs of moves A wins 4 on two of them and loses 4 on two others, wins 2 on two and loses 2 on two others, and the ninth is all square.

Using the minimax strategy A will choose move 2. B should obviously choose move 3, because then he has two chances of winning 4, and at worst can only be all square. But realizing A will choose move 2, B will see that by choosing his move 2 he will gain 2. A therefore realizing B will choose move 2 will choose his move 1. B therefore realizing A will choose move 1 will choose move 3, which logically drives A back to move 2, and the circle is completed. There is no saddlepoint. A solution for zero-sum games without a saddlepoint does however exist and can be found, although it is too complicated to set out here. The principle of the solution lies in the determination of a mixed strategy—the random choice of moves, that is to say, in such a fashion that mathematically determined ratios between the number of times each move

Figure 4.

		B		
		1	2	3
	1	4	2	-4
A	2	2	-2	0
	3	4	-2	-4

is made are maintained. In the game set out in Figure 4, for example, A would play move 1 25 per cent of the time, move 2 75 per cent of the time, and move 3 not at all; while B would play move 1 not at all, move 2 50 per cent of the time, and move 3 50 per cent of the time. Each would in effect be playing a minimax strategy, because either player varying from these ratios while the other did not would worsen his result. The game turns out not to be fair but to result over each series of four plays in —1 per play, or a gain for B of 4 over 4 plays (4 rather than 9, because A never plays move 3, and B never plays move 1). In principle all zero-sum games can be solved by the determination of a mixed strategy containing the minimax principle, but with several players or several moves the matter becomes enormously complicated.

Solutions of zero-sum games thus enable players to achieve the best possible results that the game allows, irrespective of what opponents do, only provided that players play rationally. Knowledge of opponents' strategy is therefore irrelevant. This is not to say that a player cannot improve his results if he has knowledge of his opponents' actions: quite clearly, in the game shown in Fig. 4, if A always knows when B has played move 2 or move 3 he will be able to select his move 1 or his move 2 in order to gain 2 or remain all-square. In zero-sum situations, however, information causes games to become trivial because the choice of the player with information will be determined: the zero-sum game is of interest precisely for the analysis of those situations—common enough in real life—in which participants do not have knowledge of the actions of others when they determine their own.

But does the analysis of zero-sum situations have relevance to real life? There may be a few cases of real-life games which are zero-sum in their structure (like chess) and in which each player has exactly equivalent feelings about encouraging or humiliating the other, about his reputation in the outside world, and so on, so that a loss by one causes a deprivation exactly equal to the gain resulting from a win to the other, but such situations must be the exception rather than the rule. However the differences in values attached to wins and losses in actual games like chess which are zero-sum in their structure may not be sufficient seriously to distort the solution based on a zero-sum analysis. Two other considerations are more serious. In the first place, except in very simple games of very few players, and very few possible moves, solutions are too complex to be worked out even with modern computer resources. It is known for instance that chess is a game with a saddlepoint, but it is not known from what combination of moves the saddlepoint is to be found, nor whether the saddlepoint reveals a draw, a win for white or a win for black (though the first of these seems intuitively the most likely and the last the most unlikely). Secondly the minimax mixed strategy solutions of games without saddlepoints may in many real-life situations be valueless, since they depend for their validity on the same game being played over and over again. For many actual games therefore zero-sum analysis may be of no more than theoretical interest.

But as soon as the possible relevance of the analysis to social interaction is examined, much more fundamental difficulties appear. The most obvious of them is that in almost all—perhaps in all—human situations the gain of one almost never equals the loss of another. Take the simple case of a frontier dispute between two states. Issues involved may include the strategic importance of the disputed strip of territory, its economic resources, the wishes of its inhabitants, the effects on the governments' prestige (and so on internal support) of retention or acquisition, the view of other states, the military and other costs of defence of the strip by the possessing state, the effect of the dispute and of its continuation or resolution on the relations between the two states. It is virtually impossible that a settlement of the issue one way or the other will cause a net loss in each of these aspects to one side precisely equalled by a net gain to the other. There may be a heavy advantage to one side, but there will be some gain to both. Moreover the gains to both sides may be greater if the dispute is settled than if it is allowed to continue. In other words most, if not all, social situations are not accurately described in zero-sum terms.

Recognition of this fact has led to attempts to develop theories of non-zero-sum games, games that is to say which contain some element of cooperation or bargaining. Two classical non-zero-sum or mixed motive games which are superficially similar but in fact fundamentally different in their implications are those which go under the names of 'chicken' and 'prisoners' dilemma'. In both cases there are assumed to be two players, each with two possible courses of action, and in both cases two pairs of actions lead to substantial loss for one and substantial gain for the other, one pair leads to small gain or small loss for both, and the other pair leads to substantial loss for both. The difference is that in chicken the substantial loss from the last pair exceeds any possible gain from any other, so the game solution is on the pair that produce small loss or gain; while in prisoners' dilemma the substantial loss from the fourth pair is less than the possible loss from the first and second pair so the game solution is on the substantial loss. The matrices may be represented as follows:

Figure 5.   Figure 6.

Figure 5 (matrix): Columns B1, B2; Rows A1, A2. A1B1: B +10...

		B 1	B 2
A	1	−2 (top right) / −2 (bottom left)	+10 / −10
	2	−10 / +10	−100 / −100

Figure 6 (matrix):

		B 1	B 2
A	1	+5 / +5	+8 / −100
	2	−100 / +8	−20 / −20

The figures in the bottom lefthand corner of each square represent the result of that pair of actions for A, the figures in the top righthand corner the result for B.

The matrices represent situations of the following kinds. In chicken two teenagers drive cars down the middle of the road towards each other. If both swerve to avoid collisions ($A_1 B_1$) both suffer some loss of reputation for daring, but nothing worse. If both continue ($A_2 B_2$), they crash and suffer death or serious injury. If one swerves and the other continues ($A_1 B_2$, $A_2 B_1$), the one who continues gains greatly in esteem and the other is shamed. Simple inspection of the matrix shows that by the minimax principle both will select move 1—that is to say both will swerve.

Contrast the situation in prisoners' dilemma. Here the story is that the governor of a prison successively tells each of two prisoners that if he confesses to a murder that the two are supposed to have committed he will be set free and rewarded, and the other will be hanged. If neither confesses they will be freed without reward. If both confess they will both receive a ten-year sentence. They are told to think about it overnight. The last of these pairs of actions is $A_2 B_2$ in the matrix, the next to last $A_1 B_1$, and the other two $A_1 B_2$ and $A_2 B_1$. Simple inspection of the matrix shows that the minimax principle leads to the ten-year sentence, whereas if they had been able to cooperate on $A_1 B_1$ they would both have gone free.

A somewhat bizarre illustration of the chicken principle in international relations might be a trade negotiation between two states where failure to reach agreement meant the assassination of leading members of both governments $(A_2 B_2)$; the reaching of agreement involving mutual concessions caused sufficient opposition for both to fall at the next election $(A_1 B_1)$; and the reaching of agreement in which one party successfully adhered to initial demands and the other made heavy concessions caused the first government to be returned to power at the next two elections and the second immediately to fall, though without the agreement being denounced. The minimax principle says that agreement would be reached with mutual concessions. Prisoners' dilemma situations are however perhaps more common—as for instance in a disarmament negotiation where an agreement with balanced concessions would be of some advantage to both parties $(A_1 B_1)$, no agreement would involve continuing costs and perceptions of hostility for both parties $(A_2 B_2)$, but some agreements would give one party a large advantage enabling the security of the other subsequently to be threatened $(A_1 B_2, A_2 B_1)$. Because of uncertainty about existing military capabilities, about the exact effect of proposed reductions, about the future evolution of the international situation, and about future technological developments, the no agreement option may well often represent the minimax solution.

The foregoing illustrations may have suggested some of the variables that analysis of mixed motive games has highlighted.[8] In the first place

---

[8] The two leading analysts have been T. C. Schelling (*The Strategy of Conflict*, Harvard University Press, 1960) and Anatol Rapoport (*Fights, Games and Debates*, University of Michigan Press, 1960), but numerous other articles and descriptions of experiments are to be found, particularly in issues of the *Journal of Conflict Resolution*.

the outcome of the game will be profoundly affected according to whether there is only one play or whether each play is one of a series. Secondly play is quite different in the cases where communication exists from those where it does not—and communication can take a variety of forms. If communication exists, the order of moves, the possibility of making commitments, and the question of side-payments become important. Finally analysis has focused attention on the question of whether preferences are or can be known before the start of a game, and what effect the play of the game itself may have on them.

The proposition derived from prisoners' dilemma type situations is that when the possible loss from an unreciprocated cooperative or concessionary action is greater than the possible loss if both parties choose an uncooperative or hostile course of action, then the uncooperative action will be taken even though both would gain from mutually cooperative behaviour. Experiments have shown that this proposition is less likely to hold if the same game is played many times over by the same players. A typical pattern is of sporadic cooperation (A_1 B_1 plays) in the early stages, a decline to more competition for a substantial middle period during which the lesson that this way both lose gradually sinks in, and a closing period of a relatively high level of cooperation. Excessive use of cooperative moves tends to lead to exploitation, while excessive use of uncooperative moves tends to produce determined retaliation and so continuing losses for both parties. The strategy most likely to succeed appears to be early and for a few moves persistent attempts at cooperation, maintenance of cooperative pattern if established but instant retaliation if departed from, followed by a return for a few moves to cooperation to give the chance for the cooperative pattern to be re-established. The possible applicability of these findings to the conduct of international relations is obvious, for many international situations involve repeated moves in relation to a continuing, if slightly varying issue; but seductive though the findings are, clearly care must be used in applying them in real-life situations which may differ in some significant respect from the game situation.

What in effect repeated plays do is to break down the no-communication proviso of the original prisoners' dilemma. Clearly if the prisoners were able to communicate with each other, and if each were able to rely on the promises of the other, they could agree on both remaining silent. Every cooperative move in a sequence of plays communicates a willingness to cooperate if the other player will act similarly, just as retaliation serves to show that if the other player attempts to exploit cooperativeness the A_2 B_2 solution is made more likely when both will lose. Thus the ability or inability to communicate profoundly alters the play and the outcome of the game. But communication can be of many kinds. Every action, as has been seen, is a communication of some kind, although its intent may be, and frequently is, misinterpreted. A solution to a problem may so stand out that agreement on it can be tacitly reached without any formal communication at all: thus experiments have shown that if a sum of money is to be divided between two people in such a way that if without communication they agree on how it should be divided they will get the money according to their agreement, but if they disagree neither gets anything, then in the overwhelming majority of cases both propose a 50-50 split. Agreement is still likely if by some means or other a different split is made to stand out, by for instance, writing 70-30 per cent on the blackboard: the unhappy one who is to get 30 per cent realizes that his partner/opponent has now a strong expectation of getting 70 per cent and no reason for selecting any other figure, so that if he does not settle for 30 per cent neither is likely to get anything. This is the notion of salience, developed and extensively analysed by T. C. Schelling, and part of the process of bargaining may be directed towards persuading the other party that a particular solution is salient.

But communication of intention, as for instance by the prisoners talking through the walls of their cells, is almost valueless unless both parties can be confident that the other will act according to his professed intention. This introduces the notion of commitment, which was touched on in an earlier chapter.[9] If the governor required an oral confession, and if each prisoner fixed to himself a mechanism from which he could be released only by the other prisoner and which would lead to his death if he opened his mouth, each could be convinced that the other would act according to his profession, and they could solve the game on $A_1 B_1$. A commitment may be verbal, by manoeuvre, or by side-payments, but it may be effective only if it is communicated to, and believed by, the other party. If in the division of money game one party said he would take only a 70-30 per cent split, if he profoundly disliked, and was known to dislike, electric shocks, if the game were played by players simultaneously pressing buttons marked 50 per cent, 60 per cent, 70 per cent and so on, and if one player wired up his buttons so that he got a shock from all except the 70 per cent button, his partner/opponent would see him as being committed to 70 per cent (i.e. virtually unable to play anything other than 70 per cent) and would perforce settle for 30 per cent in order not to get nothing. Similarly if the first player had inescapably undertaken to pay to a third party 40 per cent of the value of the game, the second player might again be likely to

9 See Chapter 6, pp. 131-2 above.

conclude that the first meant what he said when he asserted that he would not settle for less than a 70-30 per cent split. But in both cases the commitment could be effective only if it was communicated to, and believed by, the second player. Thus in contrast to the zero-sum games with a saddlepoint, where the game always has the same result irrespective of whether or not there is communication between the parties or either knows the other's move, in the non-zero-sum game the outcome is critically affected by the order in which moves are made, by the extent and accuracy of communications and, if moves are simultaneous, by the kinds of prior commitment that can be made. Since probably all international relations questions are of a non-zero-sum character, the relevance of these derivations from mixed-motive game theory is again likely to be considerable.

The hard logic of these arguments, and the game structure to which they are related, break down in the real world because human preferences about possible outcomes from situations may not be clear or known to the participants before the situation develops, or may change in the course of its evolution. In the chicken-type situation the minimax solution is $A_1 B_1$. But if player A is able to demonstrate his commitment to A_2 (for instance by tying the steering-wheel in position, fixing the throttle and then climbing over on to the back seat and hand-cuffing his hands to the door), then player B is likely to accept the loss of face involved by swerving while A continues straight on. But if this should happen a number of times B's loss of face may become so intolerable that he comes to prefer accepting the virtual certainty of a head-on collision rather than again being shamed before his fellows. His preferences have been changed by repeated plays of the game, and the quantities in the matrix are accordingly erroneous, and the structure of the game is destroyed. Moreover A's commitment now leads not to the major gain for himself as it previously did, but to disaster for both players. This situation is evidently not an uncommon one in international relations, in small and in large issues, where repeated threats backed by commitments to carry them out lead to repeated withdrawals by the second party, until a point comes where the retreating party will stand it no longer and the outcome of least benefit to either party results. A rough example of this may be France's steady extraction of concessions from her partners in the European Economic Community until in 1965 they had at last had enough, France having committed herself in those circumstances to do so walked out, and the operations of the Community were hamstrung for six months to the disadvantage of all parties. That in real life preferences may change in the course of plays of a game seriously undermines the practical value of the analysis of mixed-motive games and limits the applicability of many of the insights that have been derived from it.

Game theory thus illustrates the method of constructing highly abstract models of interacting entities, such as states, and permits manipulation of interaction and prediction of outcomes. Prediction is valid however only within the limits of the initial assumptions upon which the models are based, and rigorous methods of analysis, leading to firm prediction even within the limits of initial assumptions, have so far been developed only for zero-sum games. Almost no international situations, however, are of a zero-sum character. Analysis of non-zero-sum or mixed motive games does not yet allow of firm prediction of outcomes. But there is no question but that exploration of game structures has led to the formulation of propositions about relationships in much more precise terms than they had previously been conceived, and the method has thus led to significant advances in understanding and in precision. Its value however has so far been heuristic rather than predictive or prescriptive.

The other method of trying to handle the problem of experimentation has been through the creation of simulated representations of international situations. They may take the form of attempts to simulate an actual or historical situation, such as the 1908-9 Bosnian crisis, or the Vietnam war, or the conflict situation in the Levant; or they may be concerned to explore the possible developments of part real, part imaginary, or wholly imaginary, relationships. Simulation may take the form of role-playing by individuals, or of role-playing under constraints programmed on a computer, or of a wholly computerized activity. The design and method of simulation will be fundamentally affected by the purpose it is intended to serve.

In a simulation without use of computers the basic procedure is to describe a situation, nominate the states or other entities acting in it, and set out in varying amounts of detail the purposes of the state actors and their capabilities. The participants are assigned decision-making roles in each of the interacting states, and the simulation is initiated by a message to one or more of the states which will provoke or require action in the form of a further message, or a proposal for negotiation, or mobilization of some capability. All messages and proposals must pass through a control centre which will reject unfeasible proposals (and may misrepresent others). The data may be actual or historical data if the simulation is of a real-life situation, or may be purely imaginary if the situation is imagined.

In a man-computer simulation the procedure is basically similar except that certain assumptions about the consequences of action and the limits of possible action are programmed into a computer, and participants thus operate within clearly defined constraints which they can override or ignore only at costs which may or may not be wholly known to them. In an all-computer simulation a complex set of variables is specified and the simulation consists in working through interaction patterns resulting from alterations in the variables.

Simulation procedures have many virtues. They require precise specification—and quantifiable specification if computers are used. They arouse an intense sense of involvement among human participants, and are thus powerful teaching and learning devices. They enable the same situation to be replicated many times: if human participants are being used the effects of varying the parameters or of using different players can be observed; and in the computer case the effects of changes in the variables may emerge which might have been not merely not anticipated but even not imagined at all.

But as a means of experimentally testing hypotheses about interaction patterns among states in the real world, and so permitting prediction about the consequences of action, simulation has as yet only limited value. The all-man simulation vividly illustrates problems of communication and perception, the effects of differential perception, the effects of time pressures and pressures of high stakes, and may afford some hints about how different kinds of persons may respond in particular situations; but it gives no effective means of measuring how these different considerations will operate, and thus offers little guide to prediction even within the framework of the simulation. If the simulation is of a real-world situation, its predictive value is further reduced by the degree to which the real world has been significantly simplified in the simulation, and by the lack of complete congruence between roles in the simulated and real worlds. In the man-computer case the building-in of parameters may permit more accurate assessment of the effect of changes in particular variables, but this assessment will crucially depend on the wisdom with which the parameters were conceived, and on the extent to which they can be quantified without damaging distortion. However, over long periods of time large numbers of runs may enable parameters increasingly to be extended and refined, and the predictive value of the simulation within the framework of its own assumptions may be significantly increased. Projection on to the real world of course would remain a hazardous operation.[10] All-computer simulations, though revealing within the framework of their assumptions, must also be treated with care as predictive guides to real-world situations; both because the

[10] For full accounts of the most ambitious simulations of this kind see H. Guetzkow et al., Simulation in International Relations (Prentice-Hall, 1963).

problem remains of defining variables in such a way that the simulation is sufficiently isomorphic to a real-world situation, and because all variables must be defined in such a way as to be quantifiable or ranked on a numerical scale, and this may lead to the exclusion of significant variables or the distortion of others that are included.[11]

In this chapter three different ways of conceptualizing and manipulating international systems conceived as state systems have been outlined. The first, verbal method, has not led to major advances since the pioneering attempt of Morton Kaplan nearly a decade and a half ago, to which reference has already been made. The second, game theory, produced little advance in its original zero-sum form (because the model was too remote from international relations situations), but its derivative, mixed motive or bargaining games, though less rigorous in their structure or certain in their solutions, have led to several new ideas and to more precise formulation of many old ones. The third, simulation, has unquestionable value as a teaching and training device, but claims made by some of its advocates for the value of the method as a hypothesis–testing, and still more as a policy–prescribing, device have provoked vigorous dissent. At this early stage in the development of the subject it would be premature to dismiss any of the three methods as certainly having nothing further to contribute: their more extreme opponents, however, would wish to do just this, on the grounds that aspirations to scientific rigour cannot be realized, that in their enthusiasm for their own toys practitioners of these methods cannot avoid making exaggerated claims, and that these claims are misleading and are made dangerous by their pseudo-scientific character.[12]

[11] The point made earlier about prediction of rates or trends as contrasted with prediction of individual events, should however be remembered here. See Chapter 1, p. 8 above.

[12] A collection of papers representing the two sides in this 'traditionalist' versus 'scientific' controversy is to be found in K. Knorr and J. N. Rosenau, eds., *Contending Approaches to International Politics* (Princeton, 1969).

10

Behavioural systems

IN CHAPTER 8 TWO different methods were suggested of conceiving manageable abstractions from 'the international system', which was defined as 'the totality of all [state-] boundary-crossing interactions of whatever kind among whatever units'.[1] The first of these methods was to select particular units, such as states, and to identify various ways in which systems conceived in terms of states, and the interactions among them may be analysed. The second was to identify particular types of interaction and to define a variety of systems, each consisting of all interactions, among whatever units, of a particular type. Using rather different language, the international system may be conceived of as a social system, the units in the system being international status roles. 'International status roles may be conceived as the outputs of the foreign-policy process of international actors.... The input of an international actor consists in the demands facing its policy-makers and the power put at their disposal; its output is in the policy-makers' international decisions or policies or, from another point of view, their international role-playing.'[2] The second type of conceptualization involves breaking down the status roles into a variety of different types of systems of action, the units in the system being the status roles in respect of a particular type of action only, together with additional originators and receptors of this type of action.

The notion of behavioural systems of this type has been most fully

[1] See p. 193 above.
[2] George Modelski, 'Agraria and Industria', in K. Knorr and S. Verba, eds., *The International System* (Princeton, 1961), p. 122.

worked out by David Easton with relation to a political system.[3] Social interactions may include behaviour of economic, legal, religious, cultural, scientific or many other kinds. A similar variety of interactions may be observed at the international level, though at this level those relating to the use of force may be thought to require separate conceptualization. It is not proposed in this introductory book to attempt a systematic exploration of international systems of this kind: no such attempt has anywhere yet been made and it must remain for a future occasion. All that is proposed in this chapter is to look briefly by way of example at possible methods of conceiving three such systems—political, military-strategic and economic—and in the next chapter to consider ways in which systems of this kind may be seen as relating to state systems.

A useful starting-point may be Easton's notion of a political system, both as the clearest exposition of the method, and to make more precise the meaning of political at the international level. Easton conceives a political system as the interactions of individuals or groups, not as biological entities, but in respect of the political aspects of their behaviour, political being defined as activity relating to the authoritative allocation of values for a society. The environment of the system consists of the other behavioural systems in the social system, the ecological, biological and personality systems within the society, and a variety of other systems outside the society. Inputs into the system are conceived of as demands from individuals or groups either within the political system or from the environment, and as support for 'the authorities', the 'regime', and the 'political community' (all precisely defined). Outputs are responses by the authorities to their perceptions of demands and of support. Feedback processes form crucial links between inputs and outputs. The ability of the system to persist depends on its capacity to handle stress, this capacity varying with the ways in which demands are processed, with the type of political system, precisely defined (change in the *type* of system may be a vital method of coping with stress, so long as *a* system of authoritatively allocating values continues), with the effectiveness of outputs in mobilizing support, with the efficiency of operation of feedback processes at crucial points in the system, and with the sense of community.[4]

What Easton is saying in his brilliant and comprehensive exposition

[3] D. Easton, A *Framework for Political Analysis* (Prentice-Hall, 1965), and A *Systems Analysis of Political Life* (Wiley, 1965).
[4] For a fuller discussion of the usefulness of the Easton model for the study of international relations see M. B. Nicholson and P. A. Reynolds, 'General systems, the international system, and the Eastonian analysis', *Political Studies*, xv (1967), pp. 12-31.

is that for there to be in society a sufficient continuing flow of decisions about who gets what, when and how,[5] certain interacting processes have to operate with a sufficient degree of effectiveness: the needs, aspirations and expectations of members and groups of members of the society have to be able to be articulated, the significant ones have to be able to be identified and formulated into manageable issues, and channels have to exist through which the issues can be made known to those with capacity to make decisions about them which will be accepted as being binding; the extent to which the decisions of these 'authorities' will be accepted as being binding will vary with the degree to which the authorities are thought to have the legal or moral right to take decisions, with their ability to reward, deprive or coerce, with the degree of satisfaction which people feel with the procedures by which decisions are made, with the extent to which people identify themselves with the society and wish it to continue, and with the degree to which they feel their aspirations to be in fact satisfied; the degree to which they feel their aspirations to be satisfied will depend on the processes through which their demands reach the authorities, how these demands are perceived by the authorities, and how effectively the decisions are perceived by members of the society to relate to the demands and so mobilize, or fail to mobilize, further support; in all the process, feedback of many kinds and at many levels is the critical linkage.

This is an illuminating analysis of a political system—but a political system of a particular kind. There is no such political system at the international level. There are no authorities with the capacity to make decisions that will be accepted as binding sufficiently frequently or sufficiently generally. There is therefore no focus to which demands may flow for satisfaction. The systemic processes identified by Easton accordingly cannot be observed. But it is true none the less that there are demands, occasionally from individuals, but more usually from groups, and it is also true that decisions are reached as to who gets what, when and how. Whether the processes by which decisions are reached are called political processes is merely a matter of definition—but an important matter of definition, for if the processes are simply called political without their nature being defined, their nature is liable to be seriously misunderstood.

Some components of Easton's system can be identified at the international level. There may be thought to be a regime, in the sense that there are some rules and some structures through which issues are regulated. Structures include, peripherally, such institutions as the

[5] H. D. Lasswell, Politics: who gets what, when, how (McGraw Hill, 1936).

International Court of Justice, the United Nations Security Council, General Assembly and Trusteeship Council, and the specialized agencies, but more centrally the diplomatic system. Rules are primarily those of diplomatic privilege and immunity within which the diplomatic system operates; but additionally expectations about the methods of handling or resolving issues may derive from explicit agreements, though these are liable to be impermanent. A political community may be observed in the sense that there is, willy-nilly, an international political division of labour, and that it is in the last third of the twentieth century all but impossible not to participate in this community. A nascent sense of community may also possibly be detected, at least to the extent that some significant members of the community recognize that cooperative action, if only in a few fields, is advantageous, desirable, or even necessary. Slowly growing recognition that we are all in the same boat, as we have never been before, induces an embryonic we-feeling.

No authorities then, but something of a regime, unavoidably a political community, and possibly an emerging shadowy sense of community. These are conditions making decisions possible and increasing the likelihood of their being acceptable, not ways in which the need for decisions is made articulate, and the decisions are made. In both these respects the international 'political' system, if it is to be so called, that appears currently to exist, is woefully weak. A few activists may formulate demands, for nuclear disarmament, for the end of United States 'aggression' in Vietnam, for the destruction of Zionism, for the overthrow of an 'illegal' government in Rhodesia; but there are no regular patterns or channels through which such demands can be formulated into manageable issues, and the point to which they may be directed for satisfaction is unidentifiable. So the majority of individuals or groups in most parts of the world remain apathetic, though dissatisfied, grumbling that they cannot do anything about it anyway. Such demands as are made are largely mediated through state authorities, and the attention paid to them will depend largely on these authorities' view of the requirements of themselves or of their peoples or of both, rather than on the significance or importance of the demand for the international system. Frustration of demands is to a slowly increasing degree leading to the predictable effect of violence, so that anti-Zionists, for instance, are making their demands on the international system known by international violence. Hijacking and bomb attacks on aircraft have had the intention of forcing international action : one response has been to increase international coordination of aircraft security procedures and to provoke further examination of international action against hijackers. This is to extend procedures for dealing with demands, even if only by suppressing them (such suppression being in this case acceptable to most peoples in the world).

'Political' decisions are thus taken at the international level, in the overwhelming majority of cases, by persons acting for units in the system directly settling between themselves, by bargaining processes, any issues that arise. This does not refer only to states, but to other units that operate in the international arena. Issues that arise are thus those that are perceived to arise by the governors of these units, and they may or may not relate closely to the aspirations or needs of peoples or groups in international society. It is a hit and miss business, because the governor of the Bank of England, say, will have some notion of what his fellow-governors think is desirable, may have some notion of what the British government thinks is desirable, may even have some notion of what may be desirable in broad terms for the British people, and will in a meeting at Basle learn of similar notions held by governors of other central banks; but there is no means by which these central bank governors meeting in conclave can be made aware, take cognizance of, and so take decisions in relation to economic or monetary requirements of international society as a whole—nor indeed would they think it their function or duty so to do, except to the extent that the welfare of their own banks or their own peoples would be affected thereby. Procedures by which allocations are made internationally are therefore made with reference to units in the system, not—or only rarely, or in small degree—with reference to the system as a whole. Demands that arise in the system have no effective way of being processed. This is a situation in which 'civil' (i.e. intrasociety) conflict is likely to break out; and indeed it may not unreasonably be hypothesized that one of the reasons why conflict, of many kinds, is increasingly becoming internationalized is that an international 'society' is developing but political processes for allocating values for that society are wholly inadequate. The Eastonian analysis is immensely useful as a means of highlighting ways in which the international 'political' system is inadequate, and prescriptions for action may readily be derived from it.

To say that 'an international society is developing' is to say that it ought to be possible usefully to conceptualize other international behavioural systems. The weakness of political procedures means that violent procedures are more likely to be in evidence, so there may be advantages in looking at a military-strategic international system. This would be a system consisting of individuals or groups interacting in respect of the military-strategic aspects of their behaviour—by which I mean behaviour relating to the mobilization and use of armed violence in an organized form.

Interacting units in such a system might be seen as the military-strategic aspects of the behaviour of such individuals or groups as the United Nations Security Council, General Assembly, or Secretary-General; alliance structures; state decision-makers; military and perhaps intelligence establishments (such as the United States Central Intelligence Agency), in so far as they may have sufficient autonomy to be analytically separable from the political structures by which they are formally controlled; internationally organized guerrillas, insurrectionists and subversive agents; internationally employable mercenaries; armaments manufacturers and salesmen; military-strategic theorists; scientists, technologists and other research workers; participants in disarmament and peace movements. It is the behavioural interactions which are at issue, not the interactions of the individuals or groups themselves.

As in the case of the international political system, the environment of this system would be all other behavioural systems that can be conceptualized in the emerging international society, systems other than social that exist at the international level such as the ecological,[6] and systems outside international society such as the meteorological system. Inputs into the system could come from any part of this environment, or from within the system itself (thus many have argued that the existence of military-industrial complexes in advanced societies leads to their having themselves an autonomous impact on the use of organized armed violence); but whether outputs in the form of the application of organized violence occur would depend on the perception of the mix of contrasting demands from various parts of the environment by those who control the means of violence. Feedback processes, as perceived by the controllers of violence, would relate the effects of outputs to the inputs that stimulated them.

'Those who control the means of violence' is the key phrase. Until recently it could have been persuasively argued that there was little point in thinking of an international military-strategic system because virtually all means of organized violence were controlled by states, and this kind of interaction was part of state interaction and could usefully be seen only in this way. The present argument is that while this view still contains a substantial measure of truth it is no longer wholly adequate, and is becoming steadily less so. This for a variety of reasons.

In the first place there have been rare occasions in the past, and there may be more in the future, when military violence has been applied by international organizations. The war in Korea in 1950-52 will

---

[6] Defined by Easton as 'the physical environment and the nonhuman organic conditions of human existence' (A Framework for Political Analysis, p. 71).

perhaps not serve as a good example because here, although action was nominally by the United Nations and under United Nations control, it was effectively directed by a particular state-member, the United States. But the Congo in 1960-63 offers a better illustration. The continuing presence of Belgian troops after the precipitate withdrawal of Belgian political authority appeared likely to provoke the strong hostility of many African states, support from the Soviet Union to them, and in the cold war context consequent counterintervention by the United States. In these circumstances the United Nations Secretary-General, Dag Hammarskjöld, obtained from the Security Council in July 1960 authority to create a United Nations army, composed of contingents from states other than permanent members of the Security Council, 'to provide ... such military assistance as may be necessary'.[7] Under the authority of this resolution (and of subsequent resolutions passed in the General Assembly and in the Security Council extracted by repeated threats of resignation by the Secretary-General), Hammarskjöld, and after his death his successor U Thant, not merely forced the evacuation of the Belgian troops, but intervened in nascent civil war among hostile factions in the Congo, and by full-scale military action in December 1961 and again in December 1962 forced Moise Tshombe of Katanga to end his attempt at secession and accept absorption into the Congo state. In this case therefore military force was applied by an army of international composition, under the direction of the agent of an international organization: this was clearly an output from an international military-strategic system in response to complex inputs from its environment.

One of the reasons for the prudence displayed by the major powers in the Congo crisis, and indeed in other crises, was their awareness of the nature and destructive power of the weapons which they possessed. This is a second reason for postulating an international military-strategic system. Weapons are not now merely local in their impact and do not affect only the targets upon which they are directed. Missile technology brings every region of the earth within reach of every other. Thermonuclear explosives do not merely devastate the area that they strike but through fallout may affect people far distant from the point of explosion, and not merely the people themselves but their children as a consequence of the genetic effects of radiation. Bacteriological and chemical weapons contain the potential of eliminating all life upon the earth, and their control if once employed—or by accident released—might be exceedingly difficult. In these circumstances international

[7] Quoted in H. G. Nicholas, *The United Nations as a Political Institution* (3rd edn, Oxford University Press paperbacks, 1967), p. 175.

military relationships acquire a different quality : it is not merely that state decision-makers may take controlling action, as for instance by the 1968 signature of the nuclear non-proliferation treaty, but that the military and the military scientists develop some traces of a transnational awareness of common expertise upon which the fate of the world may depend. This is also to be seen between political decision-makers as far as military relationships are concerned.[8] This means that military-strategic interactions are now not determined wholly (though still largely) by the perceived needs of the states to which decision-makers belong, but in part with reference to the international system as a whole.

A third reason why it may be useful to think about an international military-strategic system derives from the cost of weaponry. This cost is to be seen not merely in the high investment of financial and material resources for research and development, but in the heavy drain on scarce human scientific skills that is imposed. The unit cost of a weapon system will therefore be very high indeed unless it has a large market; but the more effective a weapon system, the fewer, other things being equal, need to be acquired. Thus one aircraft may replace nearly eight of its predecessors if it has twice the range, twice the carrying capacity, and twice the speed. In a market of unchanging size fewer of the more sophisticated systems need to be acquired. Thus for two reasons states with smaller capacity than those of the United States and the Soviet Union (and soon possibly these also) cannot afford to produce modern weapon systems : first because the economic base—in terms both of material resources and human skills—is of such a size that the proportion of its product that needs to be devoted to weaponry becomes politically intolerable; and secondly because the single-country market is so small that unit costs become intolerably high. The contrast between the British aircraft, the TSR 2, and its United States rival, the F.111 (originally known as the TFX) illustrates the problem : the costs of research and development of the two aircraft were broadly similar (though the British case required a far higher proportionate allocation of resources), but the

---

[8] 'If you have not lost your self-control and sensibly conceive what this might lead to, then, Mr. President, we and you ought not to pull on the ends of the rope in which you have tied the knot of war, because the more the two of us pull, the tighter that knot will be tied. And a moment may come when that knot will be tied so tight that even he who tied it will not have the strength to untie it, and then it will be necessary to cut that knot, and what that would mean is not for me to explain to you, because you yourself understand perfectly of what terrible forces our countries dispose.' Nikita Khrushchev to President Kennedy 26 October 1962, quoted in R. F. Kennedy, *13 Days* (Pan Books, 1969), p. 89.

Royal Air Force requirement of about 140 machines produced a unit cost of nearly £5 million, whereas the United States Air Force requirement of some ten times as many produced a unit cost of little more than half. In these circumstances other states, such as Australia, could not but choose to purchase the United States aircraft, even though for other reasons purchase of the TSR 2 might have been preferred, unless the TSR 2 price was to exclude any element relating to research and development. The Australians felt they could not contribute towards the cost of R and D. The British Labour government felt they could not carry it all alone. So the project was cancelled. The consequence of these facts is to be seen in the slowly increasing international division of labour in the production of technologically advanced weapon systems, the Anglo-French Jaguar strike-trainer being an example. The effects of this operate for the time being in restricted areas of the world today, but they form a small additional component of an international military-strategic system.

But the most important impact on military-strategic interactions perhaps derives from international ideologies and, where they exist, their institutional expressions. International ideologies reflect the decline in the overriding nature of the loyalty which used to be accorded to the nation, or to the state, and particularly to the nation-state. In many parts of the world, particularly in Africa and parts of Asia, the idea of a nation had little reality, and states did not exist, so people in these continents easily gave their loyalty to international ideologies, to Americanism, Communism, Maoism, anticolonialism, racial solidarity, nihilism, or to some combination of these. But increasing impatience with and perception of the inadequacies of nation-states in relation to the requirements and opportunities of the international system as a whole have led to decline in national and state loyalties even in the modernized, wealthy and relatively long-established states of the western world, especially among the young. An early manifestation of the effect on the military-strategic system of international ideologies was the formation of international brigades to fight in support of the Spanish government during the civil war of the 1930s; but the largely inter-state character of military-strategic interactions has been much more sharply modified in the past two decades. The internationalizing of internal war in Greece in the late 1940s, in Cyprus after 1964, in the Congo in 1960-63, in Vietnam, Laos and Cambodia intermittently since 1945, in Malaya between 1948 and 1960; the domestic pressures resulting from such conflicts as these even in states not directly involved; the international appeal of the guerrilla doctrines of Mao Tse-tung and Che Guevara; the racial and anticolonialist links between African states and organizations and the anti-Portuguese African leaders in Angola and Mozambique; the widening scope of operations of Arab guerrilla organizations, now effectively out of control of the Arab governments; even the incoherent student protest movement from the United States and Japan, through India and eastern Europe, to Italy, Germany and France—all of these in varying degrees have global military-strategic implications and point to the need for conceptualizing an international military-strategic system of which state interactions form only a part. Without such conceptualization important trends in the international arena may fail to be observed, or their significance recognized.

A third behavioural system which might be postulated, and perhaps the one which would be most easily accepted, is an international economic system. As set out in Chapter 8[9] the units in such a system would be the economic aspects of the behaviour of all individuals or groups so behaving, whether they are primarily economic in their character (international organizations such as the International Monetary Fund, banks, international enterprises, commercial operators), or whether they mainly serve other or wider functions but occasionally act economically (such as states, the United Nations Educational Scientific and Cultural Organization, or the organizers of the Olympic Games). The environment of this system would, as previously, consist of other international behavioural systems, other intra-international society systems, and extra-international society systems. Inputs would be from the environment, or from within the system. Outputs would be in the form of responses by components of the system to these inputs, and once again feedback processes would form critical linkages.

As in the case of the international political system there is no identifiable source from which outputs regularly flow, but none the less systemic processes do operate, if uncertainly, in response to inputs. The processes of international trade, for example (which may be between states, or between firms, or between individuals), depend in some degree on a measure of certainty about the exchange rates of currencies. Threats to exchange rates, from whatever source, may be met by support to threatened currencies by the International Monetary Fund, or by representatives of central banks meeting together and determining swap facilities or recycling arrangements which enable pressures to be relieved. In both cases action is being taken on behalf of the system as a whole, it is not being taken solely or even mainly by state decision-makers, and it is not being taken by the interacting units directly settling the issue between them.

Four main grounds for supposing the existence of an international

[9] See pp. 191-3 above.

economic system may be identified. The first of these is similar to one
of the elements of the military-strategic system. The problem of the
cost of advanced technology products does not arise only in connection
with weapon systems. Particle physics, civil aircraft, electronics, computers, are only a few of the fields in which the human and material
resources required for development, and the size of market necessary
for sufficient sales, cannot be found within the framework of single
state economies smaller than those of the United States and, with
severe restrictions on standards of living, of the Soviet Union. Particle
physics is a research area of which the potential is as yet not fully
known, but the research requires immensely costly accelerators: European resources accordingly are being pooled at the Conseil Européen
pour la Recherche Nucléaire. The Anglo-French Concorde, and the projected German-French airbus, illustrate international cooperative development of civil aircraft. As far as computers are concerned only
Britain and Japan among non-communist countries have so far succeeded in warding off domination by the United States International
Business Machines corporation. The formidable cost of research and
development creates the initial impetus for international cooperative
activity, but the size of the potential market is also crucial to the
chances of recovering costs: thus the British government withdrew
from participation in the European airbus project at least in part because the airlines of each of the participating countries would not
guarantee to purchase a minimum number of this rather than a United
States rival plane. This has implications not merely for international
links among producers, but for links between these producers and their
potential customers in more than one state. The market must be
unified and in some degree guaranteed as well as the production.

A related aspect of these consequences of high-cost technology is the
emergence of some degree of international division of labour. In the
nineteenth century British industry produced most varieties of manufactured products for which processes had then been invented. Only
the United States now comes anywhere near a similar comprehensiveness. Textiles for instance, which once formed a major British export,
particularly to south and east Asia, are now imported by Britain from
precisely these areas; and the international economy as a whole would
be likely to benefit if textile manufactures, not requiring a high
degree of skill, increasingly came from areas where the raw materials
are indigenous and supplies of cheap labour are plentiful, while the
economies with more highly skilled labour produced goods with a high
skill component. Attempts at such rationalization have been made
within the Warsaw Pact group of nations, and the mile after square mile

of vineyards and the cemetery of skyscraper hotel blocks on the Black Sea coast show how a major Bulgarian contribution to this rationalization has been planned in the form of wine, grapes and holidays.

But the political and social implications of such rationalization are immense, for with high-skill production goes a high standard of living, and with low-skill or agricultural production a relatively low standard of living. The early Comecon programmes accordingly produced strains within the communist group of countries; and all 'underdeveloped' countries see industrialization as part of the process of development. Division of labour within modernized state economies is politically possible only with heavy transfers of wealth to agricultural producers by subsidies, differential tax reliefs, price supports, or other means; and division of labour internationally would similarly be possible only with massive wealth transfers. Aid programmes are a tiny contribution to this requirement. But the point that is relevant here is that as the international economic system, in the search for wealth maximization, becomes increasingly characterized by international division of labour it will increasingly receive inputs from international political and social systems requiring responses in the form of international redistribution of wealth. Inadequate responses to these demands on the international economic system are likely to lead to disastrous conflict.

A third reason for postulating the existence of an international economic system may be found in the growth in the number of international firms and enterprises. In the non-communist world oil companies were among the first to develop an international character, but in the past two decades the trend has so developed that it is to be seen in most industrial fields—for example food and fats in Unilever; tyres in Firestone or Dunlop-Pirelli; pharmaceuticals in Parke Davis; radio and electronics in Philips; motor vehicles in Chrysler-Rootes-Simca-Barreiros. Moreover the practice of manufacturing under licence is being extended, and this is not restricted to transactions within the non-communist world: thus Bulgarrenaults are manufactured under licence from the French Renault car company. The effects of this internationalization of enterprises is that economic activity is not seen simply within the state context. Capital availability, tax liability, labour availability and quality, materials supply, market character, styling and design questions—all the manifold components of the production activity have to be conceived in a two-state (or more) and an interstate context. Transnational loyalties are stimulated. Economic interactions cannot be expressed within the framework of interstate interactions.

As a consequence of all the foregoing, international monetary relations have become of far greater importance than they ever were in the past. It has for much of this century been the case that currency exchange rates have greatly affected, and have been manipulated to influence, the health of domestic economies; but the emerging internationalization of research and development, of the division of labour, and of firms and enterprises, means that a dependable international means of exchange has become increasingly important. The international movement of goods and services is moreover steadily expanding, and the ratio of available credit to trading transactions has been diminishing. These are some of the reasons why the late 1960s saw first the growth of mechanisms to regulate pressure on currencies deriving from speculation or short-term fluctuations, and secondly measures to expand the supply of international credit, such as the Special Drawing Rights at the International Monetary Fund. These measures represent responses of the international economic system to demands arising from within the system itself, the agents through which the responses have evolved being representatives of international institutions, states and banks.

This chapter has contained sketches of how three international behavioural systems, political, military-strategic, and economic, might be conceived, together with some indications of why such conceptualization may be relevant and useful. Many other behavioural systems of the same type may be thought of. The main reasons for doing so are two. In the first place, conceiving international systems in terms of the interactions of identified units, the states, tends to suggest that these are the only significant units, and indeed that these units are natural and will and perhaps should continue: these are assumptions that need to be questioned and examined. The second method of conceptualization, if it can be successfully carried through, facilitates the examination of these assumptions. In the second place, and putting the same point rather differently, if it is the case that trends in international relations exist, or may exist, which will lessen the primary significance of states as units of interaction, then it becomes important for understanding, and also perhaps for regulating, international relations, to develop means of meaningfully organizing the data in which the trends are reflected. The next chapter, in outlining the complex problem of system transformation, will accordingly consider as part of its analysis the relationships that may be postulated between state systems and behavioural systems.[10]

[10] Part of the argument in this and the subsequent chapter was originally developed in an essay entitled 'Factors affecting the number of units in an international system' contained in a *Festschrift* for Dr A. Appadorai entitled *Studies on Politics—National and International*, edited by Professor M. S. Rajan (Vikas Publications 1970). Permission to use the material here is gratefully acknowledged.

I I

System transformation

WHEN IS A SYSTEM transformed so that it has become a different system?
The question in this form is misleading. It implies that there exists in
reality a system in some objective sense which when changed in some or
all of its characteristics becomes a different system. But if all systems
are abstractions from reality, are mental constructs, then the system
changes when the person who has conceived it determines that it has
changed. This is a trivial statement. The question of system transformation becomes important—its exploration may indeed become one of the
central purposes of systems analysis—when it is seen in the light of the
relationships between some observed or postulated empirical interactions
and the conceptual model of them which is the system. Take for
instance a balance of power system. This was described in Chapter 9 in
terms of certain units, and interactions among them, in a defined environment, and the conditions maximizing the likelihood of the system
continuing were explored. The system would be stated to continue unchanged so long as the essential characteristics by which it was defined
remained unchanged. The interesting and important questions about
systems transformation arise, however, when the system is compared
with a real-world situation. If the balance of power model, or conceived
system, is compared with eighteenth-century western Europe, how far
are the characteristics and processes of the model observable in that situation, how and why did they continue, how and why did they change,
and so how and why did the appropriateness of the balance of power

model break down so that a different system conceptualization is needed to describe the post-1789 situation? The question with which this chapter opens thus becomes—when do empirical processes which are seen as the referent of a system so change that a new system conceptualization becomes necessary? And the important questions are of course not just when, but how and why.

Thus a system might be conceived as consisting of five particular students each with specific characteristics, and set in a particular environment, and the interactions that would take place among them in response to various stimuli (or inputs) might be described. If five actual students, possessing the specified characteristics, were then set in the specified environment and subjected to the stimuli, one would have an empirical referent of the conceived system. (The extent to which the behaviour of the group of students resembled the postulated behaviour in the system would of course depend on the degree of isomorphism between the characteristics and environment of the actual group and the characteristics and environment in the conceived system.) If one of the five students were then withdrawn from the group, and the specification of the system (and the actual behaviour of the group) critically depended on there being five interacting units, then the system as originally conceived would be non-isomorphic in a critical dimension, and a different system would have to be conceived. The system would have to be changed. Or if one of the five students were replaced by a different student with different personality characteristics, and the specification of the system critically depended on the characteristics of the students, then again the system would have to be changed if it were to remain sufficiently isomorphic to be of value in helping to understand the real-world interactions. Similarly system changes might be made necessary by changes in the pattern of interactions (if this were a critical part of the specification), or by changes in the environment.

Clearly any attempt to examine the problem of system transformation in relation to the innumerable systems that may be abstracted from the international system would require a special methodology if the task were to be manageable. This is not the place to elaborate such a methodology. I propose here to explore the problems of system change simply in relation to one international system only. Since the majority of analysts concern themselves with state systems, and since most would agree[1] that state interactions form in 1970 an important part of significant interactions at the international level, I propose to conceptualize a state system.

[1] But not John Burton: see his *Systems, States, Diplomacy and Rules* (Cambridge University Press, 1968).

The system is conceived as one with a large number of units; in which the capabilities of the units vary, but not to the extent that any unit has no capability to influence the behaviour of any other; in which the interactions are of many kinds; and in which the responses of the system to inputs are largely the result of the autonomous action of the units themselves. This state system is a subsystem of the international system,[2] and its environment consists of all other subsystems (such as behavioural systems) of the international system, and, less importantly, of systems outside the international system.

This system may be thought to have some resemblances to, and some differences from, the states and the interactions among them of 1970. As compared with the situation in 1970 a different system would have to be conceived if there were sufficient changes in some or all of the defined characteristics—large number of units, none wholly dominant, varied interaction, and a substantial degree of unit autonomy. I propose to explore factors operating in 1970 in the direction of changing any of these characteristics; but I do not propose to indicate whether or not at one point or another a different system would need to be conceived, for this would be to speculate beyond the limits of the present analysis. It is the change factors that I wish to explore.

The factors may perhaps be classified into three groups: those that arise from within subsystems—that is to say from within the state members which are seen as the units of the system; those that derive from the interactions of which the system is presumed to be composed; and those that derive from the environment within which the system is imagined to be. Four interrelated subsystemic factors may be thought to be of primary importance, the effects of technological change, of demographic change, of increasing mass involvement in politics, and of ideology.

By interaction among states is meant the interrelationships of decisions and consequent action taken on behalf of states by those with the capacity to take them. Decisions in one state are both responses and themselves stimuli to decisions in other states, and the pattern of interactions is formed from them. In Part II of this book decisions were shown to be governed by goals, by influences (or capabilities) and means (or instruments) as perceived, and by processes, all in the context of the external environment. Technological change affects all of these, but the immediate concern is with its effect at the sub-systemic level, on capabilities, means and processes (returning to goals later), and so on the decisions that are taken and of which the interaction pattern consists.

[2] As defined above, Chapter 8, p. 193.

So far as capabilities are concerned, almost every component is affected by technological change. The strategic implications of natural geographical features, and the strategic economic significance of location, can be transformed by the development of new weapon systems and of new means of transport; natural resources previously inaccessible by reason of their climatic location or natural barriers to their exploitation may become available through the development of new means for supporting human life or new extracting techniques; raw materials may suddenly become important because of new inventions which make use of them; dependence on trade may be reduced by the discovery of processes for making substitute materials; the size, trends and structure of populations may be transformed by improvements in health and hygiene and by contraception techniques; social structure may be destroyed by industrialization, urbanization, and the emergence of new production relationships; increased specialization and division of labour creates wider and wider interdependence of different but related activities so that more and more political decisions seem to have to be taken at the centre where alone their many ramifications may be understood; these two processes may lead to mounting dissatisfaction by members of the community who cannot participate in decisions which fundamentally affect them and whose lives increasingly seem to lack meaning; all these considerations—strategic, economic, demographic, social and political— affect the military capability of the state. The kind of decisions that can or will be taken is likewise affected.

Similarly, technological change affects means of action. Speed of transportation has made possible the much greater frequency of diplomatic action by political decision-makers face to face. Speed of communication has increased the degree of control that may be exercised from the centre over diplomatic agents in foreign countries. The development of televisual as well as telephonic links will permit even more face to face discussions by decision-makers without either of them leaving their capitals. From the economic point of view the imposition of penalties or the offering of inducements is more possible on a wider scale, because of developing capabilities and developing needs among the poorer states. But the state imposing the penalty may suffer substantial losses because of the extent to which economic interdependence at the international level has grown. Propaganda has through the development of mass media for the first time become a significant foreign policy instrument, while the possible range and effectiveness of subversive action has been greatly extended. Finally, technology has transformed force as an instrument, because of the range at which it can be applied, the quality of damage that can be inflicted, and the consequent new importance of deterrence as contrasted with defence.

Likewise processes are subject to change under the influence of technology—in the quantity and quality of information that needs to be, and can be, transmitted; in the range of different communication channels that may be, or have to be, used; in the extent of repercussions of decisions and so in the number of interests or institutions that have to be brought into the decision-making process; in the complexity of interrelationship of different decisions and the impact of one upon another.

Technological developments thus affect the conditions under which decisions are made, and so affect the decisions themselves and interaction patterns. Technological change itself promotes technological change, and the exponential rate of change shows no sign of varying. The major effects are to increase the disparity of resources among units (the rich get richer faster, the poor less poor more slowly, if at all), and to decrease their capacity for autonomous action. The 1962 Cuban missiles crisis may illustrate the argument. The fate of the whole world may well have been involved, but decisions were taken in two capitals only, without consultation with others, with support if possible, but without it if it could not be mobilized. The evolution of the crisis depended critically on the means by which the United States was able to' gather precise information and display it round the world; on the variety of possibilities of counter-action made possible by technology; on the precise hour-by-hour control over naval action that was exercised from Washington; on the speed of communication between Washington and Moscow; on the precisely timed and precisely briefed diplomatic action that was able to be taken in the NATO capitals, at United Nations headquarters in New York, and at the meeting of the Organization of American States; on the perception by the chief protagonists, Kennedy and Khrushchev, that the interaction of their decisions—the necessity to avoid escalation—had to be steadily borne in mind; and on their understanding of the consequences if the situation were allowed so to get out of hand that the weapons which science and technology had placed at their disposal came to be used. Technology extended the range and speed of their actions, but, accurately perceived, limited their autonomy.

Questions of population, the second suggested subsystemic factor, are increasingly widely recognized and discussed as being among the most important influences on the world's future. Populations in most states are increasing, in some slowly, but in some, particularly in Africa, Latin America and Asia, at rates which will produce a doubling of numbers every twenty years. In mid-nineteenth century the population of the world was about one thousand million. A hundred years later it had reached about three thousand million. If current trends continued it might reach some seven thousand million by the year 2000, more than twenty thousand million by 2240 and perhaps a hundred thousand million by 2300.[3]

The forecast total for the year 2000 may now be unlikely not to be reached, but projections beyond that date are of little value because the rate of change in all aspects of life is so high that the nature of existence in the twenty-first century is impossible to foresee. But a doubling of the world's population in the last third of this century would be an event of significance enough. Most of the increase is taking place in the developing countries, and this is a second main reason why the gap between the rich and the poor is widening: the rate of growth of the developed countries, with advanced technology building on advanced technology, is higher than in the developing countries, where the expansion in gross national product is in greater or less degree absorbed by the subsistence requirements of the exploding population, so that the wealth increase *per capita* may be very small indeed. The probable significance of this for future international relations is obvious.

So far as a state system is concerned population acts as a change factor on capabilities, on instruments, and on goals, and so can profoundly affect the interaction pattern of decision. A declining population, or a population whose rate of growth is diminishing, or has become static, is an ageing population with serious consequences for capabilities. But the typical situation is the reverse of this. The effect of rapidly expanding populations beyond the rate of growth of the economy, capital availability, and technological development has already been mentioned.[4] This has implications for defence capability, because surplus capacity is not available for non-productive activity, and it fundamentally affects internal political stability. Centuries-old patterns of economic activity, social strata and customs (such as acceptance of poverty as inevitable or as punishment for past sin) are disrupted, and awareness of poverty leads to expectations of improvement which are constantly frustrated. Decision-makers are accordingly constrained to seek alleviation, whether from technical assistance or aid programmes, from encouragement to population migration, or from external adventures. Each of these expedients affects interaction patterns, the first by reducing the freedom of manoeuvre both of the donor and of the receiving state, the second by creating new elements of discord as alien groups set up tensions within

[3] N. D. Palmer and H. C. Perkins, *International Relations* (Houghton Mifflin, 3rd edn, 1969), pp. 59-60.
[4] See above, Chapter 4, pp. 73-80.

the states to which they go, and the third by provoking systemic disturbances which may or may not become significant for the working of the system.

The impact of population trends and movements as a change factor in the system as it is conceived is greatly increased by the growth of mass involvement in politics. This is the result of a wide variety of factors. They include the development of mass media possessing the capability of reaching whole populations; the evolution of technical means for organizing and sustaining mass movements; the creation or realization of real or fancied grievances such as those already referred to, to be met by mass organization; the social disintegration resulting from industrialization or changes in employment patterns with the resulting need for some compensating loyalty focus; the effect of two world wars in which populations as a whole had to be mobilized and made to endure and so had to be persuaded into the struggle; the spread of education and literacy. Some of these factors operate generally, some more in modernized and some more in developing countries; but the phenomenon to which they give rise is widespread.

The main effect of increased mass involvement is to alter the domestic environments of decision-makers. Populations generally are more concerned with day-to-day matters that are seen to affect them directly, than with distant or obscure or long-term questions, which foreign policy issues generally are. Accordingly where there is competition for scarce resources (as is almost always the case), decision-makers are likely as mass involvement develops to have less freedom to devote resources to external questions than at times or in subsystems where the masses are less involved or influential. On the other hand, if mass emotions are aroused (and such emotions may frequently be stimulated by the decision-makers themselves for other purposes),[5] the freedom of manoeuvre of decision-makers *not* to take certain foreign policy actions may likewise be lessened. Thus flexibility of response, and 'autonomous action' by decision-makers is limited in another way—by limitations imposed from within the subsystem itself.

The importance of mass involvement and its effect on the domestic environment of decision-makers is enhanced by the existence of trans-

[5] Mussolini's frequent adulation of violence and war as the context for the display of man's finest virtues meant that, at least for the faithful, the resort to war in the 1930s was the evidently proper way to get Italy out of her troubles. Some of the leaders of the new African states, having ridden to power on anti-colonialism, may have found themselves unable to resist steps which, in their new-found authority, they recognized to be economically or politically disadvantageous.

national links and by the development of the methods and facilities of propaganda. The echoes of popular movements in Africa spill over into neighbouring states, while propaganda activities become more efficacious the more the decision-makers are subject to mass influences. The clear effect of mass involvement is to lessen the freedom of manoeuvre of decision-makers: the direction of the effect is by no means so obvious. Woodrow Wilson believed that all peoples wanted peace and so if all states were so democratically governed that leaders could be called to account by their peoples there would be no more wars. The experience of mass involvement in the interwar years suggested the contrary—that hatreds arising from miseries or hardships or frustrations experienced by the masses could by skilful demagogic leadership be displaced on to external enemies and thus mass support for violent action could be mobilized, could indeed carry leaders along with its own momentum. But since the second world war mass pressures, at least in the modernized societies, have tended to be in the opposite direction, so it is possible that in some contexts Wilson's expectations may not be so ill-judged as in other circumstances they seemed to be. But whatever may be the direction of the effect of increasing mass involvement in politics, it is a factor affecting the interaction pattern of decisions that cannot be ignored.

Its connection with ideology is evident. Ideologies may be defined as sets of values serving as guides for action. They are thus closely related to goals, but not necessarily to state goals: the decision-makers of a state, for example, may see its security or the defence of its territorial integrity as a primary goal, but there may be adherents to an ideology within its border that contains as one of its aims the submergence of the state in some kind of world order. Ideologies may be transnational or international, they may be expansionist, they may look towards amalgamation or disintegration of state units, they may have as an aim the establishment of a different kind of relationship at the international level, and accordingly they may serve as a constraint in the domestic environment of decision-makers, or, if their adherents gain control of a state subsystem they may have a direct impact on state relationships.

Numerous examples of ideologies as change factors may be cited. Nationalism, together with other factors, had profound effects on relationships in western Europe in the nineteenth century. Before 1850 the western European system could have been seen as having five major units—France, Britain, Austria, Prussia and Russia—and a large number of other units of varying significance including Spain, Portugal, the Netherlands, Belgium (after 1830), Sweden, Norway, Denmark, many German states other than the big two, and several states in Italy.

By 1871 Prussia from being perhaps the weakest of the big five had become, at least potentially, very much the strongest, while a sixth major unit had emerged in Italy. By the same process the number of smaller interacting units had been drastically reduced. Nationalism had contributed significantly to this process. But the ideology of nationalism has also stimulated the reverse process. The view that every group feeling itself to be a nation should have its own state (which is the essence of many variants of nationalist ideology) contributed substantially in 1919 to the emergence or redefinition of several new states in Europe, such as Poland, Yugoslavia, Czechoslovakia, Austria, Hungary, Romania, Bulgaria, Finland, Estonia, Latvia and Lithuania; while after the second world war the ideology, frequently linked with anticolonialism, has contributed to the emergence of some seventy new states in the quarter-century since 1945, thus more than doubling the number of interacting units. Many of these units are extremely small or weak, so in order to be able to exercise some influence and to safeguard their newly won independence, many of them have entered groups or blocks of varying degrees of cohesion—the African, the Afro-Asian, the Arab League, the Commonwealth being examples. The nationalist and nationalist-anticolonialist ideologies have thus served as very significant factors in relation both to numbers of interacting units and to interaction patterns.

The structure and working of an interstate system can be even more directly affected if adherents of a particular ideology win power in one of the state subsystems. The French Revolution of 1789, as mentioned in Chapter 9, brought to power men who saw it as desirable or necessary to overthrow the monarchical states of Europe, and so brought to an end the balance of power system which is described as characterizing the relationships of the previous hundred years. The adherence of United States President Woodrow Wilson to the notion of self-determination as an expression of nationalist ideology had much to do with the shape of the Europe that emerged from Paris in 1919. The winning of power by the Bolsheviks in Russia in 1917 has greatly affected the nature of interactions, because their ideological goals include the total transformation of international relationships, the ideology claims adherents in many states, the Bolsheviks have created an institutional structure in the form of communist parties to promote the ideology, they accordingly have means for influencing the domestic environments of decision-makers in other states and so limiting their freedom of manoeuvre, and their own actions have not been restrained by any overriding desire to maintain the system. In 1956 at the twentieth congress of the Soviet communist party, however, Khrushchev recognized the technological limit on freedom to pursue these goals when he enunciated the revised doctrine of peaceful coexistence: the struggle must continue, but war was no longer inevitable, and means other than war must be used. Even more directly, Nazi ideology, claiming Teutonic domination of the world as necessary for world progress, affected the nature of state interactions, and led to alterations in the number of interacting units by conquest and absorption.

Technological advance, demographic change, mass involvement, and ideologies, can therefore each act as change factors operating on all the variables in the system as conceived. The number of units may be increased or decreased, both in formal terms, and in terms of the autonomous action which units in practice are able to take. The capabilities of units may be substantially varied. The autonomy of action of the units may be reduced, both by the greater complexity of the interaction pattern or the more serious consequences of possible or probable responses, and by limitations arising from effects on domestic environments. Sufficient change in any or all of these may clearly make the system as conceived inappropriate as a model of the emerging situation.

Change factors arising from the operation of the system itself need not detain us here as they were sufficiently explored in the analysis of a balance of power system in Chapter 9.[6] They include the number of units, which can itself have effects on the number of units and the ability of the system to survive; the flexibility of interaction; the variety of interactions; the communication flow in the system and so the perception by units of the state of the system, disturbances in it, and action necessary to preserve or destroy it. Alterations in any of these variables may have consequences leading to system transformation.

Perhaps the most significant of the factors which raise doubts about the appropriateness of the state system model are those deriving from the environment in which the system is seen to exist. This environment was described as consisting of the behavioural subsystems of the international system (political, economic, military-strategic and so on), other subsystems of the international system (such as, for example, an ideological system), and systems outside the international system. The effects of the last of these as a change factor are likely to be small: an earthquake in Turkey may well act as an input to the state system but is unlikely significantly to alter it; although a natural disaster eliminating some major unit or units, or an invasion from another planet, would each be likely fundamentally to transform the state system. Neither of these occurrences, however, appears probable.

International economic interactions can easily be seen to have effects on the autonomy, the capabilities, and even the number of units in a

[6] See pp. 202-10 above.

state system. To the Marxist–Leninist the case needs little demonstration. States are seen as expressions of the interest of the dominant class in a society. States controlled by capitalists are bound to be enemies of states controlled by the proletariat, and the states with similar social systems will be driven to band together against the states with the opposed social system. In the capitalist camp tensions necessarily exist between the greater and the lesser members, but in the interest of self-preservation against the advance of the proletariat the lesser members cannot do without the support of the more powerful. The means by which the more powerful extend their control consist of investment, both portfolio and direct, in the economies of the weaker, and the development of international combines, which gradually gain control of key enterprises in the states which increasingly become client states. Armaments production, civil aircraft, computers, motor vehicles, oil, are only a few of the fields in which United States capitalism is gaining a stranglehold over other modernized capitalist countries. The states are not therefore to be seen as autonomous units: they merely express the interests of their capitalist masters, and in so far as their mastery is increasingly being exercised from Washington, they are subordinated to the interests of United States capital.

The argument applies equally in the other camp, though here its moral flavour is good, not bad. The interests of the world proletariat require the emergence of a world communist society, just as the interests of the proletariat in a particular state are served by communism. The strength of the communist camp must accordingly be preserved and developed, and any leaders whose policies undermine it, whether by malice or misjudgment, must be removed. This is the kind of reasoning that lay behind the Brezhnev doctrine by which the invasion of Czechoslovakia in 1968 by the Warsaw Pact countries (except Romania) was justified. But if communist solidarity may at the extreme require invasion and forcible replacement of a government, it is clear that the autonomy of states in the communist camp is sharply limited.

It is not necessary to go all the way with a Marxist–Leninist interpretation of international conflict as essentially class conflict to accept that international economic interactions affect state systems. Such interactions may have industrial, commercial, financial and technological components. Without accepting the decisive influence of international companies, it is of course true that relations between Britain and Holland are affected by the existence and activities of Unilever and of Royal Dutch Shell, and the freedom of manoeuvre of decision-makers is in some degree limited thereby. French governments cannot ignore the fact that International Business Machines dominates the French computer market, and British and United States policies in the Levant are influenced by the oil companies who operate in that region. But oil is required by the British and United States economies, and so by their peoples, and interest in the Levant would therefore be substantial however the oil were being obtained; and as far as the former example is concerned, it would be difficult for France to contemplate war with the United States and so the loss of computer supply, but the interest of IBM would be against war anyway, and at levels below open conflict the effect of IBM's position is unlikely to be decisive. These transnational industrial links act as constraints, but the degree of constraint, as always, depends on the perceptions of both parties of the gains and losses that would result from various courses of action.

Commercial interactions may have wider implications. The volume and value of international commercial transactions continues to expand, and this increases the network of interconnections and the number of individuals or groups operating within it or affected by it. Increasing complexity of manufacturing processes tends to promote international division of labour, extends the range of raw materials that have to be acquired, and dictates the need for larger markets for costly, sophisticated but labour-saving products. So far as developing countries are concerned their low level of economic activity, or lack of economic viability, stimulates the flow of aid programmes, technical assistance, and loans, from international or state sources, and may encourage attempts—not usually with much success—at developing such regional cooperative arrangements as those of the East African Common Services Organization.

Growing financial interaction parallels increasing commercial activity. The spread of commercial exchanges requires not merely expansion of credit and of means of exchange (an international money supply), but confidence that international monetary arrangements will preserve sufficient stability of monetary values. Inevitably change processes, economic, political, social, technological, will lead to temporary or long-lasting alterations in costs, productivity and production in one state as against another; and resulting imbalances can be corrected only through cooperative international financial action, whether through agreed changes in exchange rates, or through loan programmes, or through central bank cooperation, or through all of these, with substantial effects on the freedom of manoeuvre of decision-makers (in domestic policies as well as in foreign policies).

Finally, the technological aspect of economic interaction imposes further constraints as state economies become increasingly unable in isolation to supply the level of capital, material and human resources required for the most advanced products. Possible effects of an international economic system developing in these ways may be illustrated from the case of Britain and Europe. Britain is a state with very few natural resources other than coal (a declining asset), recently discovered natural gas in the North Sea, and a population with a high level of technical and scientific skill. She must import half or more than half of her food and a high proportion of the raw materials for her industry. Her population is thus critically dependent on exports for employment, and indeed for survival. With a population accustomed to a high standard of living, and with the rise of industries in other parts of the world with lower labour costs and able to supply markets in their regions at lower transport costs, traditional markets for less sophisticated manufactures are steadily being lost. It appears probable that Britain may be able effectively to compete in world markets only with products of a high skill component and a relatively low import component such as chemicals, vehicles, machine tools, electronics. But markets for these goods are mainly in the developed economies of western Europe, and the United States. Moreover these goods are precisely those requiring high investment of capital and skills, too high for British resources alone to provide. In addition Britain carries heavy international financial liabilities, resulting from the range of her past international economic activities and from two world wars, while some of the European countries have high reserves in relation to their liabilities. These are economic arguments for a British association with Europe despite the substantial initial costs: if association with Europe should involve ultimately, as seems probable, the merging of the state members of the European Economic Community, at least as far as some fields of action including foreign policy were concerned, then the international economic system would have been a factor not merely in limiting the autonomy of action, and affecting the capabilities, of the units in the state system, but in reducing their number.

A similar argument may be developed with reference to an international military-strategic system. The same arguments deriving from high-cost technology apply, although the effect of cooperation in weapons production in limiting autonomy and affecting capabilities is sharply greater. Similar effects may flow from the quality of international military-strategic relationships deriving from the nature of weaponry. It is a commonplace that means are available, or within reach, that could totally destroy life on earth. These means include biological and chemical weapons as well as the more commonly talked-about thermonuclear explosives. Missile technology brings every region of the earth within reach of every other, and sufficiently effective methods of defence remain unattainable in political and economic terms, even if they may no longer be so technologically. The restraint hitherto exercised by decision-makers in states controlling these weapons demonstrates awareness of their potential, but the danger of their spread and ultimate use by miscalculation, accident or irresponsibility remains high. If it were to be the case, and it was so perceived, that the probabilities of use became high, then the pressures towards the establishment of a single global controlling authority, to perform at least this one function, would become powerful, and the relationships among states would be transformed. But even short of this the partial recognition of danger implied by the signature by most states of the non-proliferation treaty already imposes limits on the autonomy and the capabilities of the non-nuclear states. This is to be seen in the context of the international political system, as will be suggested below.

The autonomy, capabilities and indeed number of state units may be affected by a third element of the military-strategic system, the international aspects, that is to say, of subversion, insurrection and guerrilla warfare. The application of organized armed force in this form may be developed from within a state, and it may be aided, or it may have been stimulated, from outside. The activity, if successful, may lead either to the emergence of a new member, or new members, of the state system, or to the elimination of a previously existing member or members. The insurrection of the Vietcong in Vietnam, aided by North Vietnam and resisted by the United States, aimed at the elimination of South Vietnam as an autonomous actor: the conflict spilled over into Laos and Cambodia with major effects on their autonomy and capabilities. The revolt in Hungary in 1956 had as one of its objects the restoration of Hungary as an autonomous actor in the state system. Tshombe and some of the Katangese, with military aid from many quarters, similarly tried between 1960 and 1963 to establish Katanga as an autonomous unit. The internationally-aided guerrillas operating from across the border in Angola and Mozambique seek a similar end. In all these cases military-strategic interactions reduce the autonomy and capabilities of state units, and may affect their number.

The international political system, seen as a behavioural system forming part of the environment of interacting states, has much less effect because of its embryonic nature. There are no authorities to make binding allocations, as we have seen. But there are numerous international fora for discussion, which may lead to the passage of resolutions, whether in a United Nations General Assembly, or in a conference of nonaligned states at Bandung. These have no power to bind or compel, but they are political in the sense that they may influence the outcome of an issue as it is directly settled by the states concerned. The embryonic legal and ethical norms referred to earlier contribute to an international sense of community, and limit the freedom of decision-makers to ignore them: to the extent that they are widely adhered to, their breach causes loss of trust or reputation or prestige to the offender. The nuclear weapons question referred to in a previous paragraph is a case in point: the loss of autonomy and reduction in capabilities accepted by those states that have renounced nuclear weapons is less than it otherwise might be because of the strong international consensus that, while nuclear weapons exist and in present circumstances must continue for deterrent purposes, they are not to be used. Because of this consensus a non-nuclear power can with less limitation face a conflict with a nuclear power. Any threat by the latter to use its nuclear strength would be likely to provoke the intervention of another nuclear power in order to prevent the weapons being used and so to preserve the stability of deterrence which in part rests on the assumption made by the major nuclear powers that the other will not use its weapons.

As a final example of a system forming part of the environment of a state system and affecting its nature and working, the notion may be suggested of an international ideological system. Ideology has already been discussed as a change factor arising in the state subsystems. It may be seen also as a system at the international level. Communism before the death of Stalin was very largely controlled from one state centre, but this is no longer the case: the split between Moscow and Peking, and the struggle to determine whose version of the doctrine is authentic, has caused communist parties to decide where they belong, and in the process of decision links between some parties have been forged. Most have taken the Moscow line, but Maoism remains a powerful doctrine in Asia, and partly because most parties adhere to the Soviet Union, many new ideologically inspired interlinked groups have emerged in many parts of the world. Class solidarity was a Marxist slogan and expectation; but age and occupational solidarity has made sporadic appearances in international student movements, not with a clear ideology it is true, but with a common impatience with bureaucratic procedures, limited outlooks, order and tradition, and direction by the old. Some part of this impatience has derived from an instinctive judgment of the inadequacy of the interstate order and the hazards which it contains, and from an emergent sense of the community of mankind. Effects of this on state decision-makers as yet are limited, but international movements of ideas of this kind could ultimately prove a substantial change factor in an international state system.

This chapter has attempted to do no more than indicate a few ways in which a system conceived as a state system may be subject to change factors in relation to the number, autonomy, and capabilities of the state units. The purpose of systems analysis is by the elaboration of theoretical models to gain insight into the nature of real world situations. A simple model of a state system was proposed and on the assumption that the real world was accurately represented by the model, the real world was looked at with a view to determining whether change factors exist which would make the model inappropriate. Such change factors, it was suggested, might be found within the state sub-systems, in the working of the system itself, and in the environment within which the system was conceived to be. The analysis was introductory only. It was not intended to determine the question whether a state system model is or is not an appropriate way of conceiving international relations in 1970, but merely to indicate some of the considerations relevant to the making of such a judgment. Enough has however perhaps been said to indicate that analysts who think only in terms of state systems are leaving out of account questions that need some examining; and that indeed if these transformation factors are so operating as to make conceptualizations of state systems increasingly inadequate models of the real world, then they are leaving out the most important questions of all.

Conclusion

THE FUNCTION OF THEORY is to give coherence to observations. What conclusions may be drawn from this coherence will vary with the data to which the observations refer, and with the rigour with which the theory may be constructed. The most effective theory is one which states precise relationships among precisely defined, quantified variables and which accordingly permits prediction of the outcomes from the specified interactions, with a very high degree of probability that the predicted events will in fact occur. Many theories in the natural sciences are of this kind, and within their limits their predictive capabilities are high. But their effectiveness derives from the possibility of defining the limits of the observations to which the theory refers without thereby excluding variables which are of significance.

The social sciences in general, and international relations in particular, are not yet in this condition. Possibly they never can be. Theory in international relations therefore at present has much more modest aims. It has first a simple taxonomic purpose—to classify data in such a way that similar sets of data may be similarly arranged, and so in a superficial way compared. The analysis of the decision-making process contained in Chapter 7 was essentially an exercise of this kind: differences in the ways in which decisions are arrived at in different states may be observed by classifying data about the respective processes into the analytical categories of information, communication, constitution of decision-making group, and so on. Moreover a set of categories of this kind will, if well designed, ensure that the relevant questions about the decision-making process in any state will be asked.

Taxonomy is however so elementary a step, though a necessary one, that it hardly qualifies to be described as a theoretical exercise. A second and much more difficult step is to define variables into which the data may be organized. Such a definition was attempted in the micro-analysis in Part II, where it was suggested that foreign policy might be seen in terms of the four interacting variables, goals, influences or capabilities, means or instruments, and processes. This, if an effective definition of variables which successfully and meaningfully organizes data, represents a substantial step towards a theory; but one ought perhaps properly not to speak of theory until it has been specified how the variables are related. The simple statement that the choice of economic sanctions affects goals and affects capabilities in relation to other goals is worth making, but one is not taken very far until it is possible to say how goals and capabilities will be affected by the choice of economic sanctions. Unless and until it is possible to determine this with some degree of precision, and decision-makers know the result, it will not be possible to predict with any degree of probability whether or not economic sanctions are likely to be imposed. If a worthwhile degree of probability is to be achieved, then a statistical demonstration is required; but here there is the immediate difficulty that the statistical universe of the use of economic sanctions is so tiny. This suggests that the variables may not be adequately defined to form the foundation of a predictive theory.

Alternative methods of theory-building have been tried in the construction of abstract formal models, verbal or mathematical, of which a few simple examples were given in Part III. So far as verbal models are concerned, the problem of formulating abstractions which are both manageable and sufficiently isomorphic to real situations to be useful is highly intractable; while mathematical models have in some cases proved valuable within the narrow limits within which adequate quantification is possible, but on occasion the triviality of the results obtained suggests that the subjects have been chosen at least in part because quantification was possible. None the less both these methods appear to contain the potential of theory-building in the more rigorous sense of correlation of variables, and it may well be that it is along these roads that the major advances in the future are to be made.

In the meantime the beginning student needs to acquire an awareness of the nature of the whole field and its possible taxonomies. This book attempts to offer two classification schemes, one based on actors, and the other on systems. Because they are different schemes for classifying the same material, they are not exclusive, and some empirical data and illustrations have deliberately been used twice to indicate that they may be fitted into either scheme. Which scheme a student chooses to concentrate on will depend on the matters that interest him and the questions to which he seeks answers.

So far as the actors' classification scheme is concerned, the emphasis was almost entirely on states. This choice was made to keep the book down to a reasonable size; but similar analyses could—and for comprehensiveness should—be attempted of such other actors as universal institutions, regional institutions, functional or specialized agencies, and perhaps institutionalized doctrines or non-governmental organizations as well. The stage on which these actors perform was depicted as one where action was always based on uncertainty—about the nature of the set and the other players, and so about the consequence of movement, or of doing nothing; where all actors perceived their roles as being primarily in conflict with those of others, but that in reality, though it was not always so perceived, roles could in most cases be better played with some degree of cooperation, and with none at all the play could not proceed; and where actions rarely, if ever, led to clear advantage and no disadvantage, but that normally all possible actions had some elements of gain and some elements of loss, and the choice of action was to be determined by judgment of the respective mixes of gains to be won and losses to be suffered by selection of the various courses open. Action must always be seen in these terms. The student or practitioner who seeks or sees or describes action as being 'right' in anything more than a relative sense is either deceiving himself or has missed some relevant part of the total situation.

The introduction to systems analysis in Part III was more theoretical in the sense that it consisted of an exploration of some highly abstract models and related them less directly to empirical data. The contrast between the two parts in some degree exemplifies the strengths and weaknesses both of those who use 'traditional' methods of studying the subject and those who seek to develop new 'scientific' methodologies. The 'traditionalists' have been largely responsible for the great advances that have been made in understanding what goes on in the real world, and so have enabled the politician and his advisers, if they choose to read what has been put before them, to exercise their wisdom and their judgment and their intuition in a much more informed way than ever before. But judgment and intuition (or hunch and guesswork) remain central, and traditional methods of enquiry and analysis will not change this. The traditionalists know this to be so and would not wish it to be otherwise.

The new 'scientists' however—or at least some of them—seek to discover ways of determining relative probabilities of various outcomes in various situations. Fashionable futures research, for instance, is concerned to elaborate the different kinds of future worlds that are likely to emerge according to various assumptions about extrapolations of existing observable trends. A more complex version of the same activity endeavours to delineate the shape and structure of desirable future worlds and then to determine how current trends need to be modified or diverted in order to make the achievement of the desired future more probable. Enquiries of this latter kind raise the perennial questions about the purposes of political and social organization with which the political theorist has for centuries concerned himself; but they also involve formidable problems of definition and measurement of variables and thereafter immensely complex statistical procedures. The more closely a model represents the real world the less possible does its exploration and manipulation become, and for this reason most of the work of the 'scientists' has hitherto been trivial in its results or so abstract in nature as to say nothing that can be related to real-world situations. It cannot be known what may become possible through the future development of new methods and techniques. It is perhaps no less difficult—though in a different sense—to judge whether major advances in real-world manipulative capabilities are desirable.

Except from one point of view. It is a commonplace—and the evidence is everywhere—that advances in the natural sciences have outstripped advances in the social sciences, that, in other words, the capacity to understand and fashion the social and political structures which can contain and exploit, not be mastered and destroyed by, the opportunities that science has created, simply does not exist. The threats are innumerable. Pollution or destruction of the human environment through poisonous effluents, through ecological disruption, through exhaustion of natural resources, through noise, through the creation of indestructible plastic or radioactive waste, through ugliness and the spoliation of natural beauty; uncontrolled and possibly uncontrollable demographic explosions because of new and widely disseminated health and hygiene methods; undermining of social patterns, values and beliefs because of the global circulation of cultural influences, the increasingly universal acceptance of the value of wealth maximization, and the soul-destroying employment in which large numbers of humans consequently spend large parts of their lives; the looming possibility of genetic manipulation and control; the already existing destructive capability of eliminating all life from the earth—these are but a few of the menaces contained in the material and intellectual affluence which the sciences have created. In face of them human behaviour in its political and social forms appears puny and helpless. Man's capacity to survive in competition with creatures larger, stronger, swifter and better armed than he derived from his mental capacity that enabled him to adapt, and adapt to, his environment. He can now mould his physical, chemical and biological environment far more effectively than ever before. But it is his social and political environment which he now must learn to understand and appropriately to control. If his adaptive capacity is unequal to this task then he will have lost the faculty that has enabled him hitherto to survive.

Further reading

ARON, R., *Peace and War*, Weidenfeld, 1966.

BOULDING, K., *The Image*, Michigan University Press, 1956.

BURTON, J. W., *International Relations*, Cambridge University Press, 1965.

BURTON, J. W., *Systems, States, Diplomacy and Rules*, Cambridge University Press, 1968.

CARR, E. H., *The Twenty Years' Crisis 1919-1939*, Macmillan, 1939.

CLAUDE, I. L., *Power and International Relations*, Random House, 1962.

DEUTSCH, K. W., *The Nerves of Government*, Free Press, 1963.

DEUTSCH, K. W., *The Analysis of International Relations*, Prentice-Hall, 1968.

EDWARDS, D. V., *International Political Analysis*, Holt, Rinehart & Winston, 1969.

EASTON, D., *A Framework for Political Analysis*, Prentice-Hall, 1965.

EASTON, D., *A Systems Analysis of Political Life*, Wiley, 1965.

FOX, W. T. R., ed.,*Theoretical Aspects of International Relations*, University of Notre Dame Press, 1959.

FRANKEL, J., *International Relations*, Oxford University Press, 1964.

FRANKEL, J., *International Politics*, Penguin, 1969.

FRANKEL, J., *The Making of Foreign Policy*, Oxford University Press, 1963.

HAAS, E. B., and WHITING, A. S., *Dynamics of International Relations*, McGraw Hill, 1956.

HERZ, J. H., *International Politics in the Atomic Age*, Columbia University Press, 1959.

HOFFMANN, S., *Contemporary Theory in International Relations*, Prentice-Hall, 1960.

HOLSTI, K. J., *International Politics*, Prentice-Hall, 1967.

IKLE, F. C., *How Nations Negotiate*, Praeger, 1967.

KAPLAN, M. A., *System and Process in International Politics*, Wiley, 1957.

KAPLAN, M. A., *Macropolitics*, Aldine, 1969.

KNORR, K., and ROSENAU, J. N., eds., *Contending Approaches to International Politics*, Princeton University Press, 1969.

KNORR, K., and VERBA, S., eds., *The International System*, Princeton University Press, 1961.

LISKA, G., *International Equilibrium*, Harvard University Press, 1957.

MCCLELLAND, C. A., *Theory and the International System*, Macmillan, 1966.

MACRIDIS, R., ed., *Foreign Policy in World Politics*, Prentice-Hall, 3rd. ed. 1967.

MORGENTHAU, H. J., *Politics Among Nations*, Knopf, 1948.

RAPOPORT, A., *Fights, Games and Debates*, Michigan University Press, 1960.

RIKER, W. H., *The Theory of Political Coalitions*, Yale University Press, 1962.

ROSECRANCE, R. N., *Action and Reaction in World Politics*, Little, Brown, 1963.

ROSENAU, J. N., ed., *International Politics and Foreign Policy*, Free Press, 1969.

SCHELLING, T. C., *The Strategy of Conflict*, Harvard University Press, 1960.

SCOTT, A. M., *The Functioning of the International Political System*, Macmillan, 1967.

SCOTT, A. M., *The Revolution in Statecraft*, Random House, 1965.

SNYDER, R. C., BRUCK, H. W., and SAPIN, B., *Foreign Policy Decision-Making*, Free Press, 1962.

SPROUT, H., and SPROUT, M., *The Ecological Perspective on Human Affairs*, Princeton University Press, 1965.

WALTZ, K. N., *Man, the State and War*, Columbia University Press, 1959.

WRIGHT, Q., *The Study of International Relations*, Appleton-Century-Crofts, 1955.

Index

Abel, E., 172 fn. 8
Aberystwyth, 5
Abyssinia, 24, 83 fn. 22, 146, 154
Aden, 52, 102
Adenauer, K., 133
Adriatic, 62
Afghanistan, 58
Africa, 22, 24, 29, 38, 57, 61 and fn. 10, 70, 143, 236, 245, 248
Alaska, 57, 58
Albania, 62
Alexander the Great, 61
Alfred the Great, 62
Algeria, 63, 87, 144, 150
alliances, 119-20, 175, 233
Alliance for Progress, 143
Alps, 52
Andorra, 106 fn. 3
Angola, 237, 254
Antarctic, 57
anticolonialism, 53, 110-11, 140, 236, 249
antirevisionism, 54
Anzus pact, 102
Apennines, 62
Appadorai, A., 240 fn. 10
appeasement, 55, 145
Arabs, 107, 114, 139, 149, 152
    guerrillas, 237
    League, 28, 105, 249
Arbenz, J., 141
Arctic, 57, 58, 60
Aristotle, 4, 15 fn. 2, 39-40
Armenia, 76, 110

Aryan race, 43
Asia, 69-70, 75, 76, 79, 139, 143, 236, 245, 255
assassination, political, 140, fn. 9
Aswan dam, 144
Athens, 114
Atlantic, 52 and fn. 1, 56, 60, 65, 69
Attolico, B., 166
Australia, 57, 74-5, 102, 134, 236
Austria, 78, 210, 248, 249
    Austrians, 24
    Anschluss, 80, 175
Austria-Hungary, 22, 58, 63, 75, 77, 78, 94, 211
Azerbaijan, 76, 110

Baku, 130
balance of power, 197-212, 241-2, 249
    as policy, 199-201
    as situation, 198-9
    as system, 202-12, 215, 250
        capabilities in, 207-8
        definition of, 202
        flexibility in, 208-9
        information in, 206-7
        loss-gains calculus, 209-10
        number of units in, 203-6
        subsystem goals, 210
Baldwin, D. A., 143 fn. 14
Baldwin, S., 49, 66, 86
Balkans, 58, 144-5
Bandung conference, 134, 254
Bank of England, 232

Banks, M. H., 8 fn. 8
bargaining, 121, 122, 126ff., 145
  commitments, 130-1, 133, 223-4
  no agreement option, 113, 127-9, 131,
    133, 146
  rewards, 129-30
  threats, 130-1
  warnings, 130
Barthou, L., 178
Basle, 232
Batum, 130
Bay of Pigs, 141
Beirut, 114
Belgium, 24, 90 fn. 23, 125, 152, 248
Benelux, 192
Berdyaev, N., 62 fn. 11
Berlin, 38, 77, 126, 128, 138, 149, 166,
    167, 175, 176
  blockade, 135
  Congress of, 125
Bessarabia, 22
Bevin, E., 126, 132
Bhutan, 106 fn. 3
Biafra, 24, 150, 169
Bidault, G., 126
Black Sea, 58, 239
Bohemia, 21, 23, 77
Bohlen, C., 164
Bolsheviks, 53, 95, 101, 138, 154, 210, 249
Borah, W. E., 176 fn. 13
Bosnia, 225
Bowett, D. W., 26 fn. 6, 27 fn. 8
Brahman, 40
Brandenburg, 62, 89
Brazil, 68, 73
  Brazilians, 20
Brezhnev doctrine, 251
British Aircraft Corporation, 114
British Council, 136
Brüning, H., 49
Brussels, 28
  Treaty of, 31
Bulgaria, 58, 144, 249
  Bulgars, 23
Bulgarrenault, 239
Bull, H. 7 fn. 3, 150 fn. 17
Burnet, G., 7
Burton, J. W., 174 fn. 10, 242 fn. 1
Butler, R., 95 fn. 25, 125 fn. 3, 176 fn. 12
Butterfield, H., 148 fn. 16, 150 fn. 17
Byrnes, J. F., 132

Cairo, 139

Cambodia, 236, 254
Cambridge, 158
Campaign for Nuclear Disarmament, 37
Canada, 24, 60, 102, 152
Canning, G., 60
capabilities, 97-8, 117
  as affected by technology, 244
Caribbean, 56
Carnot, L., 211
Carr, E. H., 5
cartels, 32
Carthage, 204
Castlereagh, Viscount, 199
Castro, F., 38
Ceauşescu, N., 104
Central America, 142
central bank cooperation, 114, 192, 232,
    237, 252
Central Intelligence Agency, 141, 233
Central Treaty Organization, 105
Černik, O, 99
Chamberlain, N., 85, 118, 140, 145, 160,
    164, 165
Charles II, 139
Chiang Kai-shek, 38
China, 16, 17, 22, 58, 64, 74, 75, 79, 84,
    102, 106, 124
Chinese People's Republic, 16, 17, 73,
    99, 101, 106, 134, 136-7, 138, 143,
    149, 152, 153, 164
Chou En-lai, 134
Chrysler-Rootes-Simca-Barreiros, 239
Churchill, W. S., 133
Clarke, T. E. S., 7 fn. 4
Claude, I. L., 197 fn. 2
Clausewitz, K., v. 147
Comecon, 73, 103, 239
Comintern, 32-3
Commonwealth, 28, 37, 75, 101-3, 105,
    165, 249
  as international actor, 29
communism, 38, 81, 140
  as international actor, 32-3
  east European parties, 103
  French party, 33, 93, 94 fn. 24, 141
    fn. 10
  imperialist war and people's war, 94
    fn. 24
  Italian party, 33, 141 fn. 10
Concorde, 114, 238
Congo, 28, 107, 150, 234, 236
Connally, T., 19
Conseil Européen pour la Recherche
    Nucléaire, 238

Cornford, F. M., 39 fn. 4, 40 fn. 5
Crimean war, 58, 200
Cripps, S., 168, 171
Croatia, 77
  Croats, 94
Cromwell, O., 62
Cuba, 68, 138, 142
  missiles crisis, 33, 55 fn. 4, 114, 117,
    125, 133, 135, 149, 164, 172 fn. 8,
    174, 245
cybernetics, 39 fn. 3, 191
Cyprus, 150, 236
Czechoslovakia, 23, 33, 58, 104, 105,
    117, 138, 141, 249
  Czechs, 21, 94
  Hitler and, 46, 77, 115, 118, 125-6, 130,
    154, 175, 178,
  Soviet invasion of, 72-3, 88, 99, 149,
    168, 251

Dalmatian coast, 94
Dante, G., 4
Danton, G. J., 54
Davignon, J., 166
decision-makers, 38, 49, 50, 51, 53, 55,
    71, 74, 78, 79, 83, 85, 86, 87, 88,
    89, 93, 96, 97, 105, 107-9, 114, 115,
    123, 124, 125, 126, 127, 132, 136,
    140, 141, 144, 150, 152, 153, ch. 7
    passim
  as a 'process', 158, 174 and fn. 10
  psychological environment of, 52 fn.
    1, 58, 60, 64, 98, 99, 121-2, 150, 172-7
  who are?, 158-65
    foreign services recruitment, 158-60
    political recruitment, 160
decision-making, ch. 7 passim
  affected by technology, 245
  communication in, 169-71, 174
  execution of decisions, 174-7
  information in, 165-72, 174
  institutionalization of, 161-4
Declaration of Human Rights, 16 fn. 3,
    100
demography as influence on foreign
    policy, 73 ff., 117, 118
  age-structure, 78-9
  changes in Europe, 78
  composition, 76-7
  demographic transition, 79
  effect on other influences, 80, 92-3
  optimum population, 73-4
  size, 73-5

skills, 75-6
states' rank order, 73
trends, 77-80
Denmark, 248
Der Spiegel, 140 fn. 9
destroyer-bases deal, 56
deterrence, 148-51, 207, 255
Deutsch, K. W., 39 fn. 3, 170 fn. 4, 191
Diem, N. D., 141
diplomacy, 123, 124 ff., 153-4
  diplomatic immunities, 9, 10, 98-9,
    124, 231
  history of, 124-5
  techniques of, 128-32, 143
  types of, 126, 132-5
Directory, the, 54
disarmament, 127-8, 175
Dodd, W. E., 166
Dominican republic, 149
Dover, 66
Drummond, D. F., 171 fn. 6
Dubček, A., 33, 99, 104
Dulles, J. F., 126, 133, 140, 144
Duncan report, 166 fn. 3
Dunlop-Pirelli, 239

East African Common Services Organ-
    ization, 192, 252
Easton, D., 9 and fn. 12, 192 and fn. 6,
    229 and fn. 3, 230, 233 fn. 6
economy as Foreign policy instrument,
    123, 131, 142-7, 153-4
  sanctions, 146-7, 154
  as influence on foreign policy, 67 ff.
    117
    aid, 38, 70-1, 143-4
    opportunity cost, 72
    strategic implications, 90-2
    trade, 38, 67-9, 91-2
Eden, R. A., 61, 133, 146, 164
Edward VII, 120
Egypt, 5, 61 and fn. 10, 65, 138, 152
Eisenhower, D. D., 36, 71, 132, 164
El Al, 114
English Channel, 52, 63
equilibrium, 199, 202, 210
Erzgebirge, 23
Estonia, 76, 110, 141, 249
Ethiopia, see Abyssinia
Euratom, 30, 104
European Coal and Steel Community,
    30, 104
European Commission for the Danube,
    26

European Defence Community, 105, 140

European Economic Community, 19, 21, 30, 46, 69, 103, 104, 105, 128, 157, 192, 224, 253
  as international actor, 30-1
  and bilateral trade agreements, 105 fn. 2
  Commission of, 30
  Council of Ministers of, 30, 104

F.111, 235-6
Far East, 58, 133
Fascists, 43, 53, 93, 138
federations, 29, 30 fn. 10
feedback, 189-90, 208, 209
Finland, 58, 76, 249
Firestone, 239
First International, 32
Flemings, 24
Food and Agriculture Organization, 111, 192
force as foreign policy instrument, 123, 141, 147-54
  deterrence, 148-51
foreign policy
  action relates to future, 71
  as executive activity, 18
  as a process, 55-6
  at elections, 82-3
  constant-volatile scale, 66-7, 118
  constitutions and, 156-7
  definition of, 13 ff., 35 ff., 48, 51
  democratic control of, 141-2, 159, 160-1
  four-component model of, 179
  instruments of, Ch. 6 passim
  interaction of influences upon, 59-60
  limits upon, 56-7
  means-ends relationship, 120-1, 154
  power in, 115 ff.
  stimuli to, 56-7
Formosa, see Taiwan
Foxcroft, H. C., 7 fn. 4
France, 5, 6, 27, 33, 63, 73, 75, 90 fn. 23, 106, 110, 117, 139, 147, 162, 164, 168, 200, 210, 211-12, 237, 248, 252
  and Britain, 52, 120
    Europe, 30, 36, 105, 128, 224
    Germany, 72, 95
    Hitler, 115, 125, 130, 146, 154, 173, 175
    Marshall Plan, 126, 141

NATO, 175
natural frontiers, 52 and fn. 1
nuclear weapons, 152
Suez, 61, 65, 88, 149
United States, 55-6
French, the, 89, 93, 138, 150
influence of Quai d'Orsay, 159
Maginot line in, 178-9
political opinion in, 87
population, 78
François-Poncet, A., 166
Franco-Prussian war, 95
Frankel, J., 116 fn. 1, 172 fn. 7
Frederick the Great, 92, 147
French Revolution, 249

game theory, 215 ff.
  non-zero-sum games, 220-5
    commitments in, 223-4
    communication in, 222-4
  saddlepoint, 216
  zero-sum games, 215-20
Gandhi, Mrs I., 13, 14
Gaulle, C. de, 71, 85, 87, 93, 103, 104, 128, 133, 140, 150, 168
General Agreement on Tariffs and Trade, 105, 111, 134
geography as influence on foreign-policy, 57 ff., 117
  change in, 65-6, 118 fn. 13
  climate, 63-4
  economic, 64-5
  location, 60-1, 118 fn. 13
  size, 58-9
  topography, 61-3
Georgia, 76, 110
Germany, 23, 27, 49, 52 and fn. 1, 63, 65, 75, 77, 80, 88, 97, 150, 172, 173, 178, 200, 211-12, 237
  and Czechoslovakia, 115
  Federal German Republic, 30, 72, 73, 105-6, 147
  German Democratic Republic, 73, 124, 126
  Germans, 92, 93
  Nazi Germany, 6, 55, 58, 130, 144-5, 146, 154, 163, 164, 166, 168, 173
    ideology, 43, 250
  Nazis, 6, 49, 53, 60, 93, 100, 101, 103, 138, 141, 166, 176
  population, 78
  Prussia and, 62, 90
  strategy, 77, 90 fn. 23

Gibraltar, 52, 110
goals, 36 ff., 48-9, 51-5, 118, 126, 150, 154, 179, 195
  short-term and long-term, 55, 115
Goebbels, J., 138
Goering, H., 162
Goldman, M. I., 144 fn. 15
Gomulka, W., 104
government, definition of, 17 ff.
Great Britain, 6, 15, 20, 33 and fn. 14, 37, 49, 55, 73, 75, 77, 105, 106, 115, 117, 138, 140, 162, 163, 164, 238, 248, 251
  and Abyssinia, 83, 146
  anticolonialism, 110
  appeasement, 55, 82, 145, 154
  balance of power, 199-200, 210-12
  Commonwealth, 102
  European Coal and Steel Community, 30
  European Economic Community, 19, 37, 46, 54, 69, 157, 253
  France, 120
  Hitler, 115, 125-6, 130, 175-6
  Levant, 107
  Manchuria, 80
  Marshall Plan, 126
  nuclear weapons, 71-2, 152
  Rhodesia, 29, 146-7
  Suez, 61, 65, 88, 109, 144, 149
  traditions, 88
  United States, 166
  U.S.S.R., 168
  Western European Union, 31, 105
  as an island, 62-3
  British, 33 fn. 14, 89
  defence, 52, 56 and fn. 5, 66, 69, 89, 90, 94-5
  dispersed interests, 58
  economic problems, 70, 146
  effect of war on, 91-2
  executive and legislative relations, 18
  foreign policy and Crown prerogative, 156
  Foreign Office, influence of, 159-60
  recruitment, 158
  party politics, 86
  population, 74, 78
  skill, 75
Greece, 40, 144, 236
  guerrillas, 141, 150
Greenland, 59
Gromyko, A., 125
Grotius, H., 4

Guatemala, 70, 141
Guetzkow, H., 226 fn. 10
Guevara, C., 236

Haas, E. B., 197 fn. 2
Hacha, E., 46
Halifax, Viscount, 165, 166
Hammarskjöld, D., 28, 107, 234
Henderson, A., 160
Henderson, N., 125, 130, 166, 167, 175-7
Henlein, K., 154
Hess, R., 162
Hindus, 40, 44
Hiroshima, 152
Hitler, A., 23, 37, 46, 59, 60, 74, 77, 82, 90 fn. 23, 92, 93, 94 fn. 24, 95, 118, 125, 129-30, 138, 140 fn. 9, 141, 145, 154, 156, 162, 166, 168, 173, 175, 177, 178, 185, 196, 210
Ho Chi Minh, 150
Hoare, S., 86, 165
  Hoare-Laval pact, 83 and fn. 22, 86
Hobbes, T., 4, 41
Holland, 63, 152, 248, 251
Holsti, K. J., 126 fn. 4
Hoover, H., 164
Howard, M. E., 148 fn. 16
Hungary, 88, 104, 109, 138, 144, 149, 249, 254
  Hungarians, 23
Huntington, E., 57 fn. 6

Iceland, 56 fn. 5
ideology, 140, 236, 248-50, 255
Iklé, F. C., 127 fns. 5, 6, 130 fn. 8
images, 135, 138
India, 6, 13, 14, 22, 24, 30 fn. 10, 61 fn. 10, 73, 75, 88, 102, 130, 149, 152, 190, 237
  Indian Ocean, 102, 130
individual
  as international actor, 33, 114
  rights of, 42, 45-7
  security of, 41, 45-6
Indonesia, 19, 54, 73, 149
informal penetration, 123-4, 142
information, 99, 125, 135, 151, 158-9, 162, 165-72, 200, 206-7
Intergovernmental Maritime Consultative Organization, 111
international, meaning of, 24 ff.
International Atomic Energy Agency, 111

International Bank of Reconstruction and Development, 111, 192
International Business Machines, 238, 251-2
International Civil Aviation Organization, 111
International Chamber of Commerce, 112
international companies, 32, 38, 85, 114, 239, 251
International Court of Justice, 99-100, 106, 109, 231
International Development Association, 111
international ethics, 9, 97-100, 101
international institutions, 26 ff., 101 ff.
International Labour Organization, 27, 111
international law, 9, 10, 99-100, 101
International Monetary Fund, 28, 111, 112, 192, 237
    Special Drawing Rights, 240
international political parties, 32
International Political Science Association, 112
international politics, 10
international relations—
    compared with history, 7 ff.
    compared with politics, 8 ff.
    definition of, 10
    history of subject of, 4 ff.
    micro- and macro-, definition of, 7
    scope of subject of, Ch. 1 passim
international system—
    definition of, 193
    economic, 237-40
    military-strategic, 232-37
    political, 230-32
    state, change factors in, 243 ff.
        demography, 245-7
        ideology, 248-50
        mass involvement in politics, 247-8
        stresses from environment, 250 ff.
        technology, 243-5
International Telecommunications Union, 111
International Telegraphic Union, 27
International Trade Organization, 111
international trade unions, 32
Inter-Parliamentary Union, 112
Invergordon, mutiny at, 80
Iran, 58, 76, 83, 114-15
Isergebirge, 23
Islam, 22

Ismay, H. L., 28 fn. 9, 31 fn. 12
Israel, 38, 77, 84, 107, 114, 139, 149, 152
Italy, 33, 52, 61, 62, 83 fn. 22, 88, 94, 115, 130, 141 and fn. 10, 146, 152, 175, 237, 248-9
    Italians, 20, 93, 124

Jaguar strike-trainer, 236
Japan, 5, 52, 58, 59, 61 fn. 10, 63, 67-8, 69, 73, 74, 77, 91, 115, 130, 152, 154, 156, 176, 190, 237, 238
    Japanese, 93, 100
Jews, 20, 74, 84, 114
Joffe, A., 166
Johnson, L. B., 83, 165
Jowett, B., 15 fn. 2
Joyce, W., 138

Kamenev. L., 168
Kant, I., 4
Kaplan, M. A., 9 and fn. 11, 191 and fn. 4, 196 and fn. 1, 197, 227
Kashmir, 149
Katanga, 234, 254
Kazakistan, 110
Kellogg-Briand Pact, 100
Kelsen, H., 100 fn. 1
Kennedy, J. F., 55 fn. 4, 85, 114, 125, 133, 165, 172 fn. 8, 235 fn. 8, 245
Kennedy, R. F., 164 fn. 2, 174 and fn. 9, 235 fn. 8
Kenya, 24
Khrushchev, N., 114, 126, 132, 133, 235 fn. 8, 245
    and 20th Party Congress, 249
Kiesinger, K.-G., 168
Kirghizia, 110
Knorr, K., 227 fn. 12, 228 fn. 2
Kollontai, A., 168
Korea, 106, 108, 109, 135, 149, 233
Kosygin, A., 13
Kremlin, 104

Labrador, 64
Lagos, 169
Laos, 236, 254
Lasswell, H. D., 230 fn. 5
Lateran Treaties, 32
Latin America, see South America
Latvia, 76, 110, 141, 249
Laval, P., 83 fn. 22
Law Society, 14
League of Nations, 27, 83 fn. 22, 110, 146, 154, 176 and fn. 13, 201

League of Nations—*cont.*
  Commission on Disarmament, 27
  Commission on Mandates, 27
  Committees, 27
Lebanon, 71
Lend-Lease, 56, 92
Lenin, V. I., 4, 32, 197
Leningrad, 66
Leslie, M., 49 fn. 9
Levant, 37, 61 and fn. 10, 65, 107, 114,
    139, 172, 225, 252
Libya, 63
Lie, T., 109
Liechtenstein, 106 fn. 3
Lippmann, W., 84
Lithuania, 76, 110, 141, 249
Little Entente, 178
Lloyd, S., 86
London, 5, 103, 164, 165, 168
  Treaty of, 94
Louis XIV, 52
Louis XV, 54
Louis XVI, 54
Louis Philippe, 52
Low Countries, 200
Luxembourg, 125

McCarthy, J., 159
MacDonald, M., 166
MacFarlane, M., 140 fn. 9
Machiavelli, N., 4
Macmillan, H., 54, 86
Maginot line, 178-9
Magyars, 77
Malaya, 150, 236
Malaysia, 19, 54, 149
Maleter, P., 99
Malta, 52
Manchuria, 68, 80, 176
Mao Tse-tung, 17, 138, 197, 236
Marshall, G. C., 126, 171 fn. 6
Marshall Plan, 117, 141, 143, 168
Marx, K., 4, 32,
  Marxism-Leninism, 43, 167, 251
Mathisen, T., 201 and fn. 6
Mediterranean, 52
Mendès-France, 38
Mercator's projection, 66
Mesopotamia, 61
Middle East, *see* Levant
Minnesota, 64
Modelski, G., 228 fn. 2
Mohammed, 190
Mollet, G., 61

Molotov, V. M., 130, 132, 168
Monaco, 106 fn. 3
Mongolia, 58
Monroe Doctrine, 60
Moravia, 21, 77
Morgenthau, H. J., 5, 6 and fn. 3, 45 and
    fn. 7, 120 fn. 14
Moscow, 60, 61, 92, 104, 128, 151, 153,
    167, 168, 198, 207, 245, 255
Mozambique, 237, 254
Mukden incident, 80
Munich agreement, 115
Muscat and Oman, 106 fn. 3
Mussolini, B., 32, 83 fn. 22, 93, 94, 154,
    156-7, 162, 175, 247 fn. 5

Nagasaki, 152
Nagy, I., 99, 104
Napoleon, 52, 54, 59
Napoleon III, 52
Nasser, G., 65, 67 and fn. 14, 138-9,
    144, 196
nation, definition of, 20 ff.
  race and language as basis of, 23-4
national character, 88-9
national interest, Ch. 3 *passim*, 142,
    169, 174, 197
  and global community, 48
  and national objectives, 38
  and sub-national interests, 36-7
  as the general and the long-term,
    49-50
National Security Council, 165
nationalism, 22, 53, 67 and fn. 14, 81,
    140, 142, 248-9
nationality, 33 fn. 14
nation-state, 21
  spread of, 22, 24
  loyalty to, 236
NATO, 28, 31, 38, 72, 73, 102, 105, 110,
    149, 175, 245
  Council 6th Session, 28 fn. 9
natural frontier, 52 fn. 1
Nauru, 106 fn. 3
Nazi-Soviet pact, 58, 115, 138, 178
Nehru, J., 102, 166
Netherlands, *see* Holland
Neurath, C., v. 162
Neutrality Acts, 55-6, 178
Nevada, 84
New York, 66, 135, 245
New York State, 84, 114
New Zealand, 102

Nicholas, H. G., 106 fn. 4, 108 fn. 6, 234 fn. 7
Nicholson, M. B., 25 fn. 5, 229, fn. 4
Nigerian Federation, 24, 169
nine power pact 176 and fn. 13
non-alignment, 13, 144
non-governmental organizations, 31, 85, 112-14
non-recognition, 176 fn. 13
North, R. C., 171 and fn. 5
North Sea, 64, 74, 253
Northern Hemisphere, 57
Norway, 58, 74, 113, 248
nuclear non-proliferation treaty, 38, 127, 254
Nuremberg, 125
  trials, 100

Oder, 52 fn. 1
Ojukwu, C. O., 150
Olson, W. C., 45 fn. 7
Olympic Games, 33, 112, 192-3, 237
omniscient observer, 38, 48, 173, 177
Organization for African Unity, 105
Organization for European Economic Co-operation, 141
Organization of American States, 28, 105, 245,
Organski, A. F. K., 116 fn. 12
Oxford, 158

Pacific, 60, 64
Pakistan, 13, 21, 73, 102, 149, 152
Palestine, 61, 74
Palmer, N. D., 112 fn. 8, 246 fn. 3
Panama, 66
Paris, 52, 168
  Peace Conference, 22, 23, 249
Pearl Harbour, 56, 171 and fn. 6
Peking, 16, 17, 255
Penrhyndeudraeth, 114
Perkins, H. C., 112 fn. 8, 246 fn. 3
Persia, 61
Persian Gulf, 130
Philips, 239
Plamenatz, J., 9 and fn. 10
Plan Yellow, 90 fn. 23
Plato, 4, 39 and fn. 4, 40
Poland, 23, 52 fn. 1, 58, 63, 74, 104, 115, 117, 125-6, 168, 249
political organization, purposes of, 39 ff.
politics
  as influence on foreign policy, 80 ff,
  on strategy, 93-4, 117

chronology of domestic events, 80-1
definitions of, 8 ff.
parties, 85-7
pressure groups, 83-5
public opinion, 81-6
social moves, 87-9
Portugal, 63, 110, 248
power, 75, 98, 115-22, 173, 198
  as means, 120-1
  constantly in flux, 118-19
  definition of, 116
  elements of, 117
  great power, 119-20
  importance of perception and will, 121-2, 200
Prague, 46
Pratt, J. T., 176 fn. 13
Prince Paul, 60
propaganda as foreign policy instrument, 123, 127, 131, 135-9, 153-4, 248
Prussia, 62, 63, 78, 89-90, 92, 210, 248-9
Pyrenees, 52

Québec, 140

raison d'état, 88
Rajan, M. S., 240 fn. 10
Rakovsky, C., 168
Rapoport, A., 221 fn. 8
Red Army, 103, 135
Red Sea, 102
regional, meaning of, 26 fn. 7
Renault, 239
Reston, J., 84
revisionism, 53-4
Reynolds, P. A., 25 fn. 5, 229 fn. 4
Rhine, 52, 66, 172
  Commission, 26
Rhineland, 77, 162, 173
Rhodesia, 29, 146-7, 157, 231
Ribbentrop, J., 115, 128, 162, 176-7
Richelieu, A. J. du P. de, 95
Riesengebirge, 23
Rio de Janeiro, 66
Rivett, B. H. P., 8 fn. 6
Robespierre, M., 54
Roman Catholic Church, 32, 84
Romania, 58, 73, 77, 104, 144, 249, 251
  Romanians, 23, 77
Rome, 32, 204
  Treaty of, 104, 128
Roosevelt, F. D., 55-6, 133-4, 164

Rosenau, J. N., 227 fn. 12
Rosenberg, A., 162
Roskill, S., 52 fn. 2
Rousseau, J. J., 4, 39
Royal Dutch Shell, 251
Ruhr, 77
Russell, B., 33, 114
Russett, B. M., 26 fn. 7
Russia, 58-9, 61, 62, 76, 88, 89, 90 fn. 23,
    200, 210, 211-12, 248
Ruthenes, 23

Sahara, 64
San Francisco, 19, 134
San Marino, 106 fn. 3
Scandinavia, 5
Schacht, H., 144, 154
Schelling, T. C., 221 fn. 8, 223
Schlieffen Plan, 90 fn. 23
Scott, A. M., 124 fn. 1
Second International, 32
second strike capability, 59 fn. 9, 150-1
self-determination, 22, 23, 42-3, 53, 110,
    154, 249
self-sufficiency, meaning of, 53
Semple, E. C., 57 fn. 6
separation of powers, 18 ff.
Serbs, 77
Sherwood, R. E., 56 fn. 5
Silesia, 23, 77
Simon, J., 165, 176 and fn. 13
Simonstown, 52
simulation, 215, 225-7
Singapore, 52, 102
Slovaks, 21
Smith, I., 146, 157
Smoot-Hawley tariff, 68
Smrkovsky, J., 99
Soames, C., 168
social sciences, 6, 258
    definition of variables in, 8, 213
    laws of, 8
    models in, 214 ff.
    probability in, 8
    self-fulfilling predictions in, 213-14
Somaliland, 110
    Somali Republic, 24
    Somalis, 24
Sondermann, F. A., 45 fn. 7
Sorensen, T. C., 55 fn. 4
South Africa, 100, 102, 103, 147, 152
South America, 38, 57, 143, 245
South East Asia Treaty Organization,
    105

Southern Hemisphere, 57
South-west Asia, see Levant
Soviet Union, see U.S.S.R.
Spain, 63, 110, 138, 139, 162, 248
    Spanish, 89
    Spanish civil war, 138, 162, 236
Spartakists, 166
Sprout, H. and M., 57 fn. 7
Stalin, J. V., 58, 83, 104, 115, 130, 132,
    133-4, 164, 165, 168, 171, 178, 255
state
    as actor, 20, 31, 34, 38
    as obstacle to national interest, 45-7,
        49, 121
    autonomy of, 245
    definition of, 14, 16, 30 fn. 10
    distinguished from nation, 21-4
    generality of function, 15, 44
    interstate relations general questions,
        114-15
    recognition of, 16 ff.
    security of, 41-2, 45, 51-3
    sovereignty of, 10, 15, 16 and fn. 3,
        30 fn. 10, 31, 113
    system, types of, 195 ff.
Stimson, H. L., 176 and fn. 13
Stockholm, 168
Strabo, 52
Straits, the, 61
Strang, W., 129
strategy as influence on foreign policy,
    89-95, 117
subversion as foreign policy instru-
    ment, 123, 131, 139-42, 153-4
Sud Aviation, 114
Sudan, 24
Sudeten Germans, 21, 23, 77, 154
Suez, 37, 52, 61, 65, 66, 67, 88, 92, 102,
    109, 133, 144, 146
Sukarno, A., 54, 196
summit conferences, 132-4, 161, 175
Sumner, B. H., 76 fn. 20
supranational, 26 ff.
Sweden, 58, 152, 248
Switzerland, 52, 63, 95, 106, 152
    Swiss, 21
Syria, 61, 71
system—
    balance of power, 202-12, 215
    definition of, 183 ff., 186 fn. 2
    feedback, 189-90
    isomorphism, 197, 212, 242
    not goal-seeking, 196-7
    state systems, 195 ff.

system—*cont.*
types of conceptualization, 190-3

Tacitus, 52
Taipeh, 16, 17
Taiwan, 16, 17, 38
Tajikistan, 110
Teheran, 77
The Times, 13 fn. 1, 140 fn. 9, 141 fn. 10
thermonuclear weapons, 46, 116, 148, 234, 253-4
  as credible deterrent, 59
  non-proliferation treaty, 38, 127, 254
  second strike capability, 59 and fn. 9, 150-1, 207
Thompson, Ll., 164
Thorez, M., 33 and fn. 13, 141 fn. 10
Tibet, 149
Tito, J.-B., 33, 103
Togliatti, P., 33 and fn. 13, 141 fn. 10
Tojo, H., 197
Tokugawa Shogunate, 63
Tokyo, 168
  trials 100
transnational groups, 31-3
trans-Siberian railway, 58
Transylvania, 22, 77
Treitschke, H. v. 43
Trincomalee, 52
Tripartite Pact, 60
Tsars, 58
Tshombe, M., 234, 254
TSR2, 235-6
Tudors, 62
Tukhachevsky, M. N., 168
Turkey, 58, 61, 250
Turkmenia, 110
Tyrrhenian Sea, 62

U2 reconnaissance plane, 132
Uganda, 24
Ukraine, 74, 76
  Ukrainians, 23, 92
Ulan Bator, 168
Ulbricht, W., 73, 124
Unilever, 114, 239, 251
U.S.S.R. (Union of Soviet Socialist Republics) 6, 28, 29, 54, 105, 119, 132, 139, 143, 152, 162, 163, 164, 234, 235, 238, 255
  and anticolonialism, 110
    Comintern, 32-3
    German Democratic Republic, 124

Hitler, 60, 94 fn. 24, 115, 130, 168
Levant, 65, 107
Marshall Plan, 117
United Nations, 106-7, 108-9
United States, 38, 57, 61, 70, 91, 106-7, 115, 117, 151, 198, 204
Warsaw Pact, 71, 103-4
information flow, 167-8
invasion of Czechoslovakia, 72-3, 115, 149, 168
Marxist ideology of, 43
negotiating technique, 129
population of, 73, 77-8
pressure groups in, 83
role of communist party in, 18, 160, 165
size of, 58-9, 89
subversion by, 140, 150
United Fruit Company, 70
United Kingdom *see* Great Britain
United Nations Organization, 27-28, 106 ff. and fn. 3, 126, 131, 135, 147, 150, 166, 234, 245
  as international actor, 28-9
  Charter of, 16 fn. 3, 19, 26 fn. 7, 106 fn. 4
  Conference on Trade and Development, 111
  Economic and Social Council, 27, 106, 109, 111, 191
    Commissions, 111 fn. 7, 112
  Educational, Scientific and Cultural Organization, 31, 111, 192, 237
  General Assembly, 106, 108-10, 134, 135, 231, 233, 234, 254
  Secretariat, 106, 109, 135
  Secretary-General, 28, 107, 109, 110, 233, 234
  Security Council 27-8, 106-9, 134, 135, 231, 233, 234
  specialized agencies, 27, 111, 191, 231
  Trusteeship Council, 106, 109-10, 231
  veto, 28, 106-8, 108 fn. 5
United States, 6, 20, 30 fn. 10, 33, 37, 45 fn. 7, 61 fn. 10, 67, 73, 75, 76, 79, 91, 102, 135, 138, 139, 140, 149, 151, 152, 157, 171 fn. 6, 172, 178-9, 203, 233, 235, 237, 238, 252, 253, 254
  and China, 16-17
  Cuba, 117, 245
  economic aid, 143
  Germany, 72
  Great Britain, 36, 52, 55-6, 56 fn. 5, 92, 94-5, 146, 152, 164, 166, 176

United States—*cont.*
  Japan, 68, 176
  Levant, 65, 114
  NATO, 105, 110
  Self-determination 42-3
  Treaty of Versailles, 27, 178
  U.S.S.R., 57, 58, 70, 106-7, 114-15, 117, 119, 151, 198, 204
  United Nations, 106-9, 134
  Vietnam, 56, 81, 91, 101, 116, 117-118, 149, 151, 154, 231
  behavioural norms of, 87-8, 201
  climate, 63-4, 66
  hyphenates in, 77
  Information Service, 136
  location of, 60-1, 66
  objectives of, 38
  political system of, 83-4, 86, 141-2, 156, 160-1, 163, 164, 165
  separation of powers in, 18-19
  State Department, influence of, 159
  subversion by, 141-2
Uniting for Peace resolution, 108
Universal Postal Union, 27, 111, 113
U Thant, 109, 234
Uzbekistan, 110

Valona, 62
values, 38 ff., 42-4, 49, 53
  conflict of, 44
Vandenberg, A. H., 19
Vatican, 32, 106
Venezuela, 68
Verba, S., 228 fn. 2
Versailles, Treaty of, 27, 138, 178
Verwoerd, H., 103
Vienna, 133
  Congress of, 26, 125, 199
Vietcong, 254
Vietnam, 17, 38, 56, 81, 83, 88, 91, 101, 106, 109, 116, 117-18, 119, 141, 149, 154, 225, 231, 236, 254
Voice of the Arabs, 139
Voroshilov, K. E., 129

Wales, 5, 23
  Welsh, 20, 25, 33 fn. 14

Walloons, 24
war, 6, 9, 18, 42-3, 44, 52, 55, 69, 90, 91, 98-9, 100, 102, 127, 147-54, 156, 172, 250
  civil, 24
  Crimea, 58, 200
  first world, 5, 58, 92, 94, 136, 159, 209, 211-12
  Franco-Prussian, 95
  internal, 236-7
  of 1812, 60
  second world, 56, 60, 72, 77, 92, 136, 138, 141, 248
  Spanish civil, 138, 162, 236
Warsaw, 17
  Pact Organization, 28, 31, 71, 103-4, 105-6, 238, 251
Washington, D.C., 16, 17, 56, 61, 64, 115, 116, 139, 151, 153, 164, 165, 166, 171 fn. 6, 198, 207, 245, 251
Webster, C. K., 200 fn. 5
West Indies, 20
West Samoa, 106 fn. 3
Western European Union, 31, 105
White, L. C., 112 fn. 8
Wight, M., 148 fn. 16, 150 fn. 17
Wilson, H., 70, 147, 168
Wilson, W., 22, 42, 66, 201, 248, 249
Witte, S. Y., 76
Wohlstetter, A., 198 and fn. 3
Woodward, E. L., 95 fn. 25, 125 fn. 3, 176 fn. 12
world economic crisis, 68, 84, 138, 144, 179
World Federation of Trade Unions, 112
World Federation of United Nations Associations, 112
World Health Organization, 111
World Meteorological Organization, 111
world opinion, 73, 109
Wright, Q., 8, 9, fn. 9, 10

Yalta, 134
Yugoslavia, 33, 60, 73, 103, 144, 249
  Yugoslavs, 23

Zionism, 231